COMPASSIONATE
LIGHT IN ASIA

ECHOES AND REFLECTIONS
THE SELECTED WORKS OF DAISAKU IKEDA

Showcasing some of the most potent and far-reaching spiritual works of our times, this major new series brings together – for the first time under the banner of a single imprint – twelve classic dialogues between modern spiritual master Daisaku Ikeda and a distinguished roll-call of discussants, who are uniformly thinkers of global stature and reputation. *Echoes and Reflections* ranges widely across the fields of religion, politics, economics, science and the arts, and in each instance puts a profound and searching new perspective on some of the most pressing issues of our age. Topics covered include: the search for worldwide social justice; the challenges posed by climate change and diminishing natural resources; the perils of religious misdirection; the urgent need for inner growth and harmony; the importance of learning and education; and, above all, the significance of the human quest for meaning and value in life.

Titles in the series:

Choose Life, Arnold Toynbee & Daisaku Ikeda

Dawn After Dark, René Huyghe & Daisaku Ikeda

Human Values in A Changing World, Bryan Wilson & Daisaku Ikeda

Search for A New Humanity, Josef Derbolav & Daisaku Ikeda

Before it is Too Late, Aurelio Peccei & Daisaku Ikeda

A Lifelong Quest for Peace, Linus Pauling & Daisaku Ikeda

Ode to the Grand Spirit, Chingiz Aitmatov & Daisaku Ikeda

Human Rights in the Twenty-first Century, Austregésilo de Athayde & Daisaku Ikeda

José Martí, Cuban Apostle, Cintio Vitier & Daisaku Ikeda

Compassionate Light in Asia, Jin Yong & Daisaku Ikeda

Global Civilization, Majid Tehranian & Daisaku Ikeda

Moral Lessons of the Twentieth Century, Mikhail Gorbachev & Daisaku Ikeda

COMPASSIONATE LIGHT IN ASIA

A Dialogue

JIN YONG

and

DAISAKU IKEDA

Edited and Translated by Diana L. Bethel

ECHOES AND REFLECTIONS
THE SELECTED WORKS OF DAISAKU IKEDA

I.B. TAURIS
LONDON · NEW YORK

Echoes and Reflections is a new series of twelve classic dialogues held between Daisaku Ikeda and a variety of interlocutors, which took place from 1972 to 2001. The texts of these dialogues are presented in this series substantively in the form in which they originally occurred. For the sake of verisimilitude, and to preserve the integrity of the series, the events, persons and dates referred to in the texts reflect the original periods and contexts in which the conversations were first held, and so have not been altered or edited to mirror subsequent developments in international affairs or the changed worldwide circumstances of later years.

Published in 2013 by I.B. Tauris & Co Ltd
6 Salem Road, London W2 4BU
175 Fifth Avenue, New York NY 10010
www.ibtauris.com

Distributed in the United States and Canada Exclusively by Palgrave Macmillan
175 Fifth Avenue, New York NY 10010

ISBN: 978 1 84885 198 6

A full CIP record for this book is available from the British Library
A full CIP record is available from the Library of Congress

Library of Congress Catalog Card Number: available

Typeset in Garamond by Initial Typesetting Services, Edinburgh

Printed and bound in Great Britain by T.J. International, Padstow, Cornwall

MIX
Paper from
responsible sources
FSC
www.fsc.org FSC® C013056

Contents

Preface

by Jin Yong

On Our Dialogue

One summer, during the still ongoing war of resistance against Japan, most of my classmates had returned home while I, and several others who had no home to return to, remained at the school. The days were swelteringly hot, and the only exercise we could possibly do under the blistering sun was swimming. I resigned myself to the situation and spent my days immersed in reading books in a classroom.

The books I read were *Zizhi Tongjian* (Comprehensive Mirror to Aid in Government) and *The Outline of History* by H.G. Wells. *Zizhi Tongjian* was published by the Zhonghua Book Company as a traditionally bound Japanese book, sewn together with thread, and printed in large letters.

As I held each thin volume in my hands, the joy of reading the classics spontaneously welled up inside of me. *The Outline of History*, bound in the Western style and illustrated, was thick and heavy. It was hard to hold it up to read it, so I laid it out on a desk. I enjoyed the illustrations throughout the book while savouring the various aspects of world history that Wells portrayed so wonderfully.

When I grew tired of reading, I would lie down on a long, narrow bench for a little nap, my sweaty body curled up with arms and legs drawn in. When I awoke, I would resume my reading. The bench was only a little over a foot and a half wide, and reminded me of Tiaodeng in *The True Story of Ah Q*. I spent the whole summer in this way, alternating between reading and sleeping – thanks to the bench – and amazingly, I never fell off the bench even once.

In *The Return of the Condor Heroes*, I wrote that Xiaolongnu (Little Dragon Maiden) stretches taut a piece of rope and sleeps on it. Now that I think about it, I probably got my inspiration for this from sleeping on that bench. In any case, that summer vacation I passed the time fully enjoying the company of these two companions – excellent historical works from the East and the West.

Later on, I came across an article written by a certain British professor of history who criticized the work by Wells that I had read. He claimed that Wells's work lacked serious treatment of historical facts and that Wells had come to conclusions without sufficient evidence. Therefore, he insisted, it did not conform to generally accepted academic standards. I was completely convinced by this severe criticism, and I had an acute realization that there was a sharp distinction between academic research and eloquent writing. In the case of *Zizhi Tongjian*, I could not help feeling that, though Sima Guang wielded his brush with great ease and produced works of exquisite refinement and grace, he too may not always have adhered strictly to the facts and may have embellished them in no small measure.

After China won the war of resistance against the Japanese, I returned to my homeland from the southeast of China. At a bookstore in Shanghai, I happened upon an abridged edition of Arnold Toynbee's major treatise, *A Study of History*. At that point, I became so engrossed in the book that I went days without food or sleep. Many of the thoughts and ideas were so startling that it was as if I had entered a dazzling new world that I had never seen or heard of before. I imagined that what I was experiencing was even more amazing than what Granny Lin in *Dream of the Red Chamber* experienced when she entered the Grand View Garden and encountered sights and sounds she had never seen or heard before. I had no idea that this kind of scholarship and these kinds of views even existed in the world. Dr Toynbee explored in great depth the history of each major world civilization and the reasons for their prosperity and sustained development, and he came to the conclusion that, in every case, in spite of facing severe challenges, they had had the capability to splendidly overcome them. I agreed completely with these historical principles.

The more I read Dr Toynbee's book, deep down in my heart, a thought kept growing stronger and stronger. I felt that if I were to become Dr Toynbee's student and were able to study with him, I would be the happiest person in the world. Even if I later became impoverished and lived the rest of my life in poverty, suffering countless hardships and, in the end, collapsed and died on the roadside, with no one to collect my body and bury me – even then, I would feel that I had lived a happy and satisfying life.

When I came to Hong Kong and was working at Ta Kung Pao, a newspaper firm, I decided that I wanted to translate Toynbee's monumental work, and so I began working on it whenever I could find time outside of work – it comprises 12 volumes in total, but had not been completed at that time. I did not have an extensive background in the history of Western civilization (especially in regard to Egyptian, Babylonian, Persian, and Central Asian history), so whenever I came to difficult passages, I did my best to research the topic and compensate for my lack of knowledge. At the time, I felt that I was dealing with these difficulties as 'challenges', in Dr Toynbee's terms. Before I had finished the translation, however, I was required to do other pressing translations related to current events such as the revolution of the Communist Party of China and the Korean War, so I had to set aside Toynbee's *A Study of History*. Then I learned that Chen Xiaolin had published a translation of the book in Taiwan, so I had to abandon my dream and the manuscript I had been working on since my youth.

In the following decades, I voraciously read every book by Dr Toynbee that I could buy or somehow acquire. In the process of reading numerous works by Dr Toynbee, including *Civilization on Trial*, *War and Civilization*, and *East to West: A Journey Round the World*, I came across the dialogue between Dr Toynbee and Daisaku Ikeda entitled *Choose Life: A Dialogue*.

When I read *Choose Life*, I had already been exposed to numerous works on Marxism and Leninism, and so when I read Dr Toynbee's excessive admiration of Christianity, I lost interest in his work. After that, Dr Toynbee no longer had my unconditional respect. However, I was profoundly impressed by the extensive knowledge and deep concern for the future of humankind expressed by both of the participants in the dialogue.

When I received an honorary doctorate from the Peking University, a number of Japanese authors had also been nominated, but I heard that they did not receive the approval of the faculty association. I felt a little apologetic about this, but then I heard that Daisaku Ikeda had also received an honorary degree from the university, and I was relieved and felt an even greater sense of honour and accomplishment. Later on, I was asked, through Pan Yaoming, the general editor of the *Ming Pao Monthly*, whether or not I might engage in a dialogue with President Ikeda. Of course I agreed to do it wholeheartedly. Considering President Ikeda's fame and scholarship, I grew worried and could not shake a sense of humility and the feeling that perhaps we were ill-matched dialogue partners.

However, in the course of our dialogue, conducted in meetings in Hong Kong as well as in Japan, I was overjoyed to discover that we were engaged in more than an intellectual exchange – it was an exchange interwoven with a developing friendship and spiritual search for truth. Of course, we did not agree completely on every single issue. But I have great admiration for President Ikeda for recognizing the tragic mistake of Japan's invasion of China and calling for an official apology. He also earns my utmost respect for courageously fighting for what is right while refusing to crumble when subjected to blackmail, slander and defamation and for tirelessly promoting world peace and intercultural exchanges between the peoples of all countries.

Our dialogues were completely unscripted. Sometimes we conversed during a meal, other times over tea or while admiring outstanding landscapes or beautiful gardens. Since I have a tendency to speak without much forethought and from a base of superficial knowledge, I am sure there are many mistakes and incomplete aspects in my statements. I hope that our readers will kindly point these out. If I had not followed in the footsteps of President Ikeda, whose words are like precious jewels of wisdom, I would never have been able to appear in this centennial edition, published on the occasion of the 100th anniversary of the founding of Peking University.

President Ikeda and I share a profound respect for academic freedom, and we both believe in the value of academic research. We sincerely hope that academic research and scholarship will fulfil its mission to make a positive contribution to people, society, and the entire world. We feel that as honorary professors, our hopes resonate deeply with the spirit of Peking University.

Jin Yong

Preface

by Daisaku Ikeda

Life is a drama of encounters. Beautiful encounters. Momentary encounters. Encounters that determine the rest of our lives. Encounters that leave a bitter taste and feelings of regret. Each person's drama is unique.

Among all the encounters interwoven into the drama of one's life, nothing makes a person happier than encounters in which you immediately feel a sense of mutual understanding and the feeling that your ideas and thoughts are understood, even without speaking.

When we are blessed with encounters such as these, we feel a kind of nostalgia. This is what we might call, in Buddhist terms, a karmic relationship – a sense of being led by destiny. It is as if we have known each other a long time, and in the furthest reaches of our hearts, we have been engaging in dialogue.

I feel that my encounter with Mr Jin Yong was truly just such a relationship. It was our destiny. He is the great writer who breathed new life into traditional Chinese martial arts novels and took the genre to new heights in the modern Chinese language. He has been praised as the father of Chinese literature and the Dumas of the East, and it has been said that wherever there are Chinese, you will find Jin Yong's novels.

Jin Yong is not only an acclaimed author. He founded the major Hong Kong daily newspaper the *Ming Pao*, and has been the guiding light of good sense and a public opinion leader for the past forty-some years. Of course, there is no need to introduce Jin Yong's many accomplishments, for they are already well known, but I have been the most impressed with his determination to fight for free speech and his refusal to yield to the power and despotism of tyranny. Underlying this strength of character is his abundant love of the people. He has maintained an unwavering focus on the people: that fundamental point of reference. He is a great man of taste and refinement who told the profound and multi-layered story of over 4,000 years of Chinese history.

There is an expression 'To wield a sharp pen.' Mr Jin's pen was indeed a sharp sword. He had many enemies. When he would make a statement in a manner that Group A would express it, he would be maligned by Group B. And alternately, when he would make a statement in a manner that Group B would prefer, he would be detested by Group A. So, no matter what he did, he sparked antipathy from one side or another. He was feared, attacked, slandered, and even targeted for assassination.

We had an opportunity to engage in dialogue four times in Hong Kong and Tokyo. On one of those occasions I said to Mr Jin, 'The oppression must have been very severe'. His answer was immediate, 'Yes, but right and wrong and good and evil were clear as day. I absolutely did not buckle under to injustice and oppression.'

His kindly and gentle face, always smiling, accompanied a fierce and determined spirit – this is what his readers found so charming and captivating and is perhaps the secret behind the fiery martial arts novels that he gave birth to.

Jin Yong is a distinguished and brilliant author and also a prominent businessman. We can imagine that he has lived a tranquil and quiet life, and he probably could have had that way of life. But that is not the life chosen by Jin Yong, affectionately called Zha Daxia or the great chivalrous man (his real name was Zha Liangyong) by the people of Hong Kong. He was not one to cater to the trends of the times or to hesitate, gauging the direction of the winds. He insisted on basing his writing on a single standard: it had to benefit the people. He certainly must have known that if his writing abandoned the people as its major point of reference, then even voluminous statements would be empty and worthless verbiage.

Jin Yong was able to discern early on the intricacies and underlying forces of major events of the times, such as the Cultural Revolution and the period surrounding the return of Hong Kong to China. He remains thoroughly committed to freedom of expression, and especially to expressing the voice of the people, and I believe that this is precisely why he has such penetrating insight.

Those who speak the truth are continually the victims of conspiracies and wily machinations. It comes with the territory. Mr Jin looked down upon these thugs and he decisively broke through their malevolent schemes.

I have also experienced these trials and have survived them with the same fierce sense of justice. I keenly feel that my encounter with Mr Jin Yong was an amazing stroke of karmic destiny, revealing that our similar life experiences and beliefs resonate in perfect harmony.

During the Spring and Autumn and the Warring States periods, the great teacher and philosopher Mencius taught the principles of the noble path of righteousness. The opposing philosophy was the rule of might and military power that, through armed force and Machiavellian machinations, sought to enhance personal glory and prosperity by using others to achieve these ends. In contrast, the rule of right seeks to bring happiness to all people through the principle of fairness and impartiality and strength of character. To live by the rule of might is easy, while following the noble path is difficult. This was true in ancient times, and it is still true today.

This is to say nothing of the deep, dark abyss we face today. In response, so many people take the easy way by turning to military might to solve all problems. Through all this, though buffeted by the winds of public criticism, Jin Yong has remained strong, oblivious to the siren call of fame and fortune, choosing the difficult path of living by his convictions. He emphasized during our dialogue, 'If, on self-examination, I find that I am upright, I will go forward against thousands and tens of thousands'. Clearly, we see the radiance of a man of conviction who has walked the high and noble road in life.

Our discussion has touched on numerous topics including literary theory, issues surrounding the return of Hong Kong to China, the mentor–disciple relationship, friendship, the Buddhist perspective of life and death, theories of civilization, and memories of our youth.

The drama of our encounter will continue to unfold over time. I see the content of our discussions up to this point as an important milestone in the journey of our dialogue.

It has been over 16 years since Hong Kong became a member of the great family of China – and both Mr Jin Yong and I sincerely pray for the prosperity of China and our beloved Hong Kong.

The publication of the serialized articles of this dialogue in the *Ushio* monthly magazine and of the Japanese and Chinese versions of the book, as well as this English version were made possible by the hard work and valuable contributions of many people. I would like to send my heartfelt appreciation to them all.

Daisaku Ikeda

CHAPTER 1

The Seasons of Life: Self-Discipline and Character Development in Youth

Sensing a Karmic Bond, We Engage in Dialogue on the Spiritual Dimension

IKEDA: There may be many people in the world, but only a few that a person must seek out in search of counsel. To discuss matters with someone who shares similar views represents one of life's happiest occasions. Even as we converse, I feel like I have known you for a long time.

I recall the comment that the author Chingiz Aitmatov of the former Soviet Union made when we began our conversation, which was published with the title of *Ode to the Grand Spirit*. He said, 'I do not recall how our conversation started. Perhaps it did not start at all but only continued because we had already been talking to each other even before we met.'[1]

I have the same sense about our encounter, Mr Jin. That is, in Buddhist terms, I cannot help feeling that we share a karmic bond.

JIN: I feel exactly the same way. If we say that we are brothers, people would probably believe it.

IKEDA: I am familiar with a broad range of world literature, and in my youth I had thought that I would like to become a writer. To be able to engage in a dialogue with such a great author as you, Mr Jin, is such a joy for me.

JIN: Quite some time ago, I read the dialogue *Choose Life*, which was between you, President Ikeda, and Dr Arnold Toynbee, and I was greatly impressed.

I feel very honoured to have this opportunity to engage in our dialogue on this occasion.

IKEDA: Dr Toynbee once told me that the only way to create a path for the advancement of humanity is through dialogue. He said, 'You are still young. I would urge you to continue your dialogues with the intellectuals of the world.' This was his wish bequeath to me.

This calls to mind Socrates – the man most known for using dialogue in the search for truth, so much so that this manner of conversing is called the Socratic method. Socrates' disciple Plato continued writing Socratic dialogues after Socrates' death. Similarly, Nichiren, whom we revere, has left a record of writings in dialogue form. His work *On Establishing the Correct Teaching for the Peace of the Land*, which sounded the alarm about dangers to the country, is in the form of a dialogue between a host and a traveller.

Arcane and abstruse writing is inaccessible to most people. And the writing of some writers is simply a monologue that feeds their own ego. In contrast, the dialogue style of writing is easy to read and has a kind of universality about it.

Heart-to-heart dialogues that explore the spiritual and psychological dimensions of human experience have withstood the test of time and will remain in humanity's awareness for eternity. In one of our dialogues, Dr Toynbee related that a certain meeting of heads of state was reported in the media with great fanfare. He commented in a serious tone, 'Events in the political dimension are fleeting and ephemeral, but our dialogue, while low-key and unspectacular, will survive well into the future'.

JIN: President Ikeda, you have held many dialogues with distinguished people from all over the world. One of your dialogues was with former President of the Soviet Union Mikhail Gorbachev, a politician whom I respect greatly. Another was with the late Mr Chang Shuhong, one of China's foremost Dunhuang researchers and scholars and a distinguished artist in his own right. In the wake of your dialogues with such illustrious persons, I am truly honoured to have this opportunity to engage in our dialogue.

IKEDA: It is indeed my pleasure. My intention is to learn from you.

JIN: I was very impressed when I learned that you place great importance on dialogue. Some of the greatest works of philosophy have taken the form of dialogues, including, as you mentioned, the Socratic dialogues. *The*

Analects of Confucius, which chronicles the teachings of the great Chinese philosopher, was also written in a dialogue format.

President Ikeda, as adherents of Buddhism, we know that Shakyamuni conveyed his Buddhist teachings in the form of dialogues. In the Buddhist scriptures, the phrase 'Thus have I heard', attributed to Shakyamuni, was recorded by Shakyamuni's disciples and provides insight into the dialogue style of the teachings. Similarly, in the Lotus Sutra were written the specifics of where, to whom, and in what manner Shakyamuni expounded on the Buddhist teachings. In other words, this, too, is a record of dialogues.

IKEDA: I was well aware of your prodigious scholarship, but I would like to once again express my high regard for your erudition.

JIN: Well, I don't feel that I rise to the calibre of the distinguished people from around the world with whom you have engaged in dialogues in the past, but I am looking forward to participating in our discussion and contributing in my own way.

President Ikeda, you and I are of the same generation. We were both born in the 1920s. I was born in 1924 and you in 1928. In Chinese we have the term, roughly translated, 'age without substance', which has been used since ancient times. It means that even if a person is older, if he has made no progress or has no accomplishments to show for himself, then his time has been spent in idleness. His seniority is called an 'empty seniority' or 'seniority without substance'.

IKEDA: You are exceedingly humble. But, Mr Jin, you have the presence and bearing of a great man. You know, they say that where there are Chinese, your novels will be found. You are praised as a grand master of Chinese literature and as one of the most talented Asian writers. You have left a rare legacy that will last through the ages. You are a 'champion of the pen' and a leader of public opinion in Hong Kong, the world's harbour of peace and prosperity.

In your address at Soka University in April 1996, you emphasized in your discussion of *The Tso Chuan: Selections from China's Oldest Narrative History* that the most monumental and enduring act possible for humankind is to create spiritual value. I would like to suggest that during your life you have created much spiritual value, which will indeed be everlasting and eternal.

JIN: President Ikeda, in many of your writings you express brilliant observations and opinions in your persistent and tireless efforts to build world peace. You are the preeminent leader of Soka Gakkai, a spiritual organization that does its utmost to create value in society and in people's lives. Furthermore, I think it is important to note that you have maintained your courage in adhering to the truth and refusing to succumb to malicious and biased sentiments. For these efforts, you have my undying respect.

In the novels I write, there is a heroic central character or a group of heroes. And the primary quality of these heroes is their courage. Their courage is not just the courage to fight against physical odds. They have moral courage, and that is what is most important. I feel that you have this attribute of moral courage.

IKEDA: I sincerely appreciate your kind words of encouragement.

More than 20 of my dialogues with distinguished leaders in various fields have been published [67 as of July 2013], but relatively few of these have been literary authors. And so I am especially delighted to have this opportunity to speak with you.

I continue to pursue opportunities to engage in dialogue with leading Western luminaries in culture and the arts. However, our dialogue, Mr Jin, will set a significant precedent in the dialogue series.

Let us take our time and make this dialogue an enjoyable experience. As we continue each segment of our dialogue, may the experience give you strength to regain your health and fill you with the energy of youth – that we may benefit Hong Kong, China, and the entire world.

Memories of War and a Determination to Stand with the People

IKEDA: Mr Jin, when we speak about our youth, there is no way to discuss it without touching on our memories of the war. When you came to speak at Soka University in the spring of 1996, one of our students asked you the question, 'What was the source of your strength that enabled you to make your statement to stand with the people?'

In your response, you explained: 'The era in which I was raised had a major impact in shaping my life. During the war, people had a very difficult time just struggling to survive, and I could see how the people were suffering. That is why I determined to do whatever I could to stand with and support the people.'

Japan has certainly behaved barbarically in the countries of Asia and especially in China. During the past several thousand years, all aspects of Japanese culture have been greatly enriched by Chinese culture, but instead of acknowledging China as our benefactor and repaying this debt with gratitude, Japan inflicted unspeakable atrocities on the country that shared so much of itself. Such behaviour is deeply criminal.

JIN: When the Japanese military launched its assault on China, I was already familiar with a handful of Japanese people of conscience who were opposed to this war of aggression.

After the war, on the several occasions when I was able to travel to Japan, I met with some of those people who had opposed the invasion of China at the time and, as leaders in the new postwar Japanese society, had devoted themselves to deepening the friendship between China and Japan. One of these individuals was Kaheita Okazaki (1897–1989). I also met with a number of leaders in the world of arts and culture. They were all broad-minded and highly perceptive in their thinking.

IKEDA: Mr Jin, you are so gracious. After the war, Japan did not even apologize to China but instead joined the US and continued its hostile policies toward China. Japan also opposed China's inclusion in the United Nations to the very last. Even so, in the Chinese people's retrospective assessment of the war, it was Japanese militarism that was to blame, not the Japanese people.

The Japanese people must never forget, even in their dreams, the magnanimity of the Chinese people.

JIN: President Ikeda, you have been severely critical of the war and have expressed your conscience, despite the often hostile mood of Japanese public opinion, from that time all the way to the present. This requires lucid understanding as well as a profound concern for the welfare of all humankind. I also know very well that to take a stand like this, one must have a fearless and valiant spirit.

Indeed, this truly takes a person of great intellect, compassion, and bravery. As Mencius stated, 'If, on self-examination, I find that I am upright, I will go forward against thousands and tens of thousands'.[2] This means that upon close examination, if one believes that one's assertions are just and in accordance with sound reason – and even if one's adversaries number in the hundreds or even millions and are arrayed against one, poised to attack – ultimately, one must adhere firmly to one's beliefs and assertions. President Ikeda, you have truly lived your life in accordance with this idea.

IKEDA: Mr Jin, you are most generous. My mentor and teacher, Josei Toda (1900–58), once said, 'Only when Japan becomes a trusted neighbour to the countries of Asia – only then can it be called a country of peace'. This is the essential sentiment that has informed my every action as a leader. If Japan does not follow this advice, it will become isolated in the international sphere.

I have heard that during the war, the Japanese military invaded and destroyed your birthplace, the city of Quzhou, Zhejiang Province.

JIN: When the Japanese army invaded my hometown, I was 13 years old and just about to enter my second year of junior high school. My classmates and I followed our school as it migrated from one place to another to avoid the encroaching Japanese army. During this period, we received military training and experienced extremely harsh conditions. Because necessary medications and nursing care were lacking as a result of the wartime circumstances, my mother passed on from this world. The war completely destroyed my country, my people, and my family.

At one time, my family was relatively affluent. However, the Japanese army burned our home completely to the ground, leaving not even a trace. And my younger brother, with whom I was especially close and whom we all loved dearly, was killed in the war.

During my junior high school days, my regular school studies were frequently suspended because of circumstances related to the war. This is why I failed to acquire a strong foundation in the Chinese classics and in English language studies. It was only during my university days, and even after graduation, that I was finally able to fill this void in my knowledge.

Despite all the adversities, I do think that the war afforded me a significant opportunity for training and developing myself – a kind of training ground, in a sense. By this, I mean that throughout my life since then, I have never been afraid of any hardship or difficulty. During the war, I never had enough to eat and I became critically ill and almost died. After suffering these kinds of ordeals, what more could there be to make me fearful now?

A 'Training Ground' Necessary for Youth

IKEDA: Mr Jin, I believe that young people must use every experience, no matter what it is, as wings on which to lift themselves to greater heights in life, and to build a strong character just as you have done. For this purpose, I believe that youth definitely need an exacting and rigorous 'training ground'.

Some say that in ancient times, military training fulfilled this educational function for youth, but in the end, it forced young people to kill or be killed. In modern times, war has taken this inhumanity to levels far beyond our imagination, and so training young people for war serves all the more to demean their sense of humanity. It is just too tragic. This absolutely should not be allowed.

The American philosopher William James (1842–1910) once offered a proposal. He suggested that in order to redirect the human fighting instinct for the benefit of society, what was needed was a moral equivalent to war. In his famous 1910 essay, 'The Moral Equivalent of War', he wrote that society should establish a regiment for creating peace and for building structures. 'To coal and iron mines, to freight trains, to fishing fleets in December, to dishwashing, clothes washing, and window-washing, to road-building and tunnel-making, to foundries and stoke-holes, and to the frames of skyscrapers, would our gilded youths be drafted off, according to their choice, to get the childishness knocked out of them, and to come back into society with healthier sympathies and soberer ideas.'[3]

JIN: I am very familiar with your fervent and tireless efforts to bring about world peace, help people create spiritual value and improve their lives, and provide people with opportunities for education and training.

IKEDA: That's very kind of you to say. Our organization holds a variety of cultural events whose significance, in one respect, is to provide an opportunity, you might say 'a training ground', for young people to live their lives more fully. Other Soka Gakkai youth volunteer groups, such as Soka (Value Creation) Group, Gajōkai (Fortress) Group, and the Byakuren (White Lotus) Group who help participants at SGI meetings and events at SGI centres share this same purpose of youth development and enrichment.

Each day, as the youth work hard at their jobs or their studies, they develop character and more self-confidence by contributing to the lives of others, and so when they return to society, they are mature adults.

Returning to the subject of your life during the war, what are the most unforgettable experiences you have had? These may be painful memories, but please share them, not only for my benefit, but also for the sake of the youth, the generation that has had no first-hand experience of war.

JIN: I have two memories to tell. First, I remember when, during a Japanese air raid, a Japanese bomber dropped a bomb not too far from where I was standing. I immediately hit the ground. After the rat-a-tat-tat of machine gun fire sounded from above, the plane flew off into the distance. When I stood up, I saw two bodies lying on the side of the road. Their complexions had the taut yellow cast of death, blood was flowing from their mouths and noses, and their eyes were wide open, staring into space. Nearby a young school-aged girl was beside herself with shock and terror, crying hysterically. All I could think to do was to pat her on the shoulder to console her.

Another memory is the time when the Japanese military began to use biological warfare. There was an aerial assault on Quzhou, Zhejiang Province in which they dropped a bacteriological agent, *Yersinia pestis*. At that time, I was in high school in Quzhou and had my classes in a farming village. The bacteria spread throughout the city, creating a panic among the people because those who became infected would not survive.

When a member of a family became infected, the soldiers would put the infected person on a boat in the middle of the Quzhou River and wait for him or her to die. Seven days later, they would set fire to the boat. The family would be expelled from their home and have to leave all their belongings behind, including all their clothes. Their home would then be burned completely to the ground. The only consolation was that the family would receive some monetary compensation from the city.

IKEDA: What a tragic story. The scars inflicted by the prewar Japanese military's biological warfare unit, Unit 731, have still not healed completely.

JIN: One of my classmates, Mao Liangjie, was an athlete who became infected with the *Yersinia pestis* bacteria. When the news of his affliction became known, all the students at school ran frantically away from him.

On the last day I saw Mao, he lay on his bed crying. Our homeroom teacher, Mr Jiang Zikuang, paying out of his own pocket, hired two farmers to carry Mao to the centre of town. From there he would be taken to a boat that, as I mentioned before, was anchored in the middle of the river.

I was the class representative, so it was my duty to escort Mao to the river. In the pitch black of night, I followed along as the farmers carried Mao on a stretcher to the river's edge. I was so frightened, but as class representative,

I could not excuse myself from this responsibility. When we came to the bank of the river, Mao and I both shed tears as we parted forever.

Afterwards, my teacher and I returned to the school and washed our clothes in boiling water to kill any fleas, because the *Yersinia pestis* bacteria are spread by fleas. When I look back on that night, I am grateful that I was able to summon the courage to at least do what little I could, for Mao's sake.

IKEDA: The barbaric actions of the Japanese are shameful, but even more shameful is the way that many Japanese have forgotten their history. I have heard that in Chinese, the worst insult that can be said of someone is *wang ba* (literally 'forget eight'), which refers to a person who fails to observe the eight morals – duty, obedience, loyalty, trust, decorum, honour, moderation, and shame. To forget or disregard these traditional Chinese moral principles in one's life is to know no shame, and this is perhaps the worst offence of all. I know well how much the Chinese scorn this kind of forgetfulness and disregard.

In contrast, how forgetful the Japanese are. It is more than forgetfulness. When confronted with the topic of Japan's wartime responsibility, countless politicians react defiantly with a look of annoyance. They are unfazed by severe criticism from other Asian countries. They do not understand how their provocative remarks are irresponsible and derisive of the people of Asia. They have no empathy for those whose suffering has been caused by Japan. And they have no awareness of their own stupidity. The majority of people around the world see the Japanese in this way.

In a sense, peace is a battle against forgetfulness. As former German President Richard von Weizsäcker said, in his famous speech on the occasion of the fortieth anniversary of Germany's defeat in World War II, 'Anyone who closes his eyes to the past is blind to the present'.[4] Forgetting the past leaves no opportunity for true reflection, atonement, or commitment to peace.

The Japanese must completely denounce this historical amnesia and face their past truthfully. If they don't, the rest of the world will hesitate to engage Japan on a serious level.

Japanese Personality and the Danger of Militaristic Education

JIN: I would like the opportunity to ask you some questions, too, President Ikeda, about your wartime experiences. I have heard that your father,

Nenokichi, was a resolute man with a strong sense of responsibility and that he went into business producing seaweed products.

IKEDA: Yes. My father was such an obstinate man that his friends and family fondly called him 'Mr Diehard'.

JIN: Times were hard for your family during the war, I understand, and four of your older brothers were drafted and sent to fight on the battlefront. Your eldest brother, Kiichi, became a war casualty, dying in the war in Burma (currently Myanmar), and your other three older brothers finally returned home from China only after the war ended.

I have heard that your father as well as your brothers were all vehemently opposed to Japan's war of aggression. Although Japan was the aggressor in the invasion of China, people of both countries were victimized by the war.

IKEDA: On one of his furloughs from the war in China, my eldest brother shared with us his frustration and rage, and his words still linger in my mind. He told us, 'Japan is terrible! The way our troops are acting, I feel so sorry for the Chinese people.'

JIN: You were still young when the war was going on, President Ikeda, so you must have been exposed to and influenced by Japanese militarism in the educational system. I have heard that, at one point, you thought that you might like to volunteer for the naval air corps, but your father would not permit you to enlist. The reason you wanted to enlist was that your family was experiencing financial difficulties and you wanted to help out? Or was it that you were influenced by heroic images of soldiers?

IKEDA: To tell the truth, my answer is the latter. Just as you suggested, I was influenced, as were my classmates, by the militaristic training we received at school. We were raised in the Japanese educational environment of the time that instilled in children a warped perspective of the world and of humanity. It is so tragic to think of the countless numbers of young men who were spurred by this propaganda to make the ultimate sacrifice on the battlefield. There is nothing more frightening than this kind of miseducation. My realization of this tragedy chills me to the bone.

JIN: President Ikeda, your family struggled during the war, and since you were unable to continue your education, instead you later became a factory worker at the Niigata Steel Mill. Given that you had a weak constitution, I imagine that this hard manual labour at the factory took a heavy toll on your body. On the other hand, perhaps this was a beneficial training experience that contributed greatly to your character development.

IKEDA: One had to be very hardy to survive during the war. If you were weak like I was, you were treated as if you were unpatriotic. I was ashamed of being so frail and infirm. However, the labour I engaged in required me to push my sickly body to its limit in retrospect, and this elicited precious experiences of human warmth and kindness so rare in my life at that time.

For example, one cold winter night, one of my supervisors asked if I wanted to come a little closer to the fire and talk a bit. He knew that I had lung problems. I was so grateful for his kindness. I can still vividly remember our conversation and the faces of the people around that fire. He encouraged me, treating me almost as if I were his son, saying, 'It's only in the world of *sumo* (Japanese wrestling) that young people can advance quickly. So don't rush. Just take your time in deciding your future.'

The factory manager was also a very kind person. He would cheer me up whenever I felt sick, and whenever I had to be hauled in to the medical office, he would call a rickshaw to take me home. In those days, it was rare for people to use rickshaws, so the people in my neighbourhood were all surprised when they saw me arrive home.

Well now, let us turn to another topic. Mr Jin, since you have many acquaintances in Japan, I wonder what impressions you have of Japanese people.

JIN: Yes, I do have many Japanese friends. One trait that they all seem to share is their conscientiousness. Whether in their studies or their work, they devote themselves completely to their task, and in every endeavour, they strive to do their very best. There is one aspect of the Japanese character that we Chinese, especially those of us from Hong Kong, often find, and that is the tendency to be obstinate and overly intent on observing the rules, to the extent that there is no flexibility or even an effort to be flexible.

When a group of us from Hong Kong travel to Japan, it's always a source of hilarity for us to see how much the Japanese adhere to convention. And, at times, how they even become fixated on it to an irrational degree.

IKEDA: It seems that you have a specific experience in mind.

JIN: Yes. I am thinking of the time that seven of us from Hong Kong visited a certain Osaka restaurant. All the tables at the restaurant were small, and at the most, only four people could be seated at one. The waiter was distressed and apologized to us profusely, explaining that we would have to sit at two different tables, since none of the tables could accommodate all seven of us.

We spontaneously burst out laughing. Because we could not speak Japanese very well, rather than trying to explain, we thought it would be faster to just put two tables together and instantly create one long table. And so, with no great effort, all seven of us could sit at one table. The waiter nodded his head up and down, as if he had had a sudden epiphany, and beamed at us with a friendly smile. He seemed to be thanking us for helping him solve a difficult problem.

IKEDA: That's funny. Your anecdote illustrates a characteristic that Japanese tend to have — that is, they sometimes assume that things have to be a certain way, and so they do not have the flexibility or ingenuity to address the situation. It may also be that the waiter was slightly nervous in front of customers from abroad.

One Step Forward by 100 People is Better Than One Person Taking 100 Steps

JIN: Of course, this example is in no way meant to imply that the Japanese are foolish. Rather, I think that it illustrates how the Japanese have a strict sense of discipline and observance of rules. If a majority of the people value discipline and observe societal rules, a society is able to achieve a higher degree of organization, and benefit from the enormous power of community. Then, the entire society and nation will manifest a powerful solidarity. We Chinese excel as individuals and always have an abundance of creativity, but on the other hand, we lack solidarity and discipline and have a weak sense of the importance of harmony. For that reason, we are not very capable of manifesting and employing the power of the whole.

Let me illustrate with the example of travel package tours. It is very easy for a tour operator to lead a group of Japanese tour customers. If the tour guide just waves a little flag, everyone quickly and quietly lines up and follows.

IKEDA: The Japanese tendency to congregate is definitely a cultural trait.

Japanese are famous for sticking together in all-Japanese groups when they travel abroad. There may be commendable aspects of this group discipline, but in international society, I think it is considered to be more of a disadvantage. I believe that this is a characteristic that the Japanese must cast off.

JIN: In contrast, leading Chinese tourists must be a nightmare for the tour guide. Everyone will be going here and there, looking into stores, buying souvenirs, taking pictures, doing whatever and going wherever they like independently of everyone else. The tour guide will not be able to round up everyone and depart on schedule without considerable effort.

In contrast, leading Chinese tourists must be a nightmare for the tour guide. The source of the Chinese Communist Party's power lies in its 'iron discipline'. Once a command is handed down, the entire party observes it with determination. This reflects a change in attitude from the traditional Chinese independence and diffuse sense of civic life. And it became the main force for nation building in the new China.

IKEDA: On the long road toward building the new Chinese nation, one major reason that the Chinese Communist Party was able to win the trust of the Chinese people was its reputation for being well disciplined to the point of fastidiousness. The famous 'Three Main Rules of Discipline and the Eight Points for Attention' governing the Red Army included the saying, 'No one must take away any property of the people – not even one needle or one piece of thread'. These principles express a strong sense of mission and a concern for the people of China, and they helped open the door to a new era. I was deeply impressed.

In 1996, I received the title of Honorary Professor from Sun Yat-sen University, the university founded by the founding father of China. Dr Sun Yat-sen wrote about freedom in his primary work, *The Three Principles of the People*: 'Now, how shall the term "liberty" be applied? If we apply it to a person, we shall become a sheet of loose sand.'⁵

This statement carries a stern cautionary note pointing out that liberty certainly does not proffer licence, but rather must be accompanied by a sense of self-discipline. I am well aware that the people of China place great importance on this personal dimension and are deepening their understanding of liberty as they strive to build the new China.

JIN: Thank you for that thought. President Ikeda, you and I have visited each other numerous times over the years, and I think I know you well enough to say that I see in you a firm will and strong spirit. I have the distinct impression that you proceed courageously toward your chosen goals with a bold and invincible spirit.

But when I think about your title of Poet Laureate, I somehow sense a great contradiction. Perhaps this is because my image of a poet is a romanticist who has a cavalier attitude and does whatever he pleases. Specific examples that come to mind are George Gordon Byron and Percy Bysshe Shelley of England, Charles Pierre Baudelaire of France, and China's Li Bai, Li Yu, and Su Dongpo.

IKEDA: I am likewise puzzled and cannot imagine how a person with a mild-mannered temperament such as yours can write such fiery martial arts novels. Where on earth does that come from? It's truly amazing for me.

JIN: Your poetry, President Ikeda, is overflowing with poetic sentiment, but you strike me as the valiant soldier or entrepreneurial type. If I were to liken you to a historical figure, I would say that you resemble Tokugawa Ieyasu (1542–1616), the founder of the Tokugawa Shogunate of Japan, and poet Lu You (1125–1210) or politician and writer Xin Qiji (1140–1207) of China.

Perhaps this contradiction between your personality and your poetry stems from your faith in Buddhism and inspiration that you received from your mentor, Josei Toda, combined with the sense of mission that you inherited from him; that is, your desire to meet the heavy responsibility for the development of Soka Gakkai that you have carried on your shoulders.

IKEDA: There was a time in my youth when I wanted to become a writer. But as fate would have it, I ended up taking a different path in life. In those days, I was enthralled with the revolutionary and passionate poet George Gordon Byron. I even wrote a short essay about his life. I was thoroughly fascinated by Byron's poetic genius and the development of his brilliance at such a young age, and I pursued my interest further, plunging into a study of the Greek War of Independence and sympathizing completely with Byron's revolutionary passion.

Mr Jin, if, as you have sensed, I have developed the characteristics of a fighter and an entrepreneur, this may be attributed, as you mentioned, primarily to the fact that I find myself in a position of responsibility for such a large organization as SGI (Soka Gakkai International).

After all, the way of the bodhisattva in Mahayana Buddhism inevitably demands a peace movement led by the people, and so I have dedicated myself to wholeheartedly helping, as they say, one hundred people take one step forward, as opposed to helping one person take one hundred steps, so that we may steadily advance and continuously galvanize the organization to action.

On that point, it seems to me that Byron's life aptly illustrates an example of one person who advanced 'one hundred steps'. Of course, his life shows how the power of one person influenced the course of history; yet there are limits to one person's ability to truly shape history. I believe that when one hundred people each take one step, the ordinary becomes extraordinary, and this is a wholesome path, consistent with the spirit of Mahayana Buddhism.

Even so, sometimes I do wish that someone would take my place so I could live a carefree life without the burdens of leadership. This discussion reminds me of my mentor, Josei Toda, who was a magnanimous and free-spirited person.

Family Portrait – Father and Grandfather

IKEDA: The publication in Japanese of your long-awaited martial arts anthology was very well received. As a result, your name has become even better known in Japan, and this is certainly a cause for celebration.

For the benefit of your Japanese readers, let me now become the interviewer and ask you a little more about your life.

JIN: I would be most pleased.

IKEDA: First of all, I understand that when you were young, the person who influenced you the most was your grandfather, Zha Wenqing, who served as the governor of Jiangsu province at the end of the Qing period. In that province, an incident occurred in which some people burned down a Christian church. This event was a manifestation of animosity toward Christians, who were seen as the minions of the invading Western powers. At that time, your grandfather is said to have protected the prime suspect, who was about to be executed, and allowed him to escape. He took complete responsibility for the escape and submitted his resignation.

Your grandfather was resolved to risk his life to save someone else's. He had a strong sense of justice. His actions seem just like those of the heroes who appear in your novels. I feel that I now have a sense of the source from which you, the 'warrior of words', derive your daring and internal fortitude.

JIN: My grandfather could not bear to yield to the tyranny and oppression of the foreign imperialists. He would not keep silent to protect his position and comfortable way of life and let someone be put to death.

Unfortunately, shortly after I was born, my grandfather passed on from this world. However, the legacy of this great man brought much pride to the fellow citizens of his province as well as to his entire family.

My grandfather was known for his generosity. He bought farmland, which we called 'Yizhuang' (literally 'manor of morality'), to help our poor relatives. With the income he received from renting out the farmland, he helped the orphans and widows in our extended family. This monetary assistance allowed these people to live a hopeful and untroubled life, and for those who advanced to secondary school or to a university, he would provide an allowance twice a year. And to those who were studying abroad, he would send more financial support.

IKEDA: China is such a big and populous country. Yet family ties are deeper and stronger than we in Japan can even imagine.

JIN: Every year, during the Qingming Festival in the spring and the Double Ninth Festival in the autumn, my father would take my brothers and me on a pilgrimage to revere our ancestors at the ancestral shrine. All the people we met would invariably greet us by grasping both of our hands and bowing their heads up and down. This was the way they would greet my father, but even the grey-haired old men would also greet us children, who were only four and five years old, in this same respectful manner. From a child's perspective, it seemed so funny, and we could barely contain our giggles.

IKEDA: What kind of person was your father?

JIN: My father studied at Fudan University, but it seems that all his efforts there were for naught. He later returned home and managed Qianzhuang, an old-style Chinese private bank, a silkworm factory, and a silk textile factory, but none of these endeavours were successful. Management was not one of my father's strengths. I recall my father always being worried about business matters. I know, however, that his relationships with people were very satisfying for him. He was polite to a fault. It was almost as if his relationships with friends were more important to him than his business.

My father inherited the responsibility of managing the 'Yizhuang' land, so by definition he was a large landowner. During the post-liberation period of military control, when soldiers came from Shandong to purge the country of landowners and rich farmers, my father was among those executed.

IKEDA: Your grandfather lost his rank and position for trying to protect people, your mother died after her health deteriorated during the chaos of the war, and your father's life was stolen by those in power.

JIN: These were sad and painful experiences for me, but I never harboured any bitterness. This is because I understood. I knew that this was a generational transition period and that the foundations of society were shaking violently. It was an inevitable and universal drama, the kind that tragically plays itself out during periods of social change. Hundreds of thousands of people had lost their lives on battlefields throughout China. After that, several hundreds of thousands more died in various struggles.

In 1985, the judicial and prosecutorial authorities of the city of Haining, in Zhejiang province, testified, after a thorough investigation, that my father had been executed based on a false accusation.

IKEDA: This reminds me that in 1996, you kindly gave me the Lotus Sutra of the Wonderful Law, which Professor Zhao Puchu, then president of the Chinese Buddhist Association, and whom I greatly respect, transcribed with brush and ink.

As you know, the Lotus Sutra teaches the principle of attainment of buddhahood by father and son together. The bond between parent and child is profound. Their lives exist in eternal communion with one another. In this sense, I believe that your father lives within you, even now. He continually watches over you, and I am certain that he rejoices in your happiness.

JIN: Thank you for your kind words. My grandfather's and parents' deaths make me realize so profoundly how precious it is to live one's life in peace, free of violence and aggression. Most important is to strive to avoid war, whether it be between countries or whether it be domestic, and thus enable the people to build and improve their lives in a peaceful environment. Violence is always the source of many a misfortune.

IKEDA: The truth of your words pierces my heart.

Reading: Gateway to Creativity for Youth

IKEDA: Mr Jin, you are an erudite scholar well-read in the modern and ancient classics. They say that your creativity flows whenever you pick up your pen, making you one of the greatest writers of your time. What is it that inspires the creative process for a great literary figure?

JIN: I cultivated my creative powers and writing ability in my youth, by reading. I read mostly novels. My father was also especially fond of reading novels, and we had a large selection of books at home.

IKEDA: It must have been, as you say in China, a home with 'a bookish fragrance' – that is, a home filled with books.

JIN: I was raised in a large family. My great-grandfather had two sons. His eldest was my grandfather, who lived in the east wing of the main house; the younger son resided in the west wing. The house was constructed in five sections, and in the front was hung a large plaque on which was written the name of the hall. The name, Tanyuantang (literally 'quiet and far hall'), had been given to Zha Sheng, one of our ancestors, by the Kangxi Emperor. It was written in three large characters surrounded by nine golden dragons.

My grandfather had three sons, my father being the third. My grandfather's younger brother died young, leaving four grandchildren. They were all much older than I and were also avid readers.

IKEDA: So you grew up in an environment very conducive to the enjoyment of reading.

JIN: Yes. Our family owned land, so there was usually not much work to do and lots of time to read. And money was not an issue, so we bought all kinds of novels to read. We had traditional works from the Ming and Qing dynasties as well as comparatively newer works just published in Shanghai. Among these were the novels of Zhang Henshui (1894–1967), a variety of martial arts novels, periodicals related to recent literary works, such as *Fiction Monthly*, and literary magazines, such as *Red Magazine* and *Red Rose*, from the Mandarin Duck and Butterfly school of literature.

IKEDA: I believe that you have older brothers.

JIN: My older brother, Zha Liangkeng, was an avid reader and studied classical literature as well as newer works. He attended university in Shanghai and often got scolded by our father for buying so many books that he never had enough money to cover his food expenses.

As I recall, my older brother read many of the works of Mao Dun (1896–1981), Lu Xun (1881–1936), Ba Jin (1904–2005), and Lao She (1898–1966). Our uncle and cousins also owned many books, so we often borrowed and lent books to each other. So, beginning in primary school, I availed myself of the enormous quantity of novels accessible to me.

My mother and father noticed that I would spend all day reading and did not go outside to play and exercise, and they became concerned about me. They would take me outside and make me fly kites and ride my bicycle, but after I had played for what I felt to be the requisite amount of time, I would immediately go back inside and start reading again.

IKEDA: As they say, 'Genius displays itself even in childhood'.

I believe that in addition to being healthy, which your parents were concerned about, youth must exert themselves in reading good books and an abundance of literature. Reading broadens one's experience of life and the world. In reading, one can discover flowers, water, stars, light, enjoyment, anger, the ocean – in other words, the world is at one's fingertips.

In my youth, I also immersed myself completely in the world of books. Until shortly before he passed away, my mentor maintained a strict educational regimen for me, always asking me what I was reading that day.

Just as the growth of a tree depends on the extent to which it is nourished, so does the growth of one's spirit. The books that a youth reads during his or her teens and twenties will be treasures for life. Mr Jin, your experience reflects this. I have a sense that this overlooked secret is the key to the creativity of the great literary masters.

JIN: The library of the primary school that I attended was a veritable cornucopia of books, and the teachers encouraged students to read more than just their school textbooks. One of my teachers lent me the Frances Hodgson Burnett trilogy: *A Little Princess*, *Little Lord Fauntleroy*, and *A Lady of Quality*. Mr Zheng Xiaocang, the translator of the books, was a well-known literary figure from Haining, where I was born, and everyone was very proud to claim him as a native son. And so that is why these foreign works of literature were rather popular in our province.

IKEDA: Jiangsu and Zhejiang provinces were known as a literary oasis, and just as a deep ocean trench hosts a biologically diverse population of marine life, and just as the abundant verdant overgrowth of a marsh attracts large flocks of birds and other wildlife, Jiangsu Province and the neighbouring province of Zhejiang produced an abundance of great literary figures. Historically speaking, this area was known as the most progressive region in China from a cultural and educational point of view.

Lu Xun, Zhang Binglin, and Mao Dun were all Chinese philosophers from the modern period, great 'knights of the pen', who were also from Zhejiang Province, your homeland. I cannot help but sense the depth of tradition from which you arose.

Mr Jin, what books did you most treasure as you were growing up? I am sure there were many, but please share your three favourite books.

JIN: The books that I loved the most were *The Water Margin*, *Romance of the Three Kingdoms*, and the great Alexandre Dumas's works, *The Three Musketeers* and the sequel. Wu Guangjian translated *The Three Musketeers* and its sequel into Chinese.

Besides these favourites, the book *Deux Ans de Vacances* (Two Years' Vacation) left a lasting impression on me. It is a tale of 15 boys who set out on an ocean voyage and have many adventures on an uninhabited island.

IKEDA: That's amazing. All the works you mentioned are books that I studied under my mentor, Josei Toda. They are precisely the ones that I used as my study texts.

I still remember the works I read. In the same volume in which *Deux Ans de Vacances* was published, there was *The Story of Robinson Crusoe*. Injecting a little humour into a comparison of his life in prison with the main character's life on the deserted island in *The Story of Robinson Crusoe*, Mr Toda quipped, 'This is fiction, because nowhere does it say anything about making salt'.

JIN: Bao Tianxiao, the translator of *Deux Ans de Vacances*, rendered the tale in an old-fashioned literary style, but fortunately my language skills were relatively good, so I could understand it. Mr Bao continued writing in Hong Kong until the 1950s. He passed away peacefully past 100 years of age.

The Lost Continent of Mu, also a favourite of mine in my youth, was a science fiction novel that opened up a world of adventure and fantasy for me.

Ten and several years ago, I had the opportunity to visit with the author An Zijie at his residence, and we touched on the topic of novels for children. It was then that I first learned that he had translated this work.

Because I could recall many details of the story, Mr An and I had a very enjoyable time discussing it. In the book, there was one passage about the Chinese prime minister's activities, and I found out that this did not exist in the original work, but was added by Mr An. This, undoubtedly, greatly increased interest in the book for Chinese readers, especially young readers.

What Inspires Literary Imagination?

IKEDA: How entertaining! The special appeal of the story-lines and their development makes the works that you just mentioned stand out as exceptional. I would like to discuss specific literary works more thoroughly in another chapter, but let me say here that this element of fascination and ability to elicit interest is very important.

Someone once said that a story has the power to bring disparate entities together and also the power to make them bond. I believe that whether the entities are humans and animals; humans and outer space; spirit and the physical body; men and women; the next world and this one; the past and the present or future; and so on, the ability to inspire interest is the essence of this power to bring these entities together and construct a single cosmology.

The word 'meaning' could be interchanged with the word 'interest'. At a very profound level, underlying both is the Mahayana Buddhist notion of enjoyment, as in, 'where living beings enjoy themselves at ease' – to quote from the sixteenth chapter of the Lotus Sutra – and the reason people have been born into this world is to experience joy.

On a related note, Mr Jin, do you think that literary creativity, specifically the capacity to construct an engaging story-line, is an innate talent? Or do you think that it is developed by environmental influences and personal effort?

JIN: I believe that it is an innate gift to be able to develop interesting story-lines and create literature. When I tell a story to my wife, children, or grandchildren, they seem to be more fascinated than when someone else tells them the same story. I am able to take an ordinary event and, by embellishing it with a little creative imagination, turn it into an enchanting tale. My wife always laughingly asks me, 'As usual, you made that up, didn't you? I don't know if it's true or made up.' However, the capacity to write is, I believe, developed through reading and hard work.

IKEDA: I agree. I also believe that what a child listens to in the early years is tremendously important. As you said, the creativity required to write great literature may be definitely a natural gift; however, the actualization of that potential is most likely made possible by experiences in childhood. So a lot depends on what kind of stories a child hears and from whom they hear them.

It is well known that great writers like Goethe and Pushkin grew up listening every night to folktales and other stories, told to them by their mothers or nannies. The characteristic feature of this oral tradition was the direct heart-to-heart transmission of the story from one person to another. In the course of the story, the storyteller and the listener together experience vibrant images that shape a shared world of meaning. In this sense, the story is more powerful in its oral delivery than when simply read from the page.

This quotation by Goethe truly expresses the heart of the matter: 'Writing is an abuse of language, reading silently to oneself is a pitiful substitute for speech. Man effects all he can upon man by his personality.'[6]

When the great masters of literature were young, storytellers fascinated them with stories of long ago, making their hearts dance to the excitement in their voices and nurturing the golden seedlings of their nascent Romanticism that would eventually develop into full-blown literary genius.

But that was in the old days. Now, we continue to lose the richness of that kind of pure and genuine communication.

A Best-Selling Author at 15

IKEDA: Childhood is an impressionable period. Your days began and ended with reading great books. Mr Jin, I have read that when you were 15, you and two friends published a reference book to help students studying for their junior high school entrance exams. And amazingly, it became an instant best seller.

JIN: We called the book *A Gift for Junior High School Entrance Exam Candidates*. The content was nothing extraordinary. We just assembled entrance exam questions from previous tests and combined these with analyses and answers. The feature that made the book a great success was that students could easily search for answers to their own questions. Our reference work was published in Zhejiang Province but was also sold in Fujian, Jiangxi, and other provinces. The profits from the publication provided financial support for all three of us after high school, all the way up until we entered the university in Chongqing.

The book did not help us to cultivate our literary talents; it was simply a commercial success. It was just a matter of some 15-year-old boys accurately understanding the needs of consumers – entrance exam students just like themselves – and meeting those needs in a clear and simple manner.

The success of the *Ming Pao* newspaper, which I founded subsequently, undoubtedly can also be attributed to this intuitive insight into reader psychology.

IKEDA: My mentor was an excellent mathematician who also wrote a best-selling reference work in his youth. It was entitled *A Deductive Guide to Arithmetic* and went into over 100 printings over the course of several years. His success must also have been due to his insight into the minds of his readers.

Mr Jin, I understand that at the young age of 17 you came to a major turning point in your life in regard to writing.

JIN: Yes. My authoritarian head instructor, Chen Naichang, expelled me from school for posting a wall newspaper that had satirical content. This was one of the worst crises I ever encountered in my entire life. Not only did my expulsion mean that I would be unable to continue my studies, but it would also deeply impact my ability to take care of my most basic needs. Afterward, with the help of the school principal and my friends, I was able to enrol in another school, but this episode was a life and death crisis for me.

IKEDA: Then, when you were still in your teens, your defiant spirit which would bloom later through the publication of your *Ming Pao* newspaper was given free rein.

JIN: I was never intimidated or pressured to censor my writing, but instead wrote whatever I wanted to say. And this in itself was a feature that later led to the success of *Ming Pao*.

When I was writing editorials and desperately defending the editorial principles of *Ming Pao*, I was of the mind that all irrationality should be opposed. In contrast, what I wrote in that wall newspaper was pure youthful impulsiveness, with no thought of the consequences, and due to this lack of thought, I brought a harsh reality upon myself. In retrospect, I can see that it was nothing more than a foolish act.

Fledging Editor Mentored by Josei Toda

JIN: President Ikeda, you grew up during World War II and so were robbed of the opportunity to receive an education. However, after becoming a member of Soka Gakkai and studying under Josei Toda, you progressed rapidly in your studies.

I have heard that during this time you were in charge of editing a children's magazine. I am sure that you overcame many difficulties: while devoting yourself to your studies, you were also acquiring an enormous amount of knowledge, out of necessity, for your job.

IKEDA: The first assignment that was entrusted to me at my mentor's publishing company was editing a children's magazine called *Boy's Adventure* (later changed to *Children's Japan*). I was 21 at the time. I was responsible for all aspects of the publication, from planning to soliciting manuscripts as well as editing and proofing. At times when it seemed that a solicited manuscript would not arrive in time and there would be a lack of content, I would have to make up for it by writing material myself. In short, this was when I was pressed, by necessity, to seriously devote myself to writing. I began to develop my writing under the strict tutelage of Mr Toda, and this has been the most valuable experience of my entire life.

More than anything else, I wanted to introduce children to the best works, and so I approached many different authors. As I discovered, however, authors are an eccentric lot, and they also tend to ignore manuscript deadlines. I would become so irritated. I often thought to myself, 'Don't they know how busy we are? How many times do I have to go knocking at their door?'

In addition to my job, I also attended night school. I was so busy every day, but I felt that if I was not passionate about learning, I could not create a magazine that would inspire children. So I made sure that I at least continued reading as much as I could.

JIN: President Ikeda, I have had a very similar experience. It was when I had the chance to edit a newspaper's arts and entertainment column. In addition to planning and editing, I also had occasion to write movie and theatre reviews. Although cinema critique was completely outside of my field of expertise, I became, out of necessity, obsessed with skimming theoretical works on film and the performing arts, and in a very short period of time became a semi-professional expert of sorts in these areas.

Despite my lack of practical experience, I had more theoretical knowledge and a greater understanding of theatrical and cinematic works than most people in the film and drama arena. After that experience, my modus operandi became 'Study quickly, apply instantly'.

People who do not know me well think that I am a scholar with extremely broad and substantial knowledge in many areas. In reality, when I am faced with a need for information, I immediately set about learning about the topic until I understand it. Then I discover that I have turned myself from an amateur into a pro of sorts.

IKEDA: You truly embody the saying, 'Necessity is the mother of invention'.

JIN: Incidentally, President Ikeda, you have asked me about my childhood reading experiences and favourite books, so now may I ask you to speak a little about the kinds of books you read and your study and reading experiences in your youth?

IKEDA: It would be a pleasure. Before I met my mentor, Mr Toda, I was self-taught, primarily in the fields of literature, philosophy, and poetry – fields to which I was greatly attracted. But after the war, books were scarce, and so some friends and I started a reading circle whose members lent each other their books. And in this way, we could read all the books in each other's collections.

I recall, off the top of my head, that some of the favourite titles in Japan during that time were by authors such as Kunikida Doppo (1871–1908), Tokutomi Roka (1868–1927), Ishikawa Takuboku (1886–1912), and Yoshida Genjirō (1897–1945). Also popular were works by philosophers like Nishida Kitarō and Miki Kiyoshi. Among Western authors we liked were Victor Hugo, Johann Wolfgang von Goethe, Henri-Louis Bergson, and Ralph Waldo Emerson. I read most of the works of Leo Tolstoy and was greatly influenced by the poetry of Walt Whitman.

In retrospect, I think that my poor health may have contributed to my strong attraction to themes exploring human nature, the meaning of life, and how to lead a good life. I was drawn more to works with, shall I say, a universal consciousness that strongly affirmed human life and a belief in human potential, as opposed to works with a negative and pessimistic perspective.

JIN: I can see how your reading choices have played a major role in shaping the person you are today.

IKEDA: For better or for worse. The first time I spoke at Harvard University (September 1991), I touched on the giants of the American Renaissance, such as Whitman, Emerson, and Thoreau. Professor Harvey Cox commented that next time, if possible, he would like to hear me discuss Melville. He caught me off guard! They say that a writer's talent is evident in their first work, and so it may be that the things that people learn when they are young may determine the course of their entire lives.

Youthful Aspirations and Obstacles

IKEDA: It has been fascinating to hear about your recollections of your youth. When you were young, what did you really want to be when you grew up? Did you want to become a great writer from the very start?

JIN: Actually, in my youth, I had a strong desire to become a diplomat. So I went to Chongqing, which was the capital of the People's Republic of China in those days, to pursue a higher education. I studied at the Central University Faculty of Foreign Languages, located in Chongqing.

After entering the university, I clashed with a student who was an undercover agent of the Nationalist Party and was expelled from the university. Then, after the war, I went to Shanghai to study international law at the Dongwu University Faculty of Law and after graduation continued on to conduct research in that same department.

In 1950, I moved to Beijing with the idea of entering the Ministry of Foreign Affairs of the People's Republic of China. This was at the invitation of Mr Mei Ju-ao, an advisor to the diplomatic corps at the time. Mr Mei was an international legal scholar and had been one of the judicial officers presiding over the International Military Tribunal for the Far East, charged with investigating Japanese war crimes.

I was advised by the current administrator of the Foreign Languages Faculty, Mr Qiao Guanhua, that based on my family background (that is, I came from a landowning family) and province of origin it would be best for me to work for a time in the Chinese People's Institute of Foreign Affairs, then transfer to the diplomatic corps. It seems that some of the events that occurred during this period have been misrepresented, so I want it to be known that Mr Qiao advised me with the best of intentions.

However, I was not pleased with this advice, because I thought that the Institute of those days simply issued international declarations and hosted foreign dignitaries. That is why I decided to return to the work that I had done before at the *Da Gong Bao*, one of the earliest and most influential newspapers published in China.

IKEDA: Your dream of becoming a diplomat was cut short, and perhaps it was just one of those setbacks that occur in youth. However, as the Chinese saying goes, 'Inscrutable are the ways of Heaven'. Sometimes it is possible for good to come of misfortune.

Former President Mikhail Gorbachev once told me that he had hoped at one time to be accepted for employment in the Soviet Police Agency in Moscow, and after graduation from college he had been informally offered employment. But suddenly this offer was rescinded and he had to return home. He said that he was in extreme shock after having his hopes for the future dashed in an instant.

Yet, if President Gorbachev's hopes had been fulfilled at that time, his life would have evolved very differently. Perhaps your case, Mr Jin, is very similar. After overcoming this setback in your youth, you became an authority whose broad perspectives of developments in Asia are heeded and whose views exert significant influence on the futures of Hong Kong and China. Perhaps we can say that the dreams of your youth have been realized far beyond your expectations.

JIN: When I look back on those days, I think that it was all for the best that my hope of becoming a diplomat did not materialize. I base this on seeing the experiences of many of my classmates who later achieved high office as ambassadors and consul generals in the Chinese Nationalist Party, or Guomindang, government. One after another, they have all lost their jobs and have ended up disillusioned and withdrawn from society. They cannot even live their lives as they wish.

During the time that I served on the Drafting Committee of the Basic Law of the Hong Kong Special Administrative Region of the People's Republic of China (also simply called the Hong Kong Basic Law), and later when I was a member of the government preparatory committee, I worked with as well as negotiated with many high-level bureaucrats in the Ministry of Foreign Affairs of the People's Republic of China. At this point in my life, however, I am not even slightly envious of them.

If it were possible to trade places with them and exchange their life experiences and achievements with my work as a novelist, commentator, and researcher, I would definitely refuse the offer. But please do not mis-understand, President Ikeda. I am certainly not saying that my current success is in any way greater than theirs.

IKEDA: I am well aware that you speak with humility in your heart.

JIN: What I mean to say is that I live my life as I please, according to my conscience. I have not been subject to the commands of superiors or the shackles of the bureaucrat, but instead am free to act and speak as I wish. Basically, I am saying that I enjoy living my life in such freedom.

I feel that I can make a much more significant contribution by writing social commentary supporting the sovereignty and dignity of the people and advocating for world peace in my newspaper, than if I had become a foreign service officer.

Every activity of a foreign diplomat is subject to rigid restrictions. That kind of life is completely unsuitable for a self-reliant maverick like me who does whatever he wants and could not care less about what others might say. If I had become a foreign diplomat, my whole life I probably would have felt so constrained and I would not have the happiness and joy that I know now.

CHAPTER 2

Creating Twenty-First Century People: Deng Xiaoping and the Return of Hong Kong

Deng Xiaoping's Proposal for the Future of Hong Kong

IKEDA: Mr Jin, as you know, Deng Xiaoping, the person who built the foundation for China's dramatic development, passed away on 19 February 1997. I had the opportunity to meet this great man on two occasions. In our first meeting, Deng made this unforgettable statement about the history of Japanese militarism. He said, 'Throughout the over 2,000-year history of contact between the countries of Japan and China, we have never been at odds except for a short period of less than 100 years. The scourge of Japanese militarism devastated the lives of Chinese people, but the Japanese people were also victimized.'

By this, Deng Xiaoping indicated that we should not view the conflict as one country pitted against another; that is, China versus Japan. I was impressed by the Chinese wisdom which holds that history must be told through the eyes of the people – which is to say that one must stand on the side of the people, no matter what country it is. In his last speech, Premier Zhou Enlai firmly asserted, 'We will never vie for hegemony as a nation. . . . We will always stand up for the peoples and ethnicities throughout the world who suffer oppression.' Deng's thought, I felt, echoed Zhou's assertion in that speech.

In our second discussion, we shared our perspectives on the China–Japan Peace and Friendship Treaty. On that occasion, Deng frankly expressed China's position on the necessity for an 'anti-hegemony provision' in the treaty, saying, 'It is imperative that no country in the Asia-Pacific region, including China and Japan, seek to gain dominance over all others'.

Several years before this, in my novel *The Human Revolution*, I asserted that 'Japan should negotiate treaties of peace and amity with every nation of the world, and that the signing of such a treaty with neighbouring China should take top priority'. Three years after my conversation with Deng, the Treaty of Peace and Friendship between Japan and the People's Republic of China, which expressed the earnest desires of the peoples of Japan and China, was concluded.

Mr Jin, in your first interview with Deng in July 1981, you covered a broad range of topics, including his views on the prospects for China's economic development, the Cultural Revolution, and the relationship between China and the US.

Especially notable was this question that Deng asked of you. He asked, 'What opinion do you have, as a journalist, of us, the leaders of China?' Your response was straightforward. You said that you wanted China to keep in place its long-standing policies, without alteration.

Your answer seemed to reflect the issue that was foremost in your mind – that is, the future of Hong Kong. You explained that the most important way to alleviate the unease that the people of Hong Kong felt about their future was for China to refrain from making arbitrary policy changes. You were able to get right to the point and address the people's concerns.

Deng responded with complete agreement. This was a magnificent scene – a discussion of critical issues, with creative sparks flying, between a great author and a great politician.

JIN: Deng was very intent on establishing the Basic Law of the Hong Kong Special Administrative Region. When the Drafting Committee of the Basic Law convened our first meeting in Beijing, Deng and the other main Chinese leaders met with the committee and had a commemorative photograph taken of the entire group.

Prior to this, Deng had designed and formulated the governing principles that became the foundation of policies that would be implemented after Hong Kong's return to China, such as: (1) 'One country, two systems' in which the social and economic systems as well as the lifestyle of the people, including their civil rights and freedoms, would remain unchanged, (2) 'Hong Kong governed by the people of Hong Kong', and (3) 'High-level self-government'. These principles were incorporated into the Joint Declaration of the Government of the United Kingdom of Great Britain and Northern Ireland and the Government of the People's Republic of China on the Question of Hong Kong (Beijing, 19 December 1984), and after that, we used them in drafting the Basic Law.

Therefore, it would not be an overstatement to say that Deng himself played a major role in the establishment of the Basic Law, which was shortly thereafter implemented in Hong Kong. We members of the Drafting Committee put his proposal in writing, doing nothing more than to supplement specific content and administrative details to enable implementation.

IKEDA: So, the structure of the Basic Law of the Hong Kong Special Administrative Region legislation was built upon the solid foundation provided by Deng.

Incidentally, you mentioned the Joint Declaration agreement. The negotiations between the two countries took quite a long time, but it appeared that the guiding principles offered by Deng were accepted readily by the United Kingdom.

JIN: Yes. The task of completing the Joint Declaration was certainly an extremely lengthy process. Most of the time was spent on articulating and interpreting phraseology and terminology.

When it became clear that the Chinese negotiators were taking a reasonable and broad perspective with numerous points sympathetic to the Hong Kong people, the British were so happy, they could not help but dance for joy at this unexpected development. Their predictions were exceeded and hopes fulfiled far more than they had expected by the Chinese proposals.

IKEDA: What do you think that the British were initially expecting?

JIN: Well, first of all, since China was a socialist country led by the Chinese Communist Party, they had anticipated that after Hong Kong's return to China, it would certainly be governed in the same way as Shanghai and Tianjin.

They thought that the governor and bureaucrats who would govern Hong Kong would all be dispatched from Beijing. All businesses, both large and small, without exception, would be nationalized and placed under government control. All existing Hong Kong laws would be abolished and replaced with Chinese laws. The judicial system, consisting of the courts, judges, and lawyers, would be changed to conform to the Chinese legal system. The Hong Kong dollar would be scrapped and use of the Chinese currency renminbi would become mandatory. Banks such as the Hong Kong and Shanghai Banking Corporation Limited and the Standard Chartered Bank, many of whose investors are British, and businesses such as Jardine Matheson Holdings, Swire Group, and Cathay Pacific Airways would be taken over by the Chinese government and administration would be assigned to the state.

The market economy would be replaced with a command-control economy, and people's rights such as freedom of expression and freedom of movement, that is, the right to travel abroad, would all be severely curtailed.

IKEDA: Instead, as they discovered, the Chinese proposals were realistic and extremely flexible.

JIN: Yes. Surprisingly, China said that even after Hong Kong's return, it would support Hong Kong's capitalist economy and not insist that Hong Kong adopt a socialist system. They even announced that the people would not have to change their lifestyles and could also continue to elect their own representatives to their own government, and generally enjoy a high degree of self-government.

It is doubtful that the British would have asked for anything so ideal. Therefore, it was completely unnecessary to debate any basic principles of governance or administration. The negotiations between China and the British focused mainly on the technical issues of the transfer.

The reason that the Chinese proposed to incorporate the above principles into the Joint Declaration was not because they grew out of the negotiations. Rather, they wanted the Chinese government's policy to be clearly articulated in the context of an international treaty. Their intention was to reassure the people of Hong Kong and ensure that the world would continue to be confident in Hong Kong's leadership.

IKEDA: I see. So, Deng, the mastermind of reform and liberation, played a major role in Hong Kong's future.

JIN: Yes. That is true. If you want to understand how Deng contributed to Hong Kong and the welfare of its people, perhaps you can think about it in this way.

If Deng had not made these recommendations for the future of Hong Kong, and if he had not actively promoted these plans with his authority, personal popularity, inner strength, and insight to bring about the situation that we have today, then, following 1 July 1997, we can only imagine the scenarios that would have played out.

It is possible that, beginning several years before the return of Hong Kong, the situation would have become chaotic and spun out of control. Undoubtedly, conditions would have worsened from a lack of sound municipal management, causing people to be concerned for their safety.

The Role of Deng Xiaoping, the Master Architect of Reform and Liberation

IKEDA: With that said, Deng must have looked forward to the day of the return of Hong Kong with high emotions. As he so famously said, 'After the return of Hong Kong, I look forward to celebrating the Chinese New Year there'.

It has been fascinating to hear about Hong Kong and Deng's role in planning its return to China. To bring us to the present day, I would like to ask how you view Deng and his role in China's evolution in recent times.

JIN: If it had not been for Deng Xiaoping, China would surely not have developed to the point it has today. Shortly after the Tiananmen Square incident of 4 June 1989, I wrote an article entitled 'If This Is a Race to See Who Lives the Longest, I Want Deng Xiaoping to Win', in my *Ming Pao* newspaper (6 August issue). The gist of the article went something like this:

> Many of the powerbrokers of the Chinese Communist Party still hold on to their conservative ideas and are opposed to any reforms or freedoms. Even so, if only Deng Xiaoping stands firm on the path to reform and liberation, he can serve as that single ray of light to guide China to a hopeful future.
>
> Those who oppose this path toward reform and freedom are getting quite old. If Deng remains healthy and of sound mind, those who oppose him will not be able to interfere. I fervently wish him good health and long life so that he may outlive the old-timers making up the opposition.

An old Chinese proverb posits, 'On this one person depends the survival of heaven and earth'. The saying refers to an important figure, and the expression 'heaven and earth' here refers to the country of China in its entirety.

I believe that this expression had the same meaning in Japanese during the Warring States Period (15th to 17th centuries) in Japan. Whenever 'heaven and earth' was mentioned, this referred to all of Japan.

IKEDA: Yes. That is correct. In Japan, the expression 'heaven and earth' was meant to refer to the entire Japanese land mass. Of course, in Japan's case, this 'heaven and earth' covered a much smaller area. And even though much was made of it, the actual land area was equivalent to only about one Chinese province.

JIN: For about the last 20 years of his life, Deng Xiaoping was that one important person who literally held the future of China in his hands. If Deng had not been in the picture in China in 1978, we would have witnessed great misfortune throughout the entire country.

IKEDA: I am sure that China watchers around the world would want to know what the prospects are for China following Deng Xiaoping, and what this means for Hong Kong as well.

JIN: Deng preferred to be called 'the master architect'. Others, including myself, likened him to a standard bearer in the sense that he was the one who stood at the head of the column, pressing forward with the banner of reform and freedom. He did not relish this title, however, because he said that one of the members of the 'Gang of Four', Jiang Qing, Mao Zedong's wife, had dubbed herself 'standard bearer'. So Deng had an aversion to the image as well as the title.

The image of standard bearer brings to mind the person at the head of the column of soldiers on horseback, holding high a majestic banner, calling out loudly to the troops, leading the surge forward to strike the enemy ranks. This is clearly incongruous with the position of Commander in Chief. The aspects of this image that are most striking are the folly of rushing blindly into battle and the lack of strategic planning for a steady advance one step at a time. The title of 'master architect' seems far more appropriate for a courageous and illustrious commander.

IKEDA: I definitely agree with that.

JIN: Based on precise drawings and intricate calculations, a master architect renders plans for a massive structure, both interior and exterior, in its entirety. The architectural style that is chosen will determine the construction plans, processes, and choice of materials. Once the design plans are completed, before anything else, the architect conducts an inspection to make sure that there are no oversights, and if there are, they are addressed.

Following this, everyone involved participates in a discussion so that opinions are elicited from every perspective, with the objective being to eliminate any defects or safety issues and create a perfect plan. Then, when the design proposal is accepted, a building company is chosen to do the construction. The master architect must, even after construction begins, oversee and inspect the progress in terms of the correct sequence of tasks, conformity to code and standards, and the status of the final product.

If, by some misfortune, this master architect passes away before the project is completed, it would be a severe and unfathomable loss. However, fortunately, in that case, the entire design plan would already have been completely perfected and the appropriately skilled technical staff and workers already chosen. Also, most of the first stage of construction would already be going smoothly. All that remained to be done then would be to continue with the construction, based on the design plan.

Therefore, the builders must by no means allow themselves to become confused, argue about details, or arbitrarily change aspects of the design plan or blueprints. There should be no problem as long as they get down to work, proceed according to sequence, and advance the project one stage at a time.

IKEDA: And so if China continues on this path of reform and liberation in a calm and balanced manner, Hong Kong will undoubtedly benefit also.

JIN: Yes. It goes without saying that it is important for Hong Kong to be the object of this design. However, in contrast to the entire country of China, Hong Kong is but one tiny area. But if China, the enormous and majestic skyscraper is impeccably built on a solid foundation, then Hong Kong, a tiny room in the skyscraper will certainly not be shabby.

A Free Man: Mr Jin's First Step Toward Hong Kong

IKEDA: I see what you mean. Now, getting back to our discussion of your life story, I believe that you left the Chinese mainland for Hong Kong in 1948. You were 24 at the time, weren't you?

JIN: Yes. Two years before that, during the summer of 1946, I entered the newspaper business. First, I was employed by the *Dongnan Ribao* (Southeastern Daily) in Hangzhou where I worked as a reporter and interviewer for the English international news.

IKEDA: Hangzhou is a scenic place, known as the Venice of the East ever since the days of Marco Polo long ago. I went there once in 1974 during my second visit to China.

JIN: Is that so? During my second year there, I heard that Shanghai's *Da Gong Bao* was looking for a translator for the international news, so I immediately applied and took the application exam. Because I had been trained professionally, my score was fairly decent, and I was hired with no problem. Then, because the newspaper was no longer able to publish in Shanghai, the following year it reestablished its operations in Hong Kong. This was when I was dispatched to Hong Kong.

IKEDA: I have heard that your entry into Hong Kong was not without incident. Apparently, you boarded the Shanghai-to-Hong Kong flight in high spirits, but after takeoff, you discovered that, in your haste, you had neglected to take any money with you. You suddenly broke into a cold sweat. Coincidentally, Pan Gonbi, the president of the *Guomin Ribao* (Citizen's Daily), happened to be on the same flight, and noticing your discomfort, he asked you what was wrong. When you told him of your predicament, he lent you $10, and so you were able to make it to your newspaper office.

What an amusing episode, and what an appropriate anecdote with which to raise the curtain on the drama of your amazingly eventful life. To begin, please describe your first impressions of Hong Kong.

JIN: My very first impressions were of the stifling heat and the fact that I could not understand a thing that people were saying because they were speaking in the Cantonese. At that time, I had no idea that a town that I felt completely lost in would end up becoming my home for close to 50 years, or over half of my life.

I married my wife, raised my children, wrote novels, and established a newspaper company in Hong Kong. My family and my business were both created in Hong Kong. Having said that, however, I must admit that because I had lived in Shanghai for many years, my impression was that

Hong Kong seemed slightly behind the times in the economic as well as cultural spheres. I felt that I had arrived at a somewhat rustic and unsophisticated place off the beaten track.

Nevertheless, I felt that the people of Hong Kong were honest, and that they placed a high value on trust in their personal relationships, so you could be assured that they would stand behind their word. I immediately grew to like these people. They expressed more warmth than the people of Shanghai, and I felt that they were more like the people in small- to medium-sized cities in China's interior provinces than people living in a large international metropolis. With Hong Kong's increasing prosperity, however, it was these characteristics of the people that changed most rapidly.

IKEDA: I also am quite drawn to the Hong Kongese. My most vivid impression of Hong Kong is that it is teeming with 'real people'. I recall your editorial for the *Ming Pao* entitled 'Hong Kong Has No Treasures, Except for Its Freedom!' in which you wrote, 'The main reason that many of us love living in Hong Kong is that this is clearly a free place'.

Since your youth, you have loved freedom and have cultivated an adversarial stance toward power and authority. Perhaps Hong Kong, harbour of freedom, was perfectly suited to your temperament and perspective as a freedom-loving person.

The *Ming Pao* Daily Newspaper: Its Founding and Editorial Principles

IKEDA: Mr Jin, you gained notoriety as the 'King of Free Speech' for publishing and heading up Hong Kong's major daily newspaper *Ming Pao* for over 30 years. When *Ming Pao* was founded in 1959, you started with only four employees. It was quite a while before operations began to go smoothly, and at one point people speculated that it would not last long – perhaps only one or two more years.

As we discussed previously, I had a similar experience: I worked at the publishing company run by my mentor and later helped him found the *Seikyo Shimbun*, the daily organ of the Soka Gakkai. The harsh, rough-and-tumble newspaper and publishing industry was full of difficulties. And to think that you managed both the operations and the editing! I can imagine, based on my own experience, the travails you must have encountered.

JIN: Let's see. The *Seikyo Shimbun* was established in 1951, wasn't it? It was eight years prior to the founding of *Ming Pao*. I understand that the *Seikyo Shimbun* has grown to be the third most widely circulated in Japan. The daily circulation is now 5.5 million copies. The *Ming Pao* pales in comparison. In the past 30 to 40 years, the population of Hong Kong has more than doubled, and the circulation of *Ming Pao* has consistently remained in a range proportionate to the population. Even if we compare again in eight years, there is no way that *Ming Pao* can overtake the *Seikyo Shimbun*.

The one aspect that our newspapers share is that they both started from scratch and developed gradually after surviving periods of difficulty and struggle.

IKEDA: Thank you for your kind words of encouragement. My mentor always said that he hoped that all Japanese people would one day read the *Seikyo Shimbun*. I have taken his wish to heart and have been determined to enable people all around the world to read our newspaper. In response to your encouragement, I will strive all the harder to make our newspaper the best it can be.

JIN: I believe that our two newspapers are based on very similar principles. I recall that Mr Toda emphasized that a newspaper must inspire trust in its readers. I agree wholeheartedly.

'Ming', the first character of our name *Ming Pao*, expresses meanings such as 'clear principles', 'clearly understanding the difference between right and wrong', 'being able to distinguish fine distinctions', 'making clear impartial judgments, as if looking into a finely polished mirror', 'seeing oneself especially with unclouded eyes', and 'being fair and transparent'.

In terms of political leanings, we refrain from siding with the Communist Party or the Chinese Nationalist Party. We go to great lengths to fact-check stories, to ensure the accuracy of reporting, and to offer fair and principled analyses and commentary.

IKEDA: My mentor once said, 'Journalism without integrity is as insubstantial as smoke'. The editorial principles of *Ming Pao*, which you have just described, align closely with my mentor's beliefs. I sense a profound resonance.

The *Seikyo Shimbun* differs from *Ming Pao* in the sense that it is basically an organ publication, but we have endeavoured to position it as a people's paper rather than simply the official newspaper of a religious organization.

When I had the opportunity to speak with world-famous violinist Yehudi Menuhin (1916–99) in April 1992, he said, 'I have a question for you. I have the greatest admiration for how this lay Buddhist organization has developed. What has been the secret to its growth?'

I responded by saying, 'First of all, of course, we strictly observe the doctrine of our faith, and strive to be a people-centred organization. We have advanced our movement as a religion for the people – not simply a religion for its own sake.' We have succeeded in creating a wide-ranging and accessible humanist network founded on faith. In this sense, the *Seikyo Shimbun* is a vehicle for enlightened humanism.

In this regard, do you have any guiding principle for *Ming Pao*?

JIN: Yes. I chose the following ancient Chinese proverb for our company's guiding principle. It is, 'Be broad-minded, refrain from any hint of greed, and cultivate decisiveness'. In other words, a newspaper must accommodate many different opinions and perspectives. The editorial department must not hold any bias or refuse to print viewpoints with which it disagrees. At the same time, no one involved with the newspaper, be they president or employee, should be permitted to use the paper for fraudulent ends or to gain unreasonable and excessive profit. In addition, the newspaper must be completely fair and transparent, beyond reproach, and the employees must commit themselves to serve and benefit the readership.

IKEDA: It is easy to give lip service to the principle advising 'fairness and transparency, beyond reproach', but taking the high road is difficult. As you spoke, I sensed that your every word resonated with your conviction to take the high road, which you have done consistently throughout your career. This unwavering commitment to principle earned you the title Champion of Free Speech.

Some time ago, I posed a challenge to the reporters and correspondents of the *Seikyo Shimbun*. I told them to 'respond to our readers freely and with flexibility, address their concerns in a way that they can comprehend (exposition of the Law in accordance with people's capacities, as they say in Buddhism), by expressing empathy with their joy; by giving them encouragement to face their grief; wisdom and new knowledge when their mind becomes dull, and point the way when they digress, help articulate when there is confusion, protect the weak, cool heated tempers, and melt the resistance of the hardheads'.

I urged the correspondents, as men and women of the press, to fulfil their mission and responsibility to Soka Gakkai members as well as to all of their readers, and to always treasure the people's perspective. My desire for them has not changed.

The Mission and Responsibility of Journalists to Challenge Unbridled Power

IKEDA: During your long career as a writer and champion of the press, what is it about *Ming Pao* are you most proud of? Please share your thoughts with our readers.

JIN: *Ming Pao* progressed through a number of important stages in its development, and in each one we stood resolutely by our principles.

At the end of the 1950s, China, the USSR, and also India became mired in conflict. Military intervention was an aspect of these conflicts, causing the fires of war to burn heatedly, and *Ming Pao* chose to side with China. Then, in the mid-1960s, China tested a nuclear bomb. At that time, *Ming Pao* voiced strong opposition and therefore was the target of intense denunciation by left-wing newspapers.

In the late 1960s and 1970s, China promoted the Cultural Revolution. During that time, *Ming Pao* opposed Mao Zedong, Lin Biao, and the Gang of Four's extreme leftist policies, as well as the violence the extreme left wing threatened to foment in Hong Kong. As a result, they retaliated by trying to scare us and warned that they would assassinate me or bomb our office. In spite of this, we did our best to protect Chinese culture and support the rational course advocated by Zhou Enlai, Deng Xiaoping, and Peng Dehuai.

IKEDA: All of this will be remembered as your immortal battle with pen.

JIN: In the late 1970s, *Ming Pao* fervently supported reforms and liberalization policies advocated by Deng Xiaoping. I was fortunate to have the opportunity to make the acquaintance of leaders such as Deng Xiaoping and Hu Yaobang.

Then, in the 1980s, *Ming Pao* expressed its support for the return of Hong Kong and the restoration of sovereignty to China. I personally participated in drafting the Basic Law of the Hong Kong Special Administrative Region. During this time, *Ming Pao* opposed the construction of a nuclear power plant in Daya Bay near Hong Kong. And, in 1989, we criticized the frenzy of the student movement while also attacking the Beijing authorities for using armed force and firing on the student and democracy movement protestors.

IKEDA: Your newspaper did not simply test the wind currents of the day and side with whichever seemed most advantageous. You advocated the positions that you thought were right and opposed those that you felt needed to be opposed.

As I hear more about your life, I can understand why your writing is so well received by the people. I think it is because the standard by which you have always measured your writing is the degree to which it benefited the people. For example, at a time when the nature of the Cultural Revolution was understood only superficially, you astutely observed that it was a struggle for power and did not hesitate to say so. You were able to see the true nature of the situation before others did.

Your keen observations were even more insightful precisely because you always stood on the people's side. If one were to become detached from the people – this deep and profound terra firma – even a grand statement of one million words would be superficial and worthless verbiage. Every decision must be judged based on its contribution to the common good; that is, the welfare of the people. The reason you have been acknowledged and honoured is because you have acted on this wisdom throughout your life.

Your writings express a profound affection for the people. This tendency in your writings has undoubtedly made the pressure you have been subjected to even more severe.

JIN: I have always spoken out about my beliefs, regardless of the consequences, and so my life has been threatened and I have become a target for assassination. At times, I have had to directly stand up to enormous pressures. But the distinction between right and wrong, and between virtue and malevolence, has always been obvious to me. And so I never buckled under the pressure of unjust and irrational power, no matter how threatening.

IKEDA: I have a profound respect for people who have struggled against severe oppression and been persecuted for their beliefs. This is because I feel that to be persecuted is itself evidence of a person's commitment to a just cause and that those who do not experience persecution must be compromising or deceptive in some way.

I wonder how many champions of the press such as yourself there are, Mr Jin. I wonder how many there are, especially in Japan. In a *Ming Pao* editorial, you explained the meaning of freedom of expression as follows: 'Freedom of expression means that people are allowed to express all kinds of opinions without government restriction, intervention, or punishment.'

In other words, the underlying principle is that the people's freedom of expression is protected from authoritarian pressure. Writers and journalists are the ones who fight against the unjust and powerful. The fundamental mission of the press is to fight to protect the people from the arbitrary abuse of power.

Mr Jin, you also admonished writers and journalists on what the stance of the press should be. 'Just as there are limits to the freedoms that individuals have, freedom of expression is also restricted by law. The most general limitation is that when a person exercises his or her right, another person's freedoms are not infringed upon. The mass media must not engage in mudslinging, character assassination, demagoguery, or distortion or falsification of the facts. This is because these acts infringe on the rights of others and are offensive to a sense of public dignity and decorum.'

I believe that this is an enduring principle recognized by all journalists and members of the media.

JIN: Yes. I have based my career on this conviction.

IKEDA: A seventeenth-century man of letters, Gu Yanwu, declared forcefully, 'Writing must be, in all cases, a benefit to heaven and earth.' In other words, he meant that the ability to express one's opinion must never vanish from society. Freedom of expression is what helps clarify the direction in which humankind must proceed, makes governments just, provides insight into the suffering of the people, and leads the way to human virtue. And, if expression takes these forms, it is a benefit to all heaven and earth. It leads to a better future. The more writing there is – even one work more – the better.

If, however, the content is fantasy, mimicry, or flattery, such kinds of writing should not exist. Such writing only leads one to decadence and debauchery. It provides no benefit to society. The more there is of it, the greater the damage to society (*Ri Zhi Lu* [Daily Accumulation of Knowledge], summary).

Free speech is an act that bears a heavy responsibility to benefit society. An enlightened sense of self-awareness is required for this task. Those who call themselves journalists and writers must carry within their hearts a fiery flame, a mission to create value for society.

Speak with Wholesome Words from a Wholesome Heart for a Wholesome Future!

JIN: President Ikeda, your contribution to world peace is so outstanding. There may be people who fail to appreciate the importance of what you have done, but I believe that the truth, in the end, is still the truth. No matter how much someone tries to denigrate and paint another with lies, ultimately the truth will be known.

Shakyamuni also endured envy and entrapment by lies. There is a well-known story in which a woman came to Shakyamuni when he was preaching, and intending to malign him, she said, 'Shakyamuni, this is your child', pointing to her large stomach, which was actually large because she concealed a large bowl under her clothes.

IKEDA: Regarding the anecdote of Shakyamuni, I would like to introduce the following word, 'A lie written with charcoal cannot hide the facts written in blood.'[1]

As you said, no matter how you look at it, a lie will always be a lie. So, when people lie and intend to deceive someone, before long, unbeknownst to themselves, they have inflicted damage upon themselves. They have destroyed their integrity, that part of themselves that is most pure. And finally, this leads to great unhappiness.

I do not care what people write about me. What I fear the most is that writers who deceive people will go unchallenged, and before we realize it, people will, over time, begin to have less trust in language.

Some people feel no joy upon seeing another's happiness. Rather, for some reason, they are enlivened by the misfortunes and scandalous rumours they hear about others. Perhaps this is one dimension of human nature. Nonetheless, I feel that there is too much of this kind of writing that stirs up these unhealthy sentiments.

Most of the writing people encounter is like that, and so they begin to see words as injurious to people and a means to denigrate them. They end up viewing language in those terms. This is a serious problem.

Just as Socrates associated misology, or hatred of language, with misanthropy, or hatred of human beings, originally language and people were closely related. Words or language represented human expression and feeling. The decay of language contributes to the depravation of the human heart, and depraved and decadent language surely leads to decadence of the human spirit. Loss of trust in language is equivalent to a loss of trust in humanity.

For this reason, what is needed at this point in time is to recover our trust in language. We must return to a sense of wholesomeness of mind and spirit, by recovering a sense of wholesomeness in language.

Members of the mass media must be the ones to stand on the frontlines of this effort and proclaim a bright and wholesome future for humankind through wholesome language and sincere expression.

In a sense, words and expression are like a sword. A sword that is used to protect people and save those in danger is a sacred treasure. However, a sword that is used to defame and hurt others is a weapon of malice and cruelty. And there are so many of these kinds of swords. I wonder what the heroes in your novels would do, Mr Jin, if they found themselves in the Japan of today.

JIN: I am sure that the last thing they would do is remain silent.

I always find myself using the characters that I have concocted in my martial arts novels as models of behaviour, and I tell myself, 'When confronted with imminent danger, I must not behave cowardly or shrink from it, even if I feel terrified inside. If I do, I won't be able to look the heroes in my novels in the eye.'

President Ikeda, you were opposed to the invasion of China, and I have heard that, because of your advocacy for world peace, you have suffered much intimidation and have received threats on your life from violent elements of the opposition. I greatly admire your daring spirit and courageous refusal to be intimidated by anyone.

IKEDA: Thank you for such generous praise, but now let us turn to the issue of living a life of principle. Perhaps the most noble human life is one in which a person sacrifices his life for his convictions.

Those who devote themselves to freely expressing their views are, in a sense, representatives of the people. In China there is an expression 'Wenzhang Xingguo', or 'a written work founds a nation'. This suggests that written expression can at times form the foundation of a nation and help establish a society. That is how powerful the act of expression can be. Those who make their living by the pen have taken on a mission of great responsibility. The highest honour is surely reserved for those who are prepared to die for their convictions and to advance the cause of justice.

JIN: Certainly, in the history of China and Japan there are many loyal warriors who sacrificed their lives rather than abandon their convictions. Every time I read their writings, I am captivated by this written legacy, and hold these heroes in the highest esteem.

IKEDA: Focusing in on the Chinese historical record, we find it engraved with the writings of many courageous writers who laid their lives on the line to write what they believed to be true.

I once told this story to a group of youths. I told them that in the Spring and Autumn Period of Chinese history (770–403 BCE), Cui Zhu, the ruler of the kingdom of Qi, killed his Lord Duke Zhuang. The historian of Qi recorded this fact in his historical records; that is, that Cui Zhu had killed Duke Zhuang in an act of treachery. The historian was unafraid of retribution from the powerful ruler and did not falsify his historical writing. He recorded the facts as they were. But this angered Cui Zhu and he had the historian killed.

Then, the historian's younger brother wrote of the same historical event. And Cui Zhu killed him too. Next, another younger brother stepped up and wrote about the same incident. When other historians from the countryside heard about the travails of the historian and his brothers, they rushed to the capitol to themselves insist on the truthful recording of the event.

So after going to such lengths to suppress the truth, the proud and powerful Cui Zhu was forced to accept failure, and the historical record remained as it was written for future generations.

To be willing to give one's life to write the truth . . . This takes fierce and single-minded determination. For those who follow this code of honour, every word is like a drop of blood written upon the slate of one's life. To falsify the record, even in the face of power and intimidation, would incur shame for generations to come.

Stories such as these impress upon us the kind of profound courage and determination that it took to be a writer in those days.

JIN: Writers and journalists today should sincerely take to heart these examples of courage.

IKEDA: When we consider the state of the mass media today, it is clear that we cannot rely only on the capacity of people working in the industry to reform it. This is also a problem for average citizens who are consumers of media information.

We are currently overwhelmed by massive amounts of information. However, we cannot say with any certainty that human beings have become any wiser because of this abundance of information. Rather, the reality is that people are drowning in a surge of information. It may be that people's lives have been enriched by access to so much information, but conversely, it also may be that the human spirit has become ineffectual and weak.

My mentor, Mr Toda, would encourage young people by telling them, 'Youth are the eyes of Japan. You must have sharp powers of perception.'[2] He felt that young people must discern the truth with their own eyes and cultivate the capacity to distinguish right from wrong. If people, and especially the young, are unable to develop this ability, they may forever drift like rootless weeds on the tide.

Recent human rights abuses reported in the mass media have come to light thanks mainly to citizen-based movements in the US and Europe. Greater access and development of public media infrastructure is continuing. I am in favour of this. However, in order for this structure to function effectively, it is essential that citizens conducting oversight be able to distinguish truth from falsehood.

It is therefore necessary, ultimately, for the average person to develop the discernment necessary to the task. So, each person must have the wisdom and clarity of purpose to assess societal trends and the direction in which society must proceed.

When I spoke at Harvard University on the role that Mahayana Buddhism must play in the twenty-first century, I suggested that, 'In an age marked by widespread religious revival, we need always ask: Does religion make people stronger or weaker? Does it encourage what is good or what is evil in them? Are they made better and wiser by religion?'[3]

I maintained that it is necessary to gauge the impact of a religion. I believe that a true religion is one that provides a steadfast moral compass for the development of a strong and courageous human character.

JIN: As I mentioned in my lecture at Soka University (April 1996), in today's world, technological innovation and productivity are advancing at a phenomenal rate. However, I cannot help thinking that humankind has not advanced at all since the ages of great teachers such as Shakyamuni,

Confucius, Socrates, Plato, all of whom lived 2,500 years ago, and Jesus, in terms of the principles, wisdom, and insight required for harmonious human relationships. Moreover, they still do not understand the fundamental principles expressed by these sages of old and are not even open to learning about them. As things stand now, humankind is not up to the challenge of dealing rationally and safely with the advanced technology we have acquired. It is as if we are a child of eight or nine years of age that has been given a machine gun or a hand grenade. This creates an extremely dangerous situation because we have no concept of how much damage we can do.

When we discuss the meaning of 'value', most people do not go beyond immediately thinking, 'I wonder how much that costs?' or, 'If I bought this, how much would I have to pay?' Their understanding of value is basically limited to the cost of a product.

Our current situation is that people do not fully utilize the spiritual resources available to them, or they lack the capacity to do so.

Friendship: Life's Ultimate Treasure and Testament to one's Humanity

IKEDA: If I were to draw one conclusion from all my experiences during a somewhat turbulent and eventful life, I would say that friendship is life's ultimate experience. Marcus Tullius Cicero wrote in his well-known work entitled *On Friendship*, 'It is like taking the sun out of the world to bereave human life of friendship'.[4] Indeed, true friendship permeates our lives with the warmth and brilliance of the sun. It is the greatest treasure of our lives.

JIN: I agree completely. I know that in my life, the spirit of friendship is a very important and precious sentiment. It is as important to me as my relationships with my parents, my brothers and sisters, and my wife.

IKEDA: Zhu Xi expounded on the nature of friendship in these terms. He stated, 'Friendship is not simply for the purpose of relaxation and enjoyment. It is to assist people in achieving their highest potential.' (*Jin Si Lu* [Reflections of Things at Hand])

Sima Guang, in his historical work *Comprehensive Mirror to Aid in Government*, said of friendship, 'When friends converse, each one challenges the other to be the best that he can be'. Of course, in a casual relationship or one in which one blindly follows the other, this does not apply. Nothing is more beautiful than a friendship in which both people encourage each other toward greater development and fulfilment.

Let me relate a story about deep friendship that I once heard. It seems that in Chinatown in Los Angeles, during several days of riots sparked by the Rodney King verdict on 29 April 1992, the people of Chinatown all stood up as one to protect their neighbourhood, and consequently the rioters were unable to cause mayhem and destruction in the area. This is a display of the power of racial solidarity, but even more, I believe it shows the close bonds of friendship in the Chinese community and the spiritual character of the Chinese people.

Mr Jin, I think that the martial arts novels you write have an aspect to them that honours friendship between warriors. In fact, isn't the Chinese character 'kyo', used in the word 'martial', in a certain sense, a synonym for 'friendship?'

JIN: Yes. You are absolutely correct. Friendship does constitute a major aspect of the meaning of this character. If I may add to this, the character is always associated with the word 'chivalry'. The Chinese have an especially high regard for a chivalrous spirit. This is the reason that General Guan Yu, a character in *Romance of the Three Kingdoms*, was so highly revered. Chivalry also led the heroes in the novel *The Water Margin* to take an oath, as blood brothers, to live and die together.

IKEDA: To express this thought in a word more familiar to the Japanese, we would say *shingi* or loyalty. In *Romance of the Three Kingdoms*, Cao Cao fled after he was beaten at the Battle of the Red Cliff, but Guan Yu blocked his escape route. Under ordinary circumstances, Guan Yu would have readily slain his opponent. But he remembered the debt of gratitude that he had incurred, and because of this, he forgave Cao Cao and let him go free. Stories that emphasize this sense of honour and obligation to reciprocate for kindnesses received seem to me to illustrate the moral character of the Chinese people.

Mr Jin, many of these kinds of stories exploring the nature of loyalty and friendship can be found in your work.

JIN: Yes, that's true. For example, the blood brothers of The Red Flower Society, who appear in *The Book and the Sword*, share deep feelings of affection for each other and express a profound sense of chivalry in their relationships.

The Legend of the Condor Heroes pits friendship against ethnic allegiance, and the hero takes a stand to honour his friendship. *Fox Volant of the Snowy Mountain* is the story of bitter enemies who become friends, and *The Heavenly Sword and Dragon Slaying Sabre* is about the friendship between seven fellow apprentices. *The Deer and the Cauldron* depicts the unlikely friendship between an emperor and a teenage scamp. On the whole, one could say that my work frequently overly romanticizes and idealizes the virtues of friendship.

IKEDA: May I ask you to share some memories of your own friends?

JIN: In my own experience, it seems that it has become more difficult for me to make truly close friends as I become older. With age, it seems that forming deep and sincere friendships with mutual understanding and without calculated self-interest has become more difficult than it was in my youth. And the reason seems to be that it is harder for older people to have heart-to-heart conversations about their true feelings.

Most of my closest friendships were formed in my junior high school days. In those days, my friends and I would eat together, sleep together in the same dormitory, go to the same classes, and do our homework together. We were always together, and so we got along very well. My friends from those days keep in touch even now, and we try to make a point of getting together now and then.

IKEDA: That is very similar to the pattern of friendships in Japan. When people are in their 40s and 50s, all of a sudden the number of class reunions increases, perhaps because people grow nostalgic for the uncomplicated and pure friendships of their student days.

JIN: The person with whom I founded the *Ming Pao* newspaper, my friend Shen Pao Sing, was a classmate of mine in my third year of junior high school. We met in 1938 and together founded *Ming Pao* 21 years later in 1959. We trust each other completely, and worked together for over 30 years to put out our newspaper. Our long friendship has indeed been a great blessing in my life.

Over the years, as Shen Pao Sing and I worked together on the newspaper, there was no end to the number of people who spread false rumours and schemed to try to drive a wedge between us. Even so, we never once doubted or harboured ill will against each other. When I went into the hospital for heart surgery, my 'older brother Pao Sing', as I fondly called him, waited at the hospital for eight and a half hours, from the beginning to the very end of my surgery.

IKEDA: What a marvellous friendship! Would you tell us about some of your other friends?

JIN: Among the friends I have made since going into the newspaper business, Xu Dongbin was the most dear to me and had my greatest respect. He passed away in the US in 1995. I mourned his passing for days and days. I grieved deeply, as if he had been my own brother.

Friends I have come to know in my role as a writer include Dong Qianli, Ni Kuang, Cai Lan, and Feng Qiyong. I also have friends whom I have met while playing the game of Go, and even some foreign friends with whom I have collaborated in scholarly research projects. Among my close friends in the Hong Kong business community are Feng Jingxi and David Li. When I participated in drafting the Basic Law of the Hong Kong Special Administrative Region, I became friends with a number of legal scholars. We would chat during work breaks and got along very well. They are Professor Xiao Weiyun, Mr Xiang Chunyi, and Professor Xu Congde.

IKEDA: Just as I expected, you indeed have many good friends. How precious good friends are to us. This reminds me of the question that Ananda, one of the Buddha's disciples, asked Shakyamuni. His question was, 'It seems to me that by having good friends and moving forward together with them, one has already halfway attained the Buddha way. Is this way of thinking correct?' To which Shakyamuni replied, 'Ananda, this way of thinking is not correct. Having good friends and progressing together with them constitutes not half the Buddha way, but all of the Buddha way.'

Those who we call 'good friends' and 'good companions' are, broadly speaking, those who travel together with us on our quintessential life journey. Friendship is, indeed, the tide, the boat, the gateway leading to the true path of our fulfilment as human beings.

On the subject of peace, its true nature lies in the reliance and trust between people. When bonds of friendship are created, peace begins to flow. This I believe strongly.

This is why I want this peaceful tide of humanity to flow throughout the world. And I want to unite the entire world with the precious gem of friendship, linking one person to the next. I will do this together with treasured friends throughout the world, including you, Mr Jin.

A Fundamental Principle of Life:
The Mentor–Disciple Relationship and the Path of Learning

IKEDA: Mr Jin, you have splendidly depicted feelings of love and affection between your characters in their various encounters with each other. In addition to friendship, you have also portrayed the ideal human character in which *On*, in Japanese, or a debt of gratitude, is emphasized. In one scene in your work *The Book and the Sword*, the main character who is releasing a captured enemy soldier says, 'I owe a debt of gratitude to this guy's senior. I am sure that the Red Flower Society will understand why I am honouring this debt of gratitude and not taking revenge on the enemy.'[5]

To feel a strong moral obligation to repay debts of kindness is an extremely important quality of a chivalrous person, as you have emphasized in your works. One must never forget these moral obligations. Even if it takes an entire lifetime, one must never lose the desire to somehow repay them. Buddhist teachings emphasize four kinds of debt: the debt of filial piety toward one's parents, the debt of gratitude toward one's teachers, the debt one owes to the three treasures of Buddhism (the Buddhas, the Law, and the Buddhist group), and the debt to one's country. To acknowledge one's obligations of gratitude and to repay them is the ultimate expression of one's humanity.

JIN: That's exactly right. Among the four types of debt, the debt to the three treasures of Buddhism is especially important for Buddhists to honour.

IKEDA: Mr Jin, who are the people who have made a difference in your life? Of course, I imagine that they span many fields.

JIN: First of all, one of the most influential people in my life was my fifth-grade homeroom advisor and Chinese language teacher, Mr Chen Weidong. In 1995, I had the opportunity to meet and become reacquainted with him in Hangzhou after 60 years. On that occasion, in our conversation I reminisced about the mistakes that he had corrected in my writing compositions and which specific characters he had corrected. He laughed and praised my good memory. He remarked that understanding and remembering one's mistakes was the key to self-development.

Another person very important to me was Mr Chang Yintong, the principal of my junior high school. In the incident I mentioned before where I had criticized my curriculum teacher in a wall newspaper and got expelled for it, Principal Chang did his utmost to lighten the punishment. But the curriculum teacher was a member of the Republic of China's Guomindang (Chinese Nationalist Party), and so he was able to overrule the principal. Later, Mr Chang was instrumental in helping me gain admission to another school. This was a great blessing for me and had a major impact on my entire life. In 1996, a bronze statue of Principal Chang was unveiled at a ceremony in his honour, and I was asked to write the inscription.

IKEDA: No matter how old we become, those who have contributed to our lives are still our benefactors and we still hold them in high esteem. I still maintain contact with my primary school teacher, and whenever I have the opportunity I go to visit him. In response to the small tokens of my gratitude, he always sends a thank-you note. Once he wrote in a letter, 'Your life has been filled with ups and downs, and as they say, "The tall tree is envied by the wind." . . . I feel sorry that I cannot do anything to protect you.' I greatly respect this teacher, and I have written about him in some of my essays out of gratitude for his benevolence.

Are there any other teachers besides Mr Chen and Mr Chang that you would like to mention?

JIN: Another teacher to whom I am greatly indebted is my junior high school Chinese language teacher, Mr Wang Zhi. Mr Wang taught me, by example, the virtues of resolve and perseverance, honesty, courage, and love for humanity – all the characteristics of a chivalrous spirit. When I look back on my life, I believe that I have been guided, without being fully aware of it, toward a true and upright path by these lessons from Mr Wang. Unfortunately, having been raised in my home province of Jiangnan, a blessed natural setting, and in a wealthy family, I led an extravagant and idle life of leisure as a youth. So, I deeply regret that I was unable to learn as much as I could have at the time from my teacher, a man of great integrity and inner strength.

Then, during my days at the *Da Gong Bao* newspaper, I studied translation under Mr Yang Liqiao, the department director. But now all of these wonderful benefactors in my life have passed on, and I am unable to repay them for all their kindnesses to me.

IKEDA: Buddhists believe that life and death are one and inseparable. I am sure that all of these people who have contributed so much to your life are, even now, watching over you and rejoicing in your accomplishments.

I view the great benevolence that I received from my mentor, Mr Toda, as my life's, or perhaps I should say, as my eternal and supreme, treasure. Repaying this great debt is a task to which I devote my all.

Mr Jin, you have superbly represented this theme – the mentor–disciple relationship – as the fundamental core of life. For example, in *The Heavenly Sword and Dragon Slaying Sabre*, one of your characters, a disciple, describes the brilliance of his teacher. He declared, 'A length of one thousand *ri* (1 *ri* = approx. 3.92 km) is insufficient to express his greatness. And one thousand *jin* (1 *jin* = 1 fathom) are also inadequate to express his profound depth.'[6]

This student devoted himself every day to studying under his teacher and had felt that he was not making any progress, and instead was regressing. It was not that he felt that he was lazy and neglecting his studies. Rather, he felt that the more he dedicated himself to his studies, the more he understood the greatness of his teacher. He was overwhelmed by his teacher's eminence and came to feel that his own capacity was not sufficient to achieve that level. Every single day the student studied with his teacher and had his eyes opened to new discoveries. And while being painfully aware of his own limits, he was determined and driven by a deep thirst for learning to expand the breadth and depth of his knowledge.

The 11 years that I spent studying with my mentor were very similar. I could not have been happier to be blessed with such a wonderful mentor in my youth. Yet how awesome and solemn is the bond between mentor and disciple. Having travelled on this path, I can say unequivocally that there is nothing more noble or sublime than the mentor–disciple relationship. Mr Jin, you have depicted it splendidly.

JIN: You must be truly happy, President Ikeda. You had a remarkable mentor. Both your remarkable character and life circumstances were greatly impacted by Mr Toda.

I had the pleasure of reading your novel *The Human Revolution*. You describe how you entered Soka Gakkai at the age of 19 and were taught every day by a magnificent mentor. I was very impressed and envious of your experience.

In China we say that there are two ways to learn from a teacher. One is to be taught through words, and the other is to be taught by example.

President Ikeda, you had the good fortune to learn many things from Mr Toda's example.

IKEDA: Yes, and thank you for your kind words. I appreciate them very much.

Mr Jin, in April 1996, you came to visit us at the Makiguchi Memorial Hall in Hachioji, Tokyo. I cannot express how happy I was to meet you there, the place that we regard as the castle of the mentor–disciple relationship, and to hear your insights on the essence of the teacher–student relationship.

JIN: The spirit of your first president, Tsunesaburo Makiguchi, lives on in you, President Ikeda. Even though I did not have the opportunity to meet President Makiguchi, I have a sense of his greatness through knowing you. During my visit, in honour of the anniversary of President Toda's death on 2 April, you yourself kindly planted a cherry tree in honour of me in the Makiguchi Memorial Hall garden. I was very moved by this and will treasure this memory for as long as I live.

President Ikeda, I think that successors are extremely important in every respect, and especially so in the mentor–disciple relationship. The incredible development of Soka Gakkai today is due, I believe, to the fact that Mr Toda discovered an excellent successor.

IKEDA: I am humbled by your kind words. The rapid development of Soka Gakkai was impressive, but as a result, jealousy and persecution became pervasive.

JIN: I understand what you are saying. There is an old Chinese adage which says, 'Those who do not experience persecution from others are simply ordinary'. In other words, those who are not hated by others or who do not provoke envy in others are not extraordinary individuals.

IKEDA: In the Buddhist scriptures there is a passage that observes, 'Iron, when heated in flames and pounded, becomes a fine sword. Worthies and sages are tested by abuse',[7] which means that the way to judge the authenticity of a sage or holy man is to curse and swear at him. To receive verbal abuse is an indicator of personal greatness.

I believe that whatever happens around me, I always have my mentor as my role model. I live every day of my life asking myself the question, 'How would my mentor address this situation?' It has been over half a century since I first met my mentor. And I have thought about him every single day since then. And I believe that I will continue to do so.

Qualities of a Twenty-First Century Person

IKEDA: The world we live in is gradually becoming smaller and smaller. It is becoming more integrated and unified. The central focus of such an integrated world is human beings. But what kind of person will be essential in this kind of world? Unless we foster a continuous flow of internationally minded world citizens – people with intellectual, spiritual, and physical strength; people who are broad-minded and big-hearted – our future will be limited. How can we nurture this kind of person? This is an issue to which we must all give serious thought.

JIN: That's exactly right.

IKEDA: This is something I think about every time I visit Hong Kong. I feel that Hong Kong is truly blessed. It has a geographical advantage as an international city.

Similarly, I recall President Mikhail Gorbachev telling me about his birthplace in Stavropol in the North Caucasus, a thriving area with a prosperous business and trading sector and a teeming social centre. He described the character of the area as a place where 'The people . . . are sociable and inclined to compromise since, for the nations of the Northern Caucasus, agreement has long been a major means of survival. As a result of this cast of mind and the nature of our interpersonal relations, we were fated to be internationalists.'[8]

Perhaps we can say the same of Hong Kong, in the sense that it is a cradle for nurturing international citizens.

JIN: Certainly, longtime residents of Hong Kong have cultivated a kind of international perspective. They have been blessed with opportunities to travel abroad in their childhood and to develop insights and understanding about the world. They have a broader perspective.

One thing they lack, however, is a love and affinity for the culture and traditions of China, their homeland. This is probably because they do not have the cultural and historical depth that provides for a strong Chinese identity.

IKEDA: This is an aspect that will undoubtedly undergo a major change over time after the return of Hong Kong to China. I believe that we will see a mutually beneficial merging of the strengths possessed by the people of Hong Kong and those of the mainland Chinese.

JIN: The Chinese have traditionally not been exclusive with respect to foreigners. One of their strengths has been the readiness with which they have accepted other cultures. Hong Kong, which has been influenced by British rule, has no discrimination based on racial differences. We do not perceive any difference between Westerners, Japanese, Indians, Pakistanis or blacks, nor do we interact with any of them differently from the rest. Accordingly, people form friendships, date, and marry people from other ethnicities with absolutely no problem.

Many of my friends are people who have what you might call a 'United Nations family'. For example, the daughter has married into the family of her foreign husband, and the son has taken a foreign bride, and they all get along with, enjoy, and appreciate one another. Even though their mother tongues are different, they were raised in different religions, and they have different lifestyle patterns, their harmonious relationships are based on their love for each other, and this makes it possible for them to live happily together in an intergenerational household.

IKEDA: What we need to do is to abandon our obsession with differences such as language, religion, and customs that tend to alienate people from each other, and to instead embrace a universal and all-inclusive love, for all humankind. In other words, one must have a heart of compassion.

JIN: People, no matter who they are, as well as countries, both great and small, are all equal. It is incumbent upon us all to get along with one another. Shakyamuni demonstrated compassion not only to fellow human beings, but also equally to our fellow creatures who inhabit the earth with us.

IKEDA: Equality and compassion – these are indeed prerequisites for becoming twenty-first century global citizens. And to the extent that many more people cultivate a 'heart of compassion', peace becomes a more achievable reality throughout the world.

When I was young, I was enamoured with the words of Zhuang-zi, who said, 'The Great Man has no self'.[9] I think that what he meant by the word 'self' is not the self of self-interest. Rather, I think he was referring to the small-minded self that is withdrawn inside a small cocoon: a small vessel that refuses to accept values different from its own.

The Japanese have a special term by which they refer to their own insular and provincial national consciousness. They call it an 'island country mentality', which makes people unable to be open-minded and tolerant of differences. In other words, they are unable to abandon the 'small self'. This may be the fate of the Japanese. This is why I continually urge young people to turn their eyes toward the world and boldly become international citizens. This is an absolute prerequisite for participating actively in the life of the twenty-first century.

JIN: Indeed! In this sense, the influence that you and Soka Gakkai have had on Japan has been of critical importance. Even though Japan excels in many areas, its people are sorely lacking a cosmopolitan sensibility.

I once received a survey from a major corporation. One of the questions was, 'Why is Japan's image so negative?' My answer was, 'It may be because the Japanese are not good at drawing attention to their strengths'. Because of this, their strengths may actually appear as weaknesses. So, this is an area in which the Japanese could do better. For example, a person may be an excellent scholar but have poor social skills. And because of that, he could be misunderstood and judged poorly.

IKEDA: I always tell Japanese that they must speak more. They must socialize and converse with others. They must not be stingy with words when it comes to speaking with others, especially when they live or travel abroad. They must not remain silent. If they do, they will never be able to establish rapport and get along with others.

The old saying, 'Silence is gold, and eloquence is silver', which elevates silence to a virtue, is a tendency that is still deeply rooted in the Japanese consciousness. But this principle will not serve the Japanese well in the international society of the future. Rather, it is fluency and expression that is gold today.

JIN: To become a true twenty-first century citizen, one must be able to open one's heart, rather than discriminate or hold prejudices against those different from oneself. Through interaction and mutual understanding, we will share our intentions and wishes and nurture compassion and love. One must think in terms of what one can do for the other person. This is the only way that we can ever expect to create a harmonious society and a peaceful world.

IKEDA: To have a heart of compassion – to always think of others in all of one's actions – this is the true practice of the bodhisattva.

We are called to bring people together – the people of Hong Kong and Japan, China and Japan, and Asia and the world – with hearts of compassion, by practising the way of the bodhisattva. And it will be through this great social and cultural exchange between peoples that the truly internationally minded citizens of the world will emerge.

CHAPTER 3

Friendship, Spirit, and Character: An Encounter with Buddhism

Reverence for Friendship in the Chinese Ethical Worldview

JIN: I have found our discussion about the nature of friendship profoundly interesting, and so I would like to continue a bit more. President Ikeda, after reading many of your works, I was struck by the fact that you seem to place a great emphasis on friendship. And it occurred to me that perhaps one could say that Soka Gakkai itself is a massive organization made up of friends who share a great love and affection for each other.

IKEDA: That is exactly the case. Soka Gakkai is not based on hierarchical relationships or those seeking their own self-interest. Rather, it is an organization that transcends self-interest and status and unites people through love and profound friendship among equals.

JIN: In Chinese ethics, friendship begins in sibling relationships. In relatively large households, the people a newborn baby has contact with, after the baby's parents, are the siblings.

In ancient China, relationships in the household were characterized by the expression, 'Compassionate father, filial child, elder brother as friend, respectful younger brother'. And so it was thought that siblings, related by blood and sharing the affection of family ties, also related to each other as friends.

IKEDA: It is quite different in Japan. In China, the ties between blood relations are remarkably strong.

JIN: Yes. Traditionally, the Chinese have placed more emphasis on affection between siblings than the relationship between husband and wife. Proverbs expound on the relationships in terms such as, 'A wife is like a change of clothes, while one's siblings are like your own hands and feet. When a piece of clothing is torn, it can be sewn up, but if a hand or foot is severed, it cannot be reconnected.'

We cannot deny this indicates that the status of wives, and women in general, was of little account. On the other hand, it also makes very clear the importance of relationships between siblings in Chinese society.

IKEDA: The Quatrain of Seven Steps is a poem introduced in *Romance of the Three Kingdoms*. The emperor of Wei, Cao Pi, is suspicious that his brother, Cao Zhi, is trying to usurp his throne. He calls his brother to come before him and demands that he compose a poem of seven verses to prove his innocence. Cao Zhi composes the following poem, which is famous for its expression of affection between brothers.

> They were boiling beans on a beanstalk fire;
> Came a plaintive voice from the pot,
> 'O why, since we sprang from the selfsame root,
> Should you kill me with anger hot?'[1]

Cao Pi was so moved by this poem that he refrained from exacting a harsh punishment on his brother. Throughout the course of history we see brothers vying for power, and in the ensuing power struggle their relationship is torn asunder. This poem teaches us the foolishness of this struggle.

JIN: Let me offer a different angle on this matter. The Chinese sometimes use the term 'brother' to refer to a good friend. When a Chinese person writes a letter, it is customary for the recipient to be addressed with a term of endearment meaning 'my elder brother', and for the writer to refer to himself as 'younger brother'. Close friends may take a vow to become blood brothers. It also happens that opposite-sex friends pledge their friendship to each other in a special type of pledging ritual.

When a vow of friendship is made, this is the kind of oath that is taken: 'Though we could not be born on the same day of the same month of the same year, by this oath we signal our desire to die on the same day of the same month of the same year.'

In the West, only passionate lovers would share this kind of vow to end their lives together. However, in China, in a world defined by a sense of moral obligation and human relationships, a priority is placed on friendship rather than the love relationship.

IKEDA: The words of the oath – 'desire to die on the same day of the same month of the same year' – bring to mind the Peach Garden Oath in *Romance of the Three Kingdoms*.

JIN: Yes. The oath taken by Liu Bei, Guan Yu, and Zhang Fei, the three sworn blood brothers appearing in *Romance of the Three Kingdoms*, has come to symbolize a deep and enduring friendship. There is also a passage in *The Water Margin* in which 108 characters take an oath of eternal friendship and brotherhood. This form of relationship has been used as a model in secret societies in China in more recent times.

In *Romance of the Three Kingdoms* as well as in *The Water Margin*, the virtue of chivalry, which we touched on previously, is discussed together with the value of friendship. Friendship has its basis in the realm of emotion, and, in contrast, chivalry arises from the intellect and includes the exercise of discernment.

In short, even if a relationship is not emotionally deep, when they think it reasonable to do so, the person may be moved to make a major sacrifice for the friendship. This is an act of chivalry.

IKEDA: In the *Analects of Confucius* is the passage, 'To see what is right and not do it is cowardly'.[2] In other words, if you know what is the most righteous and correct course of action, you must take that action, even if it means laying down your life in battle or sacrificing it for the sake of another. Mr Jin, this is exactly how heroes, depicted in your martial arts novels, lived their lives.

JIN: President Ikeda, now I would like to ask your views about friendship in Japanese society. From the very beginning, I have felt strongly that you have treated me as a good friend. I feel truly happy that, even in my later years, I have been blessed with such a friend as you.

The Japanese Psyche and the Difficulty of Cultivating Friendships in Japan

IKEDA: Thank you for your kind words. In regard to your question, generally speaking, I believe that Japanese society is a difficult social context in which to make friends. Friendship is a bond that extends horizontally among equals throughout human society. However, Japanese society is a vertical society, with people relating to each other as either superiors or subordinates.

In your preface to the Japanese edition of your work *The Book and the Sword*, you wrote: 'The fundamental perspective of the Chinese martial arts differs from that of the Japanese way of *Bushido*. At the core of *Bushido* is the principle of loyalty. The warrior expresses his supreme loyalty to his master to whom he owes a debt of gratitude, and he does not hesitate to sacrifice his life for him.'[3]

As you indicated, Mr Jin, the principle of loyalty has long been considered a basic social virtue in Japan. The oft-quoted phrase from an Eiji Yoshikawa novel declares that a warrior must be loyal to his master even if the master is oppressive or unreasonable. The vertical nature of the relationship was too dominant, it seems, for there to have been an opportunity for development of friendship, which is an equal, non-hierarchical relationship.

The theme of loyalty toward one's master is romanticized in many works. It appears, of course, in the classic *Chūshingura* (literally, The Treasury of Loyal Retainers), as well as in recent literary works such as *Abe Ichizoku* (The Abe Family) by Mori Ōgai and *The Fir Trees Remain* by Yamamoto Shūgoro. In contrast, works that explore the theme of friendship are much fewer.

Some intellectuals have pointed out that, to begin with, the concept of friendship has never been very well developed in Japanese culture. In fact, it was not until after the Meiji Period (1868–1912) that the mention of the value of friendship became more widespread, and it is thought that the concept itself was adopted from Europe.

JIN: I see. That's very interesting.

IKEDA: In China, the family has traditionally predominated. It seems almost as if the family stands as the fundamental wellspring of all morality in Chinese culture.

The novelist Chin Shunshin describes this idea as follows: 'The Chinese sense of group identity begins and ends with the family. The walls of this family are high and insurmountable, making it impossible to expand this sense of belonging to larger units, such as to the village, town, and province. There is no way that this sense of group identity could ever embrace the concept of nation.'[4]

Professor Francis Fukuyama, professor at Johns Hopkins University's School of Advanced International Studies, discusses the issue this way in his book entitled *Trust: The Social Virtues and the Creation of Prosperity*. He declares, 'In sharp contrast to Japan, Chinese society is *not* group oriented. This difference is captured in the saying of Lin Yu-tang, who spoke of Japanese society as being like a piece of granite, while traditional Chinese society was like a loose tray of sand, each grain being an individual family.'5

This is the extent to which, in China, the family is presumed to predominate.

JIN: I understand completely.

IKEDA: How, then, did Chinese culture develop the cultural patterns such as those you discussed before; that is, an emphasis on the bonds of brotherhood and the practice of using familial terms such as 'elder brother' and 'younger brother' in correspondence when referring to close friends? Chin Shunshin makes the connection between this point and the virtue of filial piety toward one's parents. He writes, 'Filial piety is absolute. No matter how bad a parent is, a child must still pay his debt of filial piety to that parent. The Chinese, who place great emphasis on the family, feel that they have had more than enough of this rigid and absolutist style of familial relationship. So when they interact with others in society, they try to avoid, as much as possible, the vertical style of relationship between parent and child, and instead, model their relationships on the horizontal ties among brothers.'6

A vertical relationship pattern inspired by the moral of filial piety was much too strong. Instead, as the basis for their relationships with others in society, people chose the more horizontal style of relationship, such as between brothers.

The relationship between the characters Guan Yu and Zhang Fei in *Romance of the Three Kingdoms* is depicted as a deep and powerful bond between blood brothers, and in contrast, hardly anything is mentioned about their families of origin and other kin.

Perhaps this issue holds the key to why this work is so beloved by the Chinese people. In other words, the work departs from the rigid and formal concept of the family, and readers identify with and are drawn to the horizontal model of human relationships.

JIN: That's a very interesting point. President Ikeda, you mentioned that friendships are difficult to nurture in Japanese society. You have observed that this is intimately related to the deeply rooted traditions of Japan's vertical society. Are there any other reasons that you can identify?

The Importance of Mutual Understanding in Friendships

IKEDA: Perhaps another reason is that the identity of the individual as a distinct, free entity, in a positive sense, is rather weak in Japan.

After the Meiji Restoration (1868), the great Japanese philosopher Fukuzawa Yukichi contended that in order for Japan to become a truly independent and free country, the Japanese must honour and cultivate the freedom and dignity of the individual. I believe that the situation that elicited his admonition still stands today. Generally speaking, this attribute of independence is weak in the Japanese character.

We will not discuss this in detail at this point. However, Fukuzawa discerned that the main impediment to the formation of independence in the Japanese character was Japanese religion, especially Buddhism. He astutely observed that the Buddhist religion did not help people to develop a strong spiritual backbone. I feel that we must heed Fukuzawa's point.

When people do not have a firm sense of their identity as an individual and as human beings, they simply follow the crowd in all their actions. They have no concept of actively participating in the rough-and-tumble world of individuals interacting with other individuals. They lack a readiness to engage in a shared pursuit of character development and self-improvement, which, at times, may involve sharp interchanges and a thorough airing of opinions. Conversely, there is a dominant tendency to avoid any kind of behaviour that makes one stand out or appear too bold, and so they may try to obstruct and interfere with the efforts of a person who excels above others. Frankly speaking, they gloss over problems in relationships for the sake of appearances and would rather avoid the clash of individuals striving for greater understanding and self-improvement.

JIN: I know what you mean. When Chinese become friends, they place great emphasis on the concept of *chiki* (friendship). Most important in a relationship is mutual understanding and rapport. And it is not necessary for two people to be friends for many years for this to develop.

A passage in the *Records of the Grand Historian* emphasizes this point. 'As the saying goes, two white-haired people are like new acquaintances, while a chance encounter is like an old familiar friend.' This means that two people can know each other for years and even grow old together, but seem as if they have only met recently. Conversely, others can meet, by chance, on the street – perhaps they have just disembarked from a vehicle and exchanged a few words – but if they are of like mind, it is just as if they have been friends for years and years.

Another saying points out, 'A thousand cups of wine do not suffice when true friends meet, but half a sentence is too much when there is no meeting of minds'. So, when one meets a true friend, the conversation never ends, and a thousand cups of rice wine may be consumed before one knows it. But if the conversation does not flow, even exchanging a few words becomes annoying and troublesome.

Genuine Friendship as One's Life Treasure

IKEDA: Speaking of friendship, in the preface to *Ode to the Grand Spirit*, my published dialogue with my friend Chinghiz T. Aitmatov (1928–2008), the Kirghiz author, he wrote the following.

> I long dreamed about such a dialogue and waited for the right occasion . . . As a child, I was often surprised to hear old men in our Kirghiz village complain about having no one to talk to, no one to open their hearts to. But there were people everywhere. How could they lack somebody to talk to? Now I understand what they meant. They had in mind the thirst for that one irreplaceable companion. Sooner or later, I was certain to find the person my soul had yearned for all those years, the person in whom I could see and understand myself clearer and more accurately.[7]

Mr Jin, that is exactly how I feel about conversing with you.

JIN: I feel absolutely the same way. I believe that we have become such good friends because we share such similar thoughts in so many areas, such as world issues, life, politics, culture, society and religion. This truly is a wonderful friendship in the sense of the word *chiki*.

IKEDA: *Chiki* is a good word. It is not simply a matter of familiarity. '*Chiki*' does not involve self-interest. This is when you are known as you really are, without all the extraneous trappings of the self. It is a beautiful sentiment.

It is humanity shining at its brightest. Nothing is more precious than hearts and minds united in friendship. Friendship is something that lasts.

In all of my dealings with people, I have always tried to be honest. If I did not follow this principle of honesty, I would feel that I was being rude to those with whom I interact, and my conscience would not allow me to accept myself.

Previously, when I was giving an interview during a trip abroad, I was asked this question: 'You have met so many world leaders and distinguished people, what about them has impressed you the most?' I responded immediately with, 'It would be their frankness'.

I am attracted to people who do not hesitate to say what must be said in a straightforward and frank manner. They do not lie. They take responsibility for what they have said. This means that, even if we do not comprehend what each other is saying at first, we know that we will come to understand each other eventually. And we can become true friends.

Friendships are an aspect of my life that I take seriously. I am very proud of my friendships. And as I grow older, I feel this way all the more.

Among the few works of Japanese literature that address the subject of friendship is *Run, Melos!* (1940) by Dazai Osamu. I will never forget how moved I was when I came upon this novel. It said that status and notoriety are unnecessary and that the most important thing is to never betray a friend.

As depicted in *Run, Melos!*, the best people in the world do not betray their friends. I have had the good fortune of making friends with many people, including you, Mr Jin. I have lived a long life, but I feel almost as if I have returned to my youth, as in the world of Melos.

Toward a Hopeful Tomorrow: Hong Kong after the Return

IKEDA: Mr Jin, I really appreciated your hospitality during my visit to Hong Kong in February 1997. We were very honoured to have you and your wife join us at SGI's (Soka Gakkai International) World Peace Youth and Culture Festival. I was especially pleased that, during our meeting, we were able to exchange our thoughts regarding the imminent return of Hong Kong in July of that year.

JIN: I would like to express my appreciation to you as well. I am deeply grateful for your kind concern about Hong Kong's future and for the wonderful encouragement you have given to the citizens of Hong Kong.

Most people were concerned about the economic prospects of a post-

British Hong Kong. However, few people besides yourself, President Ikeda, focused on the cultural issues or the prospects for a peaceful transition.

IKEDA: I am afraid that was true. The return of Hong Kong to Chinese rule was an issue that attracted the attention of the people of Asia and, indeed, the entire world. The question was how Hong Kong could create a hopeful future. I was especially impressed that you raised the alarm against taking a purely mammonist approach to solve the problem.

Hong Kong will certainly continue to thrive even after the handover. Yet, when a light is shone on actual human beings, it is clear that economics alone cannot sustain human life. An aspect that must always be addressed is the desire for human fulfilment. Mr Jin, this is an issue that you brought into sharp focus.

JIN: As I mentioned when we met, compared to people in other areas of the world, the people of Hong Kong tend to be acquisitive and have a desire for material things. Perhaps this is because Hong Kong is a very small country, and everywhere you go there are endless throngs of people. So, undoubtedly, this vigorous propensity of the people to improve their lives is a direct response to their circumstances – that is, Hong Kong's small land area and its masses of people.

So, the improvement of one's life tends to be associated with having more money or gaining honour or distinction. This results in judging the viability of activities – even culture and the arts – in terms of how much profit they can generate. I am extremely worried about this.

IKEDA: Putting in perspective the spiritual and psychological outlook of the people of Hong Kong, you were optimistic about the positive influence that the transfer would have on them.

JIN: Yes. The return of Hong Kong means that it has ceased to be an overseas outpost of the United Kingdom and that sovereignty has returned to China, the homeland. I think that this has been beneficial in the sense that it provides the people of Hong Kong with a sense of belonging and a psychological underpinning as Chinese. And, I have predicted that, through contact with Chinese mainlanders, the people of Hong Kong will have increased opportunity to develop a love and appreciation for their homeland.

IKEDA: I continue to wish for a wonderful future for the people of both China and Hong Kong, but I regret that the worship of money, as you maintained, is an obstacle and is now a worldwide trend.

This trend of money worship is becoming more evident even in the former socialist countries, including Russia. Over the past several decades, the ideologies that guided people and societies have been found lacking, and though humankind has embarked on a spiritual journey, it finds itself cast adrift without a compass.

People may wonder where on earth they are trying to go, and what their destination should be. As they drift aimlessly on the open sea, the only thing that seems to provide a sense of support and security to them on their journey is money. In the dialogue between former President Gorbachev and me, he repeatedly warned of the dangers of this trend.

JIN: It is definitely a serious problem.

Contemplating the Potential of the Inner Self

IKEDA: A young friend of mine once mentioned a newspaper report about Alexander N. Yakovlev, the Russian architect of perestroika and president of the Leonardo da Vinci Club of Russia. The article was published in the *Moskovskie Novosti*, a Russian newspaper, and was entitled 'From Marx to Mahayana Buddhism: Alexander Yakovlev'.

Alexander Yakovlev was a close friend of mine, and he had a profound interest in Buddhism. When a reporter asked him why, this is how he would answer:

First of all, the Buddhists do not recognize a monotheistic and external creator of the universe, but rather, they perceive god as inside the self. In other words, they aim to achieve the Buddha consciousness through personal development and self-awakening . . . I am extremely attracted to this idea. And it is not because of the belief that anyone can become a Buddha. I am drawn to the concept that inside every person is a latent capacity for personal perfection, and each person must take responsibility for his or her own development.

One often comes across the perspective in our country that people are to look to the leaders. I find it aggravating that people think they should seek aid from people such as an emperor, a general, or a president. Why do they think they should do this? I just want to say, 'Work! Create! Believe in your own potential, and don't wait to receive favours from the powerful or some other source!'

JIN: That is a very frank declaration.

IKEDA: His statement, 'Don't wait to receive favours from the powerful or some other source!' is very aptly put. In short, if we were to distinguish between those with an internal focus versus an external focus, on the whole we would have to say that people seem to be looking more and more toward the external.

The walls of ideology have crumbled. While some religions, including the Russian Orthodox Church, are experiencing a period of revitalization, the tendency of society is still to turn toward external sources of fulfilment such as power, money, and material values. To the same extent, people have forgotten the importance of contemplation. It was about this that Mr Yakovlev felt a sense of impending crisis and to which he tried to alert people. I believe we can say that Mr Yakovlev's appreciation of Buddhism was deeply rooted in this sense of crisis.

Of course, the economy is an important issue. And money is necessary. However, the constant pursuit of material things does not provide a true sense of fulfilment. At this point, for once, we must shed light on the inner self. I believe that the time has come for us to think seriously about how to achieve spiritual fulfilment, not simply material abundance.

Mr Jin, I recall that you mentioned this point when you came to visit us at Soka University.

JIN: These days, most people are blinded by the lure of material prosperity and place great emphasis on how many material products they can accumulate and consume. As a result, they have become less concerned about spiritual values.

Certainly, compared to earlier eras, we have made great progress in meeting our daily material needs. Even so, we cannot claim unreservedly that our lives have become richer and more bountiful. This is because we cannot judge a person's happiness or unhappiness by that person's quantity of material possessions or degree of wealth. Rather, it is one's sense of satisfaction and one's spiritual values that determine happiness or unhappiness.

The values of modern civilization have gradually shifted away from an emphasis on spiritual and character development. Moreover, when acquisition of material goods becomes the lone goal, as a natural consequence, rivalry and contention, predation, conflict, and war, and eventually, world wars may arise. The only way to avoid these tragic calamities is to develop, create, and hold dear to spiritual and character-building values.

If, as I believe, the human spirit is noble and just, then more people will come to shun violent, combative behaviour, and this must be the root source of everlasting peace.

IKEDA: As an old saying goes, 'never being satisfied with what one gets, and always wanting more' (literally 'taking Gansu only to want Sichuan') – when one wish is fulfilled, another desire is immediately created. There is no end to human wants.

This reminds me of an article entitled 'Where is the Ideal Society?' which appeared in *Newsweek* Magazine just before the US presidential election of 1996. At the beginning were the words, 'Even though things are going well, no one is satisfied. This is the paradox of our time.' Given the economic prosperity, the freedom of the individual, favourable labour conditions, high standards of sanitation and public health, a good social welfare system, and strict laws against discrimination based on race and sex 'the US is a very livable country. Even so, the citizens curse their leaders and are pessimistic about the future.'[8]

This state of mind in America, the champion of materialistic civilization, reveals the poverty of the materialistic orientation and indicates a need for humanity to awaken from its illusion.

JIN: You are absolutely right. I could not agree more.

It is imperative that we conquer, in the heart of every person, that desire that craves but can never achieve an infinite and eternal fulfilment. When we speak of desire, we must distinguish between favourable desire and unfavourable desire. Unlimited desire is detrimental and unhealthy. The core of Eastern philosophy addresses the question of how to overcome this detrimental desire.

IKEDA: When we first met to hold our dialogue, this must have been what you meant when you emphasized the value of Chinese spiritual culture in relation to the return of Hong Kong.

JIN: When I refer to Chinese spiritual culture, I am talking, for example, about how we can learn much more from Confucian moral precepts. Confucian teachings espouse the values of morality and ethical conduct, wise family governance, statesmanship in national government, and peace throughout the land in heaven and earth. It is a philosophy that begins with a transformation of the self and ultimately seeks global peace.

Lessons from Buddhism are more important. If people were to learn even just the basic fundamentals of Buddhism, they would awaken to an understanding of how to be a better person and how to conduct themselves in righteousness. And perhaps they would begin to foster a wish to contribute to the well-being of others and move beyond a concern for themselves alone.

This is why I fervently hope, from the bottom of my heart, that the people of SGI, including those of SGI of Hong Kong, will demonstrate to as many people as possible these spiritual and righteous values.

IKEDA: I appreciate the depth of your understanding. I am sure that our members in Hong Kong will be gratified to receive such kind encouragement for their efforts.

Shortly before the turn of the century, we were confronted with a pressing choice – that is, to live in a society tossed about by the pursuit of superficial material values or to participate in a society guided by spiritual values that illuminate the human heart. Our choice will determine whether we leave a legacy for future generations of which we will not be ashamed.

An Encounter with Buddhism and the Issue of Life and Death

IKEDA: We have touched on the topic of Alexander Yakovlev and his views of Buddhism. Now let us turn to your religious beliefs, Mr Jin. You are a Buddhist, and you possess a truly profound knowledge of Buddhism. What led you to your encounter with Buddhism?

JIN: My conversion to Buddhism was not through the teachings of a venerable priest or layperson. It was an extremely excruciating process filled with anguish and hardship.

IKEDA: What do you mean?

JIN: In October of 1976, my eldest son, Zhuan Xia, who was studying at Columbia University in the US, committed suicide. We had no warning that there was a problem. It was like a bolt out of the blue. I was wracked with grief and even felt like committing suicide myself.

And I was haunted by the desire to understand the reason my son had killed himself. I wanted to know what caused him to throw away his life. I wanted to pursue him to the world beyond and demand that he answers my question.

IKEDA: I'm so sorry. I had no idea. It is the first I have heard of this. Only those who have lost a child can ever understand how it feels. I know because I, too, have lost a child. In his younger years, my mentor, Josei Toda, also experienced this kind of loss. His daughter passed away when she was only one year old. This happened before he came to Buddhism. He recalled that 'I spent the entire night crying while embracing my daughter's cold, lifeless body'. Shortly thereafter, his wife died, and so he was forced to deal seriously with this question of death.

JIN: For about a year after my son's death, I devoted myself completely to the exploration of this issue of life and death, poring over countless books on the subject. I read intently a British publication from cover to cover. The book contained a long section in which Arnold Toynbee, the eminent historian, discussed the topic. In the essay, Toynbee delved deeply into numerous perspectives, but did not give any answers to the major issue of life and death that had come to occupy my heart. Needless to say, only after entering the realm of religion was I able to find answers.

When I was in high school, I read the Old and New Testaments carefully from beginning to end. As I recall, at the time I would take the content of these scriptures and contemplate them again and again. However, I realized clearly that there were aspects of Christian doctrine that I could not accept. After this, I turned to the Buddhist scriptures in my search for answers.

IKEDA: At one time, after his eldest daughter and wife had passed away, my mentor also searched for a path to understanding through Christianity. However, he said that he could find nothing that resonated with him to address his questions about life. Perhaps one aspect of Christianity that you found difficult to accept was its view of life and death.

Richard Nicolaus Eijiro Coudenhove-Kalergi (1894–1972), an Austrian who advocated for the unification of Europe after World War I, observed, 'In the East, life and death are perceived to be like pages in a book. The belief is that when you turn the page, the next page begins. In other words, the life and death experience is repeated. However, in European culture, life is like a book which has a beginning and an end.'[9]

Perspectives on life and death are distinctly different in Eastern thought as compared to the West. Perhaps as you fervently contemplated the issue of life and death, you could not be satisfied with the view that life was like a book with a clear beginning and end. You mentioned that your search led you to explore the Buddhist scriptures. But Buddhist scripture consists of an immense body of literature, so I am sure that you struggled mightily in your diligent pursuit.

Discovering the Truth in Buddhism

JIN: The Chinese Buddhist scriptures are composed of a vast canon of tens of thousands of volumes. I read several introductory works, but they were heavily coloured by superstition and obfuscation, so they were not useful in understanding the true nature of this world.

Later, however, I set out to read Samyutta-nikāya, Majjhima-nikāya, and Dīgha-nikāya, and for several months I single-mindedly immersed myself in contemplation and study, oblivious to hunger and lack of sleep. As a result, all of a sudden, I was struck by a realization. I thought to myself, 'I can find the truth in Buddhism. I am absolutely certain of it.'

However, the Chinese translation of Buddhist texts was too difficult. One character can have completely different meanings, and there is no way to determine the true meaning.

Then I bought the complete volume set of the primeval Buddhist scriptures in English translation by the Pali Text Society. As you are aware, the primeval Buddhist scriptures are from the earliest period of Buddhism and, according to Buddhist scholars, are thought to be the most authentic record of the actual sermons of the Shakyamuni Buddha. They were transmitted throughout the entire region of southern India and Sri Lanka and are therefore also known as the scriptures of the Southern Transmission. Mahayana Buddhist scholars as well as followers of the various sects of Mahayana Buddhism dismiss these as Hinayana Scriptures or Scriptures of the Lesser Vehicle.

IKEDA: So, it seems that you were able to compare and contrast the Chinese and English translations of the Buddhist scriptures as you pursued your studies.

JIN: Yes. The English translations of the Buddhist scriptures were very accessible. The content of the Southern Transmission scriptures was clear and unadorned and fully expressed the true essence of life, and the translation conveyed this in a way that even I, whose mother tongue is not English, could understand without difficulty.

It is at this point that my faith was born and I became a believer. The Buddha, which means 'the enlightened one' in the Pali language, certainly awakened to the nature of truth in human life. And he made it his mission to convey this truth – in other words, the Buddhist Law – to all the people of the world.

After a long process of contemplation, study of historical evidence, repeated questioning, and continued fervent research, I finally accepted Buddhism with all my heart and soul. The Buddhist teachings helped resolve the major doubts that had lingered in my heart. My heart rejoiced as I realized, 'This is it! I finally understand!' My heart was filled with boundless joy. And so, in the space of one long year, this was how my anguish and torment was transformed to irrepressible jubilation.

IKEDA: As you speak, I can sense the feelings that you must have had at that time.

JIN: I continued my research, reading next the scriptures of Mahayana Buddhism. For example, I tackled the Vimalakīrti Sutra, the Laṅkāvatāra Sutra, and the Prajñāpāramitā sutra, also known collectively as the Perfection of Wisdom Sutras. But then, doubts began to creep back into my thinking. The content of these sutras differed from that of the Southern Transmission scriptures, and consisted of primarily mystical and inscrutable hyperbolic narrative. I could not possibly accept or have faith in these scriptures.

Then, after reading the Lotus Sutra of the Wonderful Law (*Myoho-renge-kyo*), which inspired much meditation and contemplation, it finally dawned on me. This text articulating the supreme law of the Buddha was precisely the original message of the Mahayana scriptures. The Mahayana scriptures masterfully elucidated and extolled the Buddhist law in such a way that even those of lower intelligence or comprehension, who might otherwise have difficulty understanding it, could be proselytized.

In the Lotus Sutra, the Buddha used various familiar metaphors, such as a burning house, an ox cart, and a torrential downpour, to explain Buddhist teachings to the people of the world. He felt that, on occasion, it was important to use whatever means necessary to lead the people to a better life. There is even one anecdote about the Buddha in which he pretends that he has succumbed to a poison and feigns that he is sick and close to death. This was a means he used to convey the Buddhist teachings to the people.

IKEDA: I agree that the Lotus Sutra is abundant in aesthetic content. It also has an everlasting quality and a global and cosmic consciousness. Its broad reach encompasses the dimensions of life and all of creation.

The numerous proverbs and parables that are scattered throughout the sutra are rich with visual imagery. It is as if you are reading through a magnificent pictorial odyssey of life, and the scenes that come to mind, one after another, touch your heart.

JIN: After I came to understand the true meaning of the word *myoho* or 'supreme law', my resistance to the use of illusion-filled hyperbole in the Mahayana sutras receded. By this time, nearly two years had passed and my personal anguish had turned to exquisite elation.

IKEDA: The Lotus Sutra is the Perfect Teaching. It resides at the pinnacle of the Mahayana sutras, while all of the other sutras, each espousing an aspect of truth, are subsumed under the perfect teaching of the Lotus Sutra. It is as if many rivers and streams flow toward the sea and become one great ocean.

Mr Jin, you mentioned that you studied the Theravada sutras, then next turned to the Mahayana sutras, and as a result of your studies, you determined that the Lotus Sutra contained the pure essence of Buddhism. This clearly demonstrates, I believe, how seriously you committed yourself to your exploration of Buddhism.

A Moving Encounter with My Mentor

JIN: Yes. To me it was a life and death struggle. Now, moving on, President Ikeda, may I ask you to share the motivation and circumstances by which you decided to join Soka Gakkai and become an adherent of Buddhism?

As a child, I grew up hearing my grandmother chanting the Heart of the Perfection of Wisdom Sutra and the Lotus Sutra, but it took a full 60 years and much suffering and searching before I finally chose to follow the path of Buddhism.

IKEDA: My conversion occurred not through the teachings of Nichiren at first, but from being profoundly moved upon meeting Josei Toda, who was later to become my mentor.

In the aftermath of World War II, those adults who had painted the US troops as foreign devils were now extolling the virtues of European and American style democracy. Like many of my peers, I was highly suspicious of these adults and at a loss for how to view their sudden change in values. And so it was during this time that my friends and I formed our reading circle and continued to search desperately for values that we could believe in with certainty.

And so perhaps for this reason, when I first encountered Josei Toda, I peppered him with the questions that were foremost in my mind. The three main issues I struggled with were: 'What is a well-lived life?' 'What is true patriotism?' 'How should we view the Japanese imperial system?'

To him, I was an unknown, a nameless youth, but Josei Toda answered my questions sincerely and without prejudice. His answers were straight-forward, unambiguous, and without a hint of uncertainty. I did not fully understand all of his responses to my questions, but I was definitely impressed and moved by him as a person. And I was inspired by the power-ful life force and strength of character he radiated.

JIN: In your novel *The Human Revolution*, I read with great interest the part in which you depict in detail your meeting with Josei Toda.

IKEDA: I had an inherent aversion to religion. And so, whenever I heard any-thing to do with the Nichiren sect of Buddhism, I recalled scenes from my childhood of white-robed, hand-drum beating parades of people marching through the streets. Frankly, it is not a favourable image.

JIN: Then what was the thought process that led you to the point at which you joined Soka Gakkai?

IKEDA: Actually, after I entered the organization, I had the feeling that I had really made a mistake about joining such a group, but it was the personal magnetism of such an exceptional mentor as Josei Toda that captured my imagination and would not let go.

The Perennial Questions: What is a Human Being? What is the Meaning of Life?

IKEDA: Mr Jin, perhaps you, too, keenly feel that, much more than young people today, in our youth we were very serious about seeking answers to questions regarding human nature, the meaning of life, and how to live a good life. These matters concerned me greatly, and so I tried, in my own way, to pursue these issues.

A book entitled *Sophie's World* became a major topic of conversation in Japan in the mid-1990s. Sophie is a young girl who, led on by riddles from a mysterious character, enters the 'forest of philosophy'. As Sophie navigates the thorny issues in the history of philosophy, her narrative of her journey provides the reader with an easily comprehensible introduction to these topics. The book became a best seller in Japan.

The author introduces the beginning of this journey of exploration with the following passage.

> She opened the two envelopes again. *Who are you? Where does the world come from?* What annoying questions! And anyway where did the letters come from? That was just as mysterious, almost.
>
> Who had jolted Sophie out of her everyday existence and suddenly brought her face to face with the great riddles of the universe?[10]

Questions such as 'Who am I?' and 'Where did the earth and the entire universe come from?' may seem simple, but no one really knows the answers. However, just because no one knows the answers does not mean that we should avoid thinking about these questions.

JIN: I agree. No matter how much times change and how much progress we feel we have made as a civilization, these are questions that can never be resolved.

IKEDA: These universal questions, such as the nature of existence, including the experience of existence before birth and after death, are perennial themes for all of humankind. If we do not seriously consider these propositions, life will become a shallow and superficial experience. It will be a life lived only for one's own transitory pleasure, with no thought as to anyone else's welfare, as revealed in the saying, 'It does not matter to me what happens to this place – whether it becomes a field or a mountain'.

JIN: The worship of money and materialism that you mentioned before is based, I believe, on this lack of consideration of these eternal questions.

IKEDA: Exactly. Before I entered Soka Gakkai, I devoted myself to grappling with these questions, in my own way, as much as I could. In my pursuit, I studied philosophy and read a wide range of literature. At times I was attracted to Emerson's philosophy of transcendentalism, and there was also a time when I devoured the works of Henri Louis Bergson.

One could say that it was after this earnest quest that I was meant to encounter the Buddhist law, and that is exactly what happened.

The first time that I met Mr Toda, I felt that he was surrounding me with an intense radiance, and the attraction that I had felt for Emerson and Bergson paled in comparison, as if I were seeing the contours of their images recede through the mist of a spring morning. I felt that I had given myself up to something completely beyond my control.

Inspired by the feeling that I had come upon something true and genuine, and someone that I could trust and believe in, I immediately committed my feelings to poetry and read my poem to Mr Toda.

Traveler!
Where have you come from?
Where are you going?[11]

Questions about human nature, about the origins and destiny of humanity – the perennial questions – were always at the back of my mind, and so this poem came to me on the spur of the moment. It was from this point that my quest for truth really began, and, as I have discovered, it is a journey without end.

CHAPTER 4

Beloved Books of Our Youth: Studying Human Nature in Plutarch's Parallel Lives

Our Shared Literary Favourites

IKEDA: 'A dialogue, such as we are engaged in, is somewhat akin to inviting the public to share in our private correspondence. We write about the topics, including literature, that attract our interest. And if other people find these exchanges interesting, it's so much the better that they can enjoy them together with us. That is how I see what we are doing.'

I recall this comment that you made during our discussions at your home in Hong Kong in November 1995 and am struck by how it articulates the spirit of our conversations. It is a great joy for me to be able to discuss literature candidly and freely with a giant of modern Chinese literature such as you.

JIN: I also remember that you remarked how truly amazing it was that of all the works of literature that we loved in our youth, we have so many in common.

As I mentioned in our previous discussion, there is a wise saying that is often quoted: 'A thousand cups of wine do not suffice when true friends meet, but half a sentence is too much when there is no meeting of minds.' I am sure that both Chinese and Japanese like to converse and share a laugh while drinking. They may hit it off and become completely absorbed in their conversation. Then, to express their pleasure and delight, one may say, 'Well then, let me pour you another drink'. Then, the other will reciprocate the favour. And so it goes throughout the evening, and the more they engage in their conversation, the more their spirits are lifted.

IKEDA: Unfortunately, I do not drink. But I am sure that my mentor, who was very fond of sake, would have fit right in.

JIN: True friends are those who celebrate their mutual understanding, trust, respect, and acceptance of each other.

It is often said, 'A man will die for one who understands him, as a woman will make herself beautiful for one who delights in her'.[1] This expression means that perhaps the reason that a woman puts on makeup and pays attention to her appearance is so that she may please and satisfy the man who is interested in her. Likewise, a man would feel a sense of deep satisfaction if he were to sacrifice his life for one who knows him well.

IKEDA: That is a passage from *The Records of the Grand Historian*, isn't it?

JIN: Many of the chivalrous heroes that appear throughout Chinese history gave their lives to honour a friendship. They did not, however, place great emphasis on fighting for justice or distinguishing between good and evil. These figures appeared in an era before the expansion of Confucian philosophy.

For example, take heroes such as Nie Zheng who killed Xia Lei, Zhuan Zhe who killed King Lian of Wu, Hou Ying who committed suicide for his Lord Xin Ling of Wei, and Yu Rang who tried to kill Zhao Xiangzi. All of these historical figures committed their acts of murder or suicide in order to honour and repay their debt of friendship rather than to bring about justice.

Perhaps this is similar to the philosophy of the Japanese samurai. A notable act of chivalry worth mentioning is Benkei's loyalty to his master Yoshitsune. However, it goes without saying that, compared to the bravery of the kamikaze commandoes of more recent Japanese history, this is clearly different in character.

IKEDA: The question of the nature of justice is a thorny issue. Though the subtitle of Plato's great work, *The Republic*, is 'On Justice', there is hardly any mention of justice. This reveals just how difficult it is to define. One thing that we must never forget, however, is that justice must be understood as based on intimate and candid personal experience, and if this aspect is ignored or distorted, problems inevitably develop. A classic example of this is the way that, at the peak of World War II, Japanese wartime zeal was stirred up by proclaiming that the Japanese war effort pursued a just and noble cause.

At the time, death in combat was exalted as achieving eternal life by fighting for 'the noble cause of eternal loyalty', which young people of those days, especially those who thought earnestly about things, felt was nothing more than an empty slogan.

Of course, no one can endure the thought that one's own death will be in vain. In *Listen to the Voices from the Sea: Writings of the Fallen Japanese Students* (*Kike Wadatsumi no Koe*) and other compilations, we see student soldiers grasping for the meaning of their impending deaths; their poignant concerns are, first of all, for their families and relatives, but, most of all, for their homeland, where those who are dear to them live. Because of their indoctrination, they thought they would be sacrificing their lives for their homeland, and so they went to their heroic death in battle, believing that their death had significance.

The main problem is the incompetence and folly of a leadership that would coerce young people into certain death as kamikaze pilots, justifying this nonsense by loudly proclaiming slogans urging commitment to the 'noble cause of eternal loyalty'.

This kind of thing occurs not only in wartime. This notion of loyalty to a noble cause appears in every age and must be vigilantly guarded against. The more stridently this loyalty to a noble cause is urged, the more closely the facts must be scrutinized. But I digress. Please excuse my emphatic outburst.

JIN: On the contrary, I understand exactly what you are saying.

IKEDA: In any case, as I was saying, it is truly amazing that, in our youth, we shared the same favourite works of literature, such as Plutarch's *The Lives of Noble Grecians and Romans* (commonly called *Parallel Lives*),[2] *The Count of Monte Cristo*, and *The Three Musketeers*; works that sent our young hearts and imaginations racing. I cannot help feeling that for us to meet and discuss these things reveals, in itself, a profound karmic connection.

JIN: President Ikeda, we both experienced the daily trauma of living through one catastrophe after another during the war. In those days, Japan and China were in a state of armed conflict. If we had been in the military at that time, we may have faced each other on the battlefield.

Yet despite having been on opposite sides of the conflict, there is no doubt that we have many individual characteristics in common.

IKEDA: The mere thought of encountering you on the battlefield sends chills up my spine! The fact remains, however, that the Sino–Japanese conflict was, ultimately, Japan's invasion of China. I have to admit that I, like my peers, was caught up in the excitement and the appeal of the young soldier-boy image. But as I mentioned before, when my eldest brother returned from the frontlines on the Chinese mainland, what he said made me think. His words were: 'Japan is behaving atrociously. I feel so sorry for the Chinese people.' And so I began to harbour doubts about the war.

The military authorities promoted the war as a holy crusade that would create 'a Greater East Asia Co-Prosperity Sphere and liberate the peoples of Asia from the Europeans and Americans', but this was complete propaganda. Yet how different were the 'noble cause' and the reality of the war. With the defeat of Japan, this realization only became greater.

No Greater Misfortune than Having Stupid Leaders

JIN: Since we are on this topic, we would be remiss not to discuss the horrors of war and the value of peace. Every time I visit Oxford University and the University of Cambridge in England, I see plaques made of copper or wood displayed on campus in several of the famous college buildings. On these plaques are engraved the names of countless people in row after row. If you look carefully, you can see the explanation that reads, 'The following professors and students of this college gave their lives for their country in war'. The dates are 1914–18 or 1939–45.

IKEDA: Yes. I saw that, too, when I visited Oxford University.

JIN: These people were all the cream of the crop, the elite of the English educational system. Just imagine, if all of these professors, lecturers, researchers, and students of Oxford University and Cambridge had not been sacrificed in war, they may have become eminent statesmen, scholars, scientists, and artists. Instead, their lives were all snuffed out in an instant, and now, they have all returned to dust. What an enormous waste!

And furthermore, the lists of names are even longer at large, long-established colleges. Each time I see these lists, I feel so despondent. I am tormented by sadness and can only sigh with a heavy heart.

IKEDA: It goes without saying that war is an overwhelming waste, and the higher one's status in society, the greater one's responsibility to society. This concept of *noblesse oblige* is part of the traditional culture of Europe, including the UK. I have explained this concept and its importance to the students at the Soka Schools.

In Japan, this sense of responsibility was weak among the Shōwa period leaders, especially those who dragged Japan through the quagmire of the war. The higher their position, the more protective they were of themselves and more averse to putting themselves in danger. They did not take responsibility. The resulting system of policy and decision-making was fragile and lacked accountability, as the Tokyo War Crimes Tribunal brought to light.

This historical experience should teach us that we must absolutely never wage war, and that Japanese society must nurture virtue, in the best sense, in its leaders.

JIN: Today, as we look back on those times, who would regret that they did not give their life for their country? At the time, we all wholeheartedly harboured a virulent hostility and hatred toward the enemy, and thought only of wanting to kill him. However, now we find out that that sense of enmity was completely unnecessary. It was an illusion, conjured up by those in authority who pushed the country into war – a blunder committed by politicians and military leaders.

IKEDA: I think so too. It is just as they say, 'preparing for war is always immoral, but fighting is always noble' and 'war is a lie, a system of fraud'. The military leaders of those days were such idiots. In reflecting on his own military experience, the commentator Hyōe Murakami wrote, 'Why were the generals, senior commanders, and staff composed mostly of people who can only be described as ignorant, incompetent, and arrogant idiots?'[3]

My elder brother died fighting on the frontlines of Burma (currently Myanmar). Actually, it would be more accurate to say that he was forced into a war in which he was killed. He was a victim of the notorious Burma Imphal campaign in which the Japanese tried to destroy the Allied forces and invade India. This was a reckless, ill-advised, and extreme military strategy implemented by incompetent and inferior military leadership.

Some time ago, I watched a television programme that traced the history of the Imphal Campaign. It was agonizing to learn the tragic circumstances of my beloved brother's death and to know how much he must have suffered. No greater misfortune could befall a people than to be governed by stupid leaders. I believe that we should never ever again repeat this same mistake.

The Charismatic Heroes in Plutarch's *Parallel Lives*

IKEDA: Well then, let us finally enter into a discussion of literature in this chapter. I would like to discuss our views of literature and of life through the lens of a number of literary works.

JIN: I think that the reason that we both share a love for the same books is that we possess very similar characteristics. Perhaps it would be presumptuous of me to call our association a brotherhood, in the sense of a friendship between blood brothers, but at least I think I can safely say that we are birds of a feather that flock together.

People who enjoy liquor warm up to each other quickly. Those who enjoy watching sumo wrestling, soccer, baseball, or other sports readily become friends as they chat about the games. When people share the same personality traits, their tastes are often similar.

In our youth, we were attracted to adventure stories of heroes who successfully faced overwhelming odds with a courageous fighting spirit. These kinds of reading experiences helped nurture in us a passion and desire to take action and initiative. They helped cultivate in us the strength to face life's adversities and shocks without giving up.

IKEDA: I agree. Let's see. If I were to choose one of the most influential books we both read in our youth, I believe it would be Plutarch's *The Lives of the Noble Grecians and Romans*. What do you think?

JIN: Yes. For our younger readers, perhaps a brief description is in order.

The full English title of Plutarch's work is *The Lives of the Noble Grecians and Romans*. It was translated from the French into English by Sir Thomas North. The author, Plutarchus (Plutarch) was Greek, and so the original was written in Greek. North's English translation took a long time, but is a magnificent translation filled with dramatic narrative and written in an eloquent and refined style. It continues to be widely read and appreciated. In addition, a number of Shakespeare's plays, such as *Julius Caesar*, *Antony and Cleopatra*, *Timon of Athens*, *Coriolanus*, and *Pericles*, were influenced by the biographies in this translation.

North's writing was so superb that Shakespeare included many passages

with only slight embellishment and many lines of script are taken verba-
tim from North's translation.

IKEDA: The work contains many heroes whose names the average Japanese
person has heard at least once. In Japan, between 1952 and 1956, the
Iwanami Shoten Publishers published the complete translation. The translator was Yōichi Kōno.

JIN: The original title, translated directly, was *The Lives of the Noble Grecians and
Romans*. The title reflects the fact that Plutarch first presents the biography
of a Greek hero, then that of a Roman hero, to form a pair. The two heroes
share many similar attributes in terms of their accomplishments, their social
status, and their characteristics. Then, at the end of the two biographies is a
comparison and commentary. In total, 22 pairs of biographies were included.
Four stand-alone biographies were part of the work as well.

North's translation opens with the biography of the founder of Greece,
Theseus, followed by that of Romulus, the founder of Rome. The Chinese
edition is called *Biographies of Greek and Roman Heroes*, but is not a complete
translation. And unfortunately, the translation is not polished and makes
for dull and dreary reading.

IKEDA: This work was introduced to Japan and China much later. Needless
to say, it had an inestimable influence on European literature and history.

JIN: Greek and Roman legendary heroes as well as actual preeminent historical figures are portrayed in great detail. In a number of the biographies
that primarily depict battle scenes, the battles are even more realistic and
vivid than the portrayals of the heroes themselves. The author seems to
place emphasis on the comparative aspect of the work, accentuating the
similarities and commonalities between the two heroes in each pair. He
pointed out the moral and dignified character of each figure, rather than
their great accomplishments. This approach resulted in the creation of
figures who are much more alive and human.

It is said that this work greatly influenced the French Revolution. The
German translation was a favourite of Goethe, Schiller, Beethoven, and
Nietzsche.

IKEDA: You mentioned that the appeal of Plutarch's biographies is the very
human portrayal of the heroes. I am in complete agreement.

Ever since the historicism of the nineteenth century, in the view of many historical theories, including Marxism, the focus has been to seek historical laws or claim historical inevitability, while the fact that history is actually created by people has been ignored. In other words, these perspectives dehumanize history. Historical works written from this perspective may have many noteworthy points, but even so are extremely uninteresting.

The failure of the grand social experiment of the twentieth century, which was the old Soviet and Eastern European style of socialism, decisively demonstrates that modern historical and global perspectives that abandon any recognition of human beings are now bankrupt and defunct.

The phrase 'historical inevitability' is one that has never been used more in any other period of history than in the twentieth century. However, the notion that the flow of history is predetermined, and moreover, that human beings can know this, is the height of arrogance. Even if this were so, to think that everything is determined by external factors is a kind of determinism that could not be more simplistic.

This implies that all human effort, independence, and originality are, frankly, meaningless. And, in essence, this means that no matter what they do, human beings cannot escape fate and that all their efforts will be of no use.

In this sense, it is very symbolic that the two great philosophical currents of the twentieth century are the material determinism of Marxism and the psychological determinism of Freudianism.

Incidentally, I must say, the heroes of Plutarch's biographies have such humanistic appeal. Hideo Kobayashi commented, 'the "hero biographies" of Themistocles, Pericles, Alexander the Great, and Gaius Julius Caesar are all absolutely unlike any heroes I imagined'.[4] All of the heroes are definitely so human. They possess many human shortcomings and contradictions. They also commit many mistakes and missteps. They are definitely not saints or virtuous sages.

This is what it means to be human. We have worries, experience hardships, and through trial and error, we grapple with reality, create history, and leave a historical legacy. The biographies of Plutarch portray the qualities of their subjects in all their humanness in an unvarnished and frank perspective. Based on the content of the biographies, rather than being referred to as 'biographies of heroes', they may more aptly be called 'biographies of human beings'.

The Diligence of the Orator Demosthenes
and the Character of Pericles

IKEDA: Yakovlev, the architect of perestroika, whom I mentioned previously, said, 'I am all in favour of the Buddhist perception that consciousness determines life'. He said this in opposition to the materialist concept that existence determines consciousness or that 'things' are of highest significance.

What people call 'consciousness' can be referred to, in Buddhist terms, as 'single mindedness'. What kind of mind does one have? Everything, including one's life and society, starts from there. The self is infinitely malleable. Human beings are indeed central to the historical process.

Contemporary society is struggling against indifference and apathy, or in other words, the death of passion. This is exactly why I think that Plutarch's *The Lives of the Noble Grecians and Romans* is a fine book that should once again enjoy a wide readership. I believe that it is a book that has the power to help people revive a real concern and appreciation for their fellow human beings – in a way that will make them reengage in the human experience, sharing in humanity's hardships and struggles.

JIN: The heroes who appear in the work are bold and courageous. They are especially strong-willed men who submitted to no one. For example, the Greek orator Demosthenes was unable to speak clearly, and rolling the letter 'r' was especially difficult for him to do correctly. But he was determined and spared no effort. One of his training exercises involved filling his mouth with little pebbles and practising his speeches. In order to conquer the problem of his soft voice, he would run across the plains and up a steep hill until he could barely gasp for breath, and then recite his speeches and poems. Furthermore, he also practised speaking in front of a large mirror to rehearse his body language and hand gestures. And thus through assiduous effort, he trained himself to be a great orator.

These ancient heroes continued their struggles, with an indomitable spirit of courage and triumph, to overcome their challenges. President Ikeda, I am sure that it is this portrayal that has profoundly impressed you also with this book.

IKEDA: In one anecdote, Demosthenes created a practice room in his underground cellar where he could train his voice and practise his speech performance. He shaved half of his head so that he would be too embarrassed to go out, and so he stayed cloistered in his practice room for two or three months. I often tell this story to young people. I advise them, 'If you want to achieve your goals, don't forget the importance of diligence and hard work in your youth'.

JIN: Were you impressed with any of the other figures besides Demosthenes?

IKEDA: Pericles is another favourite of mine. Pericles is the one who asked about the nature of leadership in a democracy. His biography illuminates this issue from many perspectives.

First of all, the most important aspect of leadership is presence. This is dealt with in the following anecdote.

'Once, after being reviled and ill-spoken of all day long in his own hearing by some vile and abandoned fellow in the open market-place, where he was engaged in the despatch of some urgent affair, he continued his business in perfect silence, and in the evening returned home composedly, the man still dogging him at the heels, and pelting him all the way with abuse and foul language; and stepping into his house, it being by this time dark, he ordered one of his servants to take a light, and to go along with the man and see him safe home.'5

Overlooking the stream of abusive language directed at him, Pericles quietly and calmly went about his business. He was unconcerned about his reputation in the short term. He knew the mission that he must fulfil in the present. And he knew how history would judge him. He surely had a keen awareness of these things deep down in his heart.

JIN: He exemplified the dignity and style of a true leader.

IKEDA: Another characteristic of a good leader is to be able to draw a clear line between public and private life. Leaders have to rein in their desires. Pericles knew this very well, and therefore was very self-disciplined.

'For he was never seen to walk in any street but that which led to the market-place and council-hall, and he avoided invitations of friends to supper, and all friendly visiting and intercourse whatsoever; in all the time he had to do with the public, which was not a little, he was never known to have gone to any of his friends to a supper.'6

He was high-minded and upright, standing out above all others.

JIN: Pericles is the very image of uprightness, just as is expressed in the old

Chinese saying, 'Do not adjust your sandal in a melon patch or straighten your crown under a plum tree'. This means that one must avoid doing anything that might invite suspicion.

IKEDA: On that point, the late Premier Zhou Enlai was admirable. Though he occupied one of the most important positions in the entire country, he disliked receiving preferential treatment of any kind, and, for example, at the barbershop when people waiting for a haircut invited him to cut in front of them, he firmly declined.

Pericles, through inherent genius and perseverance, ultimately rose to the highest leadership position in Athens. He held all power and authority in his hands. Even so, he did not cater to the masses.

As Plutarch writes regarding Pericles' attitude toward the people, he did not readily 'yield to their pleasures' or 'comply with the desires of the multitude, as a steersman shifts with the winds. . . . [He] uprightly and undeviatingly for the country's best interest, . . . was able generally to lead the people along, with their own wills and consents, by persuading and showing them what was to be done; and sometimes, too, urging and pressing them forward extremely against their will, he made them whether they would or not, yield submission to what was for their advantage.

'In which, to say the truth, he did but like a skilful physician, who, in a complicated and chronic disease, as he sees occasion, at one while allows his patient the moderate use of such things as please him, at another while gives him keen pains and drugs to work the cure.'⁷

Democratic politics is, in a sense, an exercise in riding fluctuations in popularity. Politics is, therefore, in danger of becoming the 'popularity business'. If a politician caters to popular will, for that moment at least, everything is good, and his position is secure. However, he will not be able to achieve the maturity of politics or maintain political longevity in the long term.

In this way, in a democracy, it is always important to be vigilant because, as Plato so superbly analyzed in his work *Republic*, there is an ever-present danger of overstepping and descending into populism.

A true leader must have clear vision and lead the people with a persuasive and affirming tenacity. At times, he must state clearly what needs to be said, even though it may sound harsh to the people. This is not accomplished easily, and so all the more, a leader who can do this will win the trust of the people.

To Accomplish Great Things a Leader Must Understand the Concept of Time

JIN: Trust underlies the social contract on which society is based. In ancient times, a disciple of Confucius asked about government. Confucius answered, 'You need enough food, enough weaponry, and the trust of the common people'.

Confucius' disciple continued, 'If you had to do without one of these, which of the three would you do without first?' Confucius responded 'Do without weapons'. This is because without the people, there would be no nation. And even if there were no military, the people must still be given food.

The disciple then asked, 'If you had to do without one of the other two, which would it be?' Confucius answered, 'Do without food'. He then explained that the people would somehow be able to manage. There would be relatively little difficulty if the government stopped stocking its warehouses. 'But without the trust of the common people, you get nowhere.'[8]

IKEDA: Indeed, a nation cannot exist without the trust of its people.

JIN: These words of Confucius apply very appropriately to the present as well. For example, incurring a loss in business is a serious blow, but to lose the trust of one's clients and associates is a fatal loss. Whether a person creates an organization, starts a business, or does any other activity, trust is the most important element.

IKEDA: Upon reminiscing about the experiences I have had in China, I wrote an essay entitled 'Country of Loyalty, People of Honour'. I am very aware that the Chinese have traditionally placed great emphasis on loyalty and trust. I, too, have made this the foundation of all my relations with China over the past two decades or more.

To add to our discussion of the important qualities of leadership, I would like to also suggest that a leader must have a keen sense of timing. For example, one must retreat when appropriate and advance when appropriate. Unless a person can observe every angle, understand the timeliness of an action, and in this context, take command, he is not a first-rate leader. Pericles is an example of a leader who understands this concept of time.

In one anecdote, there was a leader who was very pleased with his popularity and became very full of himself, so much so that he wanted to invade another country. Many of his subjects expressed their approval of his plan.

However, Pericles 'endeavoured to withhold him and to advise him from it in the public assembly, telling him in a memorable saying of his, which still goes about, that, if he would not take Pericles' advice, yet he would not do amiss to wait and be ruled by time, the wisest counsellor of all'.[9]

The situation turned out just as he had feared. Athens fell, and the lives of many citizens were sacrificed. Strength is important, as is the solidarity of the people. Yet, unless the element of timing is figured into the equation, no great accomplishment will result.

In the Buddhist scriptures is the passage, 'When it comes to studying the teachings of Buddhism, one must first learn to understand the time'.[10] In his Precepts for Youth, my mentor also admonished the youth to 'understand the times in which we live'.[11]

It seems to me that Pericles also thoroughly understood the time in which he lived.

The Courageous Alexander the Great

JIN: Many heroes appear in *Plutarch: The Lives of the Noble Grecians and Romans*, but the most famous is Alexander the Great.

IKEDA: During my youth, and perhaps it was the same for you, Mr Jin, I remember avidly reading about Alexander the Great and being thoroughly thrilled. And so later on, I was inspired to write a story for young people entitled *Alexander's Decision*.

JIN: Really? If the Chinese translation has come out, I would love to read it.

IKEDA: Literary works based on the life of Alexander the Great must be legion, but the most thorough and dramatic treatment is surely in *Plutarch: The Lives of the Noble Grecians and Romans*. The authors of all these other works about Alexander the Great undoubtedly consulted Plutarch's work to some extent. In fact, I, too, relied on it for much of the inspiration for my work.

JIN: What part from the life of Alexander the Great did you use as the basis for the subject matter of your work?

IKEDA: I used the episode in which Alexander collapses from a serious illness. His friend and doctor, Philip, prepared medicine to treat Alexander's critical condition.

At that very moment, a letter arrived informing Alexander that Philip had been bribed by one of his enemies to kill him. Alexander merely hid the letter underneath his pillow. When Philip brought the medicine, Alexander silently handed the letter to him and took the medicine that he had brought.

'This was a spectacle well worth being present at, to see Alexander take the draught and Philip read the letter at the same time, and then turn and look upon one another, but with different sentiments; for Alexander's looks were cheerful and open, to show his kindness to and confidence in his physician, while the other was full of surprise and alarm at the accusation, appealing to the gods to witness his innocence, sometimes lifting up his hands to heaven, and then throwing himself down by the bedside, and beseeching Alexander to lay aside all fear, and follow his directions without apprehension.'[12]

As the story goes, Alexander successfully recovers after being deep in a drug-induced stupor. Philip did not betray Alexander. The plot was intended to destroy the bond of friendship between the two men by casting doubt upon their loyalty to one another, but Alexander's faith in his friend proved stronger in the end.

JIN: This beautifully dramatizes Alexander's bravery and is very moving.

IKEDA: Friends and, indeed, all human beings, should trust each other unconditionally. Those with a clear conscience and courage in their heart can never be overcome by malice and evil.

I have to say that Plutarch's penetrating portrayal reveals Alexander's humanity and is so vivid and gripping that it seems almost as if you are there experiencing the moment in person. Plutarch's *The Lives of the Noble Grecians and Romans* would be an excellent model for anyone aspiring to be a writer.

A Comparison Between Plutarch's *Lives* and *Records of the Grand Historian*

JIN: When I read Plutarch's *The Lives of the Noble Grecians and Romans*, I was already living in Hong Kong and over 30 years of age. The reason for my reading it was that I was researching the origins of several of Shakespeare's plays. The North translation is rendered in the English of the Elizabethan period. And because the text is so eloquent and brilliantly written, my English was just not up to the challenge.

Even so, I combed through the text in great detail with all the diligence I could muster. Yet, because I poured all my efforts into studying the English and researching the literary aspects of the work, I feel that I did not fully grasp the rich moral significance of the book.

IKEDA: Perhaps one of the reasons this book has been so well received is that it takes the biography format. Readers can readily comprehend the intersection of one human being encountering one critical event. And in the process, the contours of history come sharply into focus.

JIN: Historians often use the biographical form for historical narrative. The world's earliest example is the *Records of the Grand Historian* by Sima Qian. The next one is *The Book of Han* by Ban Gu. Compared to the *Records of the Grand Historian*, Plutarch's diaries appear at least 200 years later.

IKEDA: What differences do you see between these two works?

JIN: *Records of the Grand Historian* is by far the shorter of the two. Also, I think that the characters appear much more vigorous and dynamic than in Plutarch's work. Sima Qian also used the convention of simultaneously presenting biographies of two historical figures in a comparative analytical style. For example, he discussed in pairs Su Qiu and Zhang Yi as well as Bai Qi and Wang Jian. In addition, he wrote *The Biographies of Mencius and Jia Sheng* and *The Biographies of General Wei and Piao Qi*. Both of these combine the biographies of two figures into one work.

Later historians of Chinese history also adopted this form. *The Book of Tang* incorporated the biographies of Li Jing and Li Ji. In the time of Plutarch, there would have been no opportunity to read or hear about the content of *Records of the Grand Historian*, and so it is believed that the form of combining commentary with paired biographies was Plutarch's own idea.

If Plutarch's work had never been written, the world would be the poorer without many of Shakespeare's important plays.

IKEDA: Sima Qian's greatness was his endurance and commitment to scholarship. Midway through his great historical work, he somehow offended the Emperor Wu Di and, instead of committing suicide as was customary for men of high status, he chose to be punished by castration and lived to finish his historical work. By deciding to live with his shame, he turned his agony into a passion for completing his great work. He died shortly after completing his work.

What does a person do when confronted with difficult circumstances? What will be that person's legacy? This is the point at which a person's true colours become evident.

Sima Qian confessed that his motivation for writing *Records of the Grand Historian* was as follows: 'When Xibo, the Earl of the West, was imprisoned at Youli, he expounded the *Book of Changes*. Confucius was in distress and he made the *Spring and Autumn Annals*. Qu Yuan was banished and he composed his poem "Encountering Sorrow". After Zuo Qiu lost his sight, he wrote the *Conversations from the States*. When Sun Wu had had his feet amputated in punishment, he set forth the *Art of War*. Lü Buwei was banished to Shu but his *Spring and Autumn of Mr Lü* has been handed down through the ages. While Han Feizi was held in prisoner in Qin he wrote "The Difficulties of Disputation" and "The Sorrow of Standing Alone." Most of the three hundred poems of the *Book of Odes* were written when the sages poured out their anger and dissatisfaction.'[13]

JIN: This is from the *Taishigong zixu* (Postface and Autobiography of the Grand Scribe), isn't it?

IKEDA: Many of the masterpieces of historical writing from ancient times are the legacy of those who endured great hardship which inspired their creative powers. The authors were able to transform their suffering into dynamic motivation with which to move forward.

Nichiren, whose teachings we follow, is one who at the height of his greatest travails penned his most important works, entitled *The Opening of the Eyes* and *The Object of Devotion for Observing the Mind*.

My mentor would often say, 'We revere Nichiren Daishonin as a great man, not simply because he was able to endure great hardships. The most distinguishing aspect of his greatness was that he was able to illuminate the most essential Buddhist teachings while in the midst of his most challenging adversities.'

This ability to transform hardship is not limited to the world of literature, but is a truth that extends to all of human life. Exceptional people have cultivated the internal fortitude to turn whatever adverse circumstances in which they find themselves into a positive stimulus that becomes a tailwind at their backs.

JIN: The Japanese edition of Plutarch's *The Lives of the Noble Grecians and Romans* must be a magnificent work that has had a major influence on Japanese writers and intellectuals. In China, many of the major military and literary figures who contributed to the founding of the People's Republic of China had deep ties with Japan. These include, for example, Sun Yat-sen, Chiang Kai-shek, Tai Chi-tao, Liao Zhongkai, Lu Xun, Zhou Zuoren, Guo Moruo, and Yu Dafu.

As a result of Japan's invasion of China and its attempt to strengthen its hand by pushing the Chinese government to accept its Twenty-One Demands, the animosity the Chinese people felt toward Japan deepened. Consequently, cultural exchanges between the peoples of both countries had to be suspended. This was most unfortunate.

IKEDA: I believe that in all of the regrettable history between China and Japan, stretching from the end of the nineteenth century to the mid-twentieth century, the Twenty-One Demands represent a major turning point that led to a sharp parting of the ways between China and Japan.

Japan attempted to expand its self-serving interests in China during World War I, a time when European and US attention to China was distracted. This is, without a doubt, the most foolish action taken by Japan in modern times.

It was such an affront to the Chinese people that the Chinese government of the time announced that 9 May, the day on which the ultimatum from the Japanese was accepted, would thereafter be recognized as the National Day of Shame. This triggered an arrogant Japan to strengthen its militaristic policies even further, and thus began Japan's slow descent down the road to hell.

I have mentioned this before in this dialogue, and I will continue to repeat my firm conviction that the Japanese people must never forget the barbaric and inhumane way their country treated China! If we truly desire amiable relations between China and Japan, we must not obscure the past!

Well, our discussion has covered a wide range of topics, from Plutarch's *The Lives of the Noble Grecians and Romans* to issues in Sino–Japanese history. In the next chapter, Mr Jin, I would like to continue to explore the literary works that you and I were drawn to in our youth.

CHAPTER 5

A Resurgence of Literature: The Appeal of The Count of Monte Cristo

The Count of Monte Cristo: A Shared Favourite

IKEDA: On 1 June 1997, a Prayer Monument for World Peace was erected in the Chūgoku Peace Memorial Park in Hiroshima, the city where the first atomic bomb was dropped. I would like to take this opportunity to again thank you, Mr Jin, for the excellent inscription that you wrote for the monument.

JIN: Please don't mention it. I filled my heart with thoughts of peace and poured all of my energy into writing the inscription.

IKEDA: The recognition of the importance of sharing the tragic story of war and the atomic bomb is beginning to diminish in Japan. And fewer people burn with anger that this is happening. Despite all this, I am sure that the inspiring inscription that you wrote, Mr Jin, will rekindle the flame of peace.

JIN: When I visited Japan, you told me the story of how the first president Tsunesaburo Makiguchi opposed the invasion of China and was arrested, and later died in prison. And you also told me how Josei Toda carried on Mr Makiguchi's legacy and heroically continued the struggle. I was filled with respect and admiration for these brave men.

President Ikeda, you have articulated your own mission as a staunch advocate for justice and world peace. This truly represents a passing of the baton of justice from your two great predecessors to you, and I cannot help being deeply impressed.

IKEDA: I am humbled by your kind words. As you mentioned, I have carried on the legacy passed on to me by Mr Makiguchi and Mr Toda. And now, it is time for the youth to step up and take the baton. It is my intention that, by engaging in these dialogues, we are leaving our knowledge and wisdom for the youth who will follow.

JIN: I absolutely feel the same way.

IKEDA: Well then, let us resume our discussion of literature. This time, shall we discuss one of the favourite works of our youth, *The Count of Monte Cristo* by Alexandre Dumas? The Japanese title, *Gankutsu Ō*, means 'King of the Grotto'.

JIN: Excellent! *The Count of Monte Cristo* is one of my favourite novels.

IKEDA: I remember that we had a good time discussing this work when we first met in Hong Kong. I mentioned that my mentor had insightfully observed, 'The success of protagonist Edmond Dantès in elite social circles was not due to his financial means or his intelligence. Rather, it was because he inspired trust.' You said that you thought his perspective was right on the mark. As Mr Toda's disciple, I could not have been happier to hear you say that.

JIN: When this book became a topic of our discussion, not only was it a shared interest, but it also provided a wonderful opportunity for you to reminisce about how your mentor, Josei Toda, perceived it. I sense that we do indeed share a deep karmic connection.

IKEDA: I am sure there are many reasons why *The Count of Monte Cristo* is so beloved by people today. One is the way it depicts the historical period. It is set against the backdrop of the early nineteenth century, a turbulent period in French history that included the restoration of the monarchy and Napoleon's Hundred Days. Another is the character of Dantès who, in the face of injustice and absurdity, with single-minded determination, never abandons his principles. Also very interesting is the fascinating and scrupulously detailed depiction of the lives of the aristocratic class. These are just a few good reasons that immediately come to mind.

JIN: Among those, which do you think has the most appeal?

IKEDA: I think the most compelling aspect of all is the interesting way the story unfolds. The fate of protagonist Edmond Dantès, a man who is completely happy with his life, changes suddenly for the worse when supposed friends conspire against him. What a precipitous development. While in prison, Dantès encounters the priest, Father Faria, who becomes his teacher and provides him with a comprehensive education. Still seething with a desire for revenge, Dantès escapes from prison after 14 years of bitter struggle and perseverance.

Next, Dantès makes his debut in the high society of Paris as the Count of Monte Cristo, and with his quick wit and the hidden treasure passed on to him by the priest, he sets out to corner those who betrayed him.

JIN: The whole book is filled with one breathtaking episode after another. Before you know it, you are drawn in and completely absorbed in the story.

IKEDA: And furthermore, precious gems of wisdom and experience are scattered throughout like glittering stars twinkling in the night sky. This work does not simply provide an entertaining distraction; it is a radiant work of great world literature that shines throughout the immense variety of twists and turns in the narrative.

A Visit to the Chateau d'If

JIN: Three years ago [in 1995], my wife and I and several friends visited Marseilles. One of our friends was the unit commander of the marine firefighters of Marseilles, and so he served as our guide.

The island of If rises out of the ocean across from Marseilles, and the fortress on the rocky islet, known as the Chateau d'If, was a famous site that we were very eager to visit. According to our friend, the island gained notoriety from Dumas's novel, and the site of the story is now visited by hordes of tourists each year.

In actuality, however, since *The Count of Monte Cristo* is a fictional work, the claim that Dantès was imprisoned on the island is pure fantasy.

IKEDA: When I visited Marseilles in 1981, I was able to view the island from a distance. It was much closer to the continent than I had imagined, and I had the feeling that a good swimmer such as Dantès probably could have swum the distance easily.

Bathed in the blindingly brilliant sunlight of southern France, the white island was afloat in the distance on an ocean of cobalt blue. The hardships that the character Dantès suffered there reminded me of the struggle my mentor endured during his own imprisonment.

Often, when a book becomes a bestseller, the setting in which it takes place also becomes well known.

JIN: Yes. I had a similar experience. In my novel, *The Legend of the Condor Heroes*, I wrote about Taohua Island (literally 'Peach Blossom Island'), the setting where the female protagonist Huang Rong and her father Huang Yaoshi lived. This was an actual small island east of the Zhoushan Archipelago. Due to the exposure from the novel and television drama, the island became very well known and developed into a tourist destination.

When I visited the island, the village chief and party leaders asked that I write a few words to commemorate my visit and firmly establish the locale as the former residence of the character Huang Yaoshi, known as Dong Xie, or Eastern Heretic.

An arbour had been erected on a small hill and was named Sword-Testing Pavilion after the arbour described in the novel. In concert with this, a newly purchased boat for ferrying tourists back and forth to the island was named 'The Jin Yong'.

IKEDA: This must be the cost of fame for a popular novelist.

JIN: This kind of thing does not bother me. I am truly grateful for their goodwill. Whether or not the novel is based on fact, I do not think that this kind of notoriety ever diminishes the quality of a work. Furthermore, if readers think that something in the book is factual, this simply means that their imagination has been exercised. And, you could say that the region has just been enriched by another element providing local colour.

The world is populated with many scenic and historical sites, and undoubtedly many of them are based on far-fetched tales of imagination. For example, legend has it that the Duanqiao Bridge on Xi Hu Lake, in Hangzhou, is the place where the mythological white snake spirit and her husband Xu Xian met. Of course, such a thing as a romance between a white snake spirit and a human being is quite a fantasy.

IKEDA: A similar example in Japan is *The Fir Trees Remain* by Shūgoro Yamamoto. After it was broadcast as an NHK television drama, the Sendai area, which was the setting of the drama, became instantly popular, and it seems that sites claiming to be related to scenes in the drama popped up all over.

This may be a slight divergence, but speaking from a religious perspective, I do not think that it is very meaningful to make a pilgrimage to so-called scenic sites and historic places. To leave the place where one lives and to seek truth in some distant holy or mysterious sacred site should not be a universal practice of faith.

The late Professor Bryan Wilson, professor at Oxford University and former president of the International Society for the Sociology of Religion, with whom I have engaged in dialogue, made an interesting comment. He stated that a 'living faith' should no longer be constrained by 'the sanctification of one particular place', but rather must transcend this mentality of 'sacred geography' and affirm the original essence of religious faith and spirituality. Accordingly, he maintained, temple construction is relatively unimportant in comparison.[1]

In *The Geography of Human Life*, the great work of Tsunesaburo Makiguchi's early life, Makiguchi wrote candidly that a mature, culturally developed people do not necessarily make pilgrimages to sacred places; rather it is through an inner faith that they fulfil their sense of religious piety. I really believe that this is the case.

Portrait of Dumas, the Prolific Author

JIN: Incidentally, did you know that nearly 300 novels are attributed to Dumas, but that many of these were actually written by imitators? Some are by authors who falsely used Dumas's name, while others were mass-produced by second- and third-rate writers hired by Dumas to help him pay off his debts.

IKEDA: I have heard that his rivals maligned him by calling him 'the boss of a novel production factory'.

JIN: As a result, many of the works are of poor quality, with weak composition and shallow character development. I have been thoroughly taken in by numerous Dumas imitations.

Of course, all the works written by Dumas himself are superb, but these are just a handful, including *The Three Musketeers* trilogy, *The Count of Monte Cristo*, *The Black Tulip*, and *Queen Margot*.

IKEDA: Unfortunately, *The Black Tulip* and *Queen Margot* are not very well known in Japan. What are they about?

JIN: *Queen Margot* is the story of the mother of King Charles IX of France. She plotted to kill her son-in-law, Henri IV, by spreading poison on the pages of a book he was reading. However, it was her son, King Charles IX, who picked up the book first, and so she ended up poisoning her own son.

IKEDA: I see. Do you have a similar story-line in Chinese literature?

JIN: Yes, we do. Wang Shizhen, a great man of letters during the Ming dynasty (1368–1644) planned to take revenge on the enemies of his father by writing a superb romance novel, *Jin Ping Mei* (Golden Lotus). He saturated every page of the novel with poison, and devised an intricate scheme to ultimately put it in the hands of Yon Song's son, Yan Shifan.

Yan Shifan started reading the book and was immediately captivated by it. He became completely engrossed in it and kept reading more. The poison acted as an adhesive, and so when Yan Shifan came to pages that were stuck together, he moistened his fingers with saliva, simultaneously ingesting the poison on his fingers. The poison was weak and so he did not die, but he suffered brain damage.

Yan Shifan had always been his father's advisor. He was brilliant at writing the ritual Taoist prayers that were offered by the emperor. Because of this, the father, Yan Song, enjoyed the trust and good graces of the ruler of the time, Emperor Jiaqing. Therefore, after Yan Shifan's mental capacity declined, Yan Song fell from favour. He and his son were put into prison and that is where they died.

IKEDA: Is this a true story?

JIN: I would say that it is very questionable. According to the historical evidence, Wang Shizhen is not the author of *Jing Ping Mei*. However, it is a fact that the idea of applying poison to the pages of a book is a device that was used in both East and West, undoubtedly with the intent of captivating readers with an engrossing and suspenseful plot.

IKEDA: Since ancient times, poison has been associated with magical powers that entice people to commit evil deeds. Even in *The Count of Monte Cristo*, the use of poison enters into the story in the scene where the wife of Royal Prosecutor Villefort appears.

Many stories in the West include poisonings in their plots. Take, for example, the somewhat eerie story of the legendary Borgia family, which was alleged to have used poison to depose their relatives as well as enemies.

I recall when Umberto Eco's novel *The Name of the Rose*, which was set in a medieval Christian monastery, became a best seller. It was made into a movie. Here also we see the device of coating pages in a book with poison.

JIN: In *The Black Tulip*, Dumas paints a picture of the period of time when the Dutch were enchanted with tulips. A romantic young couple successfully raise a variety of tulip that has black petals, and it becomes extremely popular. But then, others appear who try to steal everything they have, either through force or deceit, and so the story flows from one thrilling scene to the next.

Abbé Faria, the Philosopher

IKEDA: Dumas's finest work is surely *The Count of Monte Cristo*.

JIN: The greatest appeal of *The Count of Monte Cristo*, just as you suggested, is how the story unfolds in the most captivating and unexpected ways. Moreover, the story remains completely true to the overall logic and sentiment of the narrative, down to the very last detail. This work is definitely a masterpiece.

As I was writing my novel *The Deadly Secret*, it suddenly dawned on me – the part of the story about the imprisoned Di Yun, who was orally taught the secret martial arts lore and techniques of the Shen Zhao Sutra, almost exactly replicates the part in *The Count of Monte Cristo* where, while in prison, Dantès learns from the Italian priest, Abbé Faria. I did not intentionally try to imitate this story-line. Rather, I unconsciously pursued the same idea.

IKEDA: Mr Jin, you are a preeminent writer who has been called the Dumas of the East. I think that, basically, the issue is that your ideas are quite similar to those of Dumas.

JIN: You are too kind. I could have changed the part that was similar, if I had wanted to, but I noticed the similarity after I had already written the entire book. To make the revisions would have been a painstakingly laborious effort.

To add to that, Ding Dian, who teaches the *Shen Zhao Jing*, has a distinctive manner characterized by refinement and depth and differs slightly from Faria, the priest in *The Count of Monte Cristo*. Among all of the romantic novels that I have written, the characters in this work are especially outstanding and can be counted among my best. Therefore, I thought it would be a great waste and that I may regret it if I were to omit this element.

IKEDA: When the Japanese translation comes out, I would really like to compare it to *The Count of Monte Cristo*. Father Faria has the presence of a philosopher. This is evidenced in the passage in which he tells Dantès, 'To learn is not to know; there are the learners and the learned. Memory makes the one, philosophy the other.'[2] Underlying that philosophical countenance is a profound scholarship. Father Faria continues, 'Human knowledge is confined within very narrow limits; and when I have taught you mathematics, physics, history, and the three or four modern languages with which I am acquainted, you will know as much as I do myself. Now, it will scarcely require two years for me to communicate to you the stock of learning I possess.'[3]

Though he downplays the depth of his knowledge to Dantès, he is indeed a great intellect with a considerable store of knowledge. And because he is such an intellectual, he is able to distinguish between what knowledge is essential to possess and what is not.

JIN: He makes a very profound statement.

IKEDA: Father Faria's words remind me of my dear mentor of long ago. He would often challenge us by saying, 'Just tell me what field of scholarship is your specialty, and if I have the time to devote three months to studying it, I'll learn enough to rival you, no matter what the field!' He, too, was quite an excellent scholar.

JIN: Incidentally, President Ikeda, you have been comparing me to Dumas. I am truly humbled by this. However, Dumas's splendid literary skills were so superb that I am no match for such excellence. Our literary styles are certainly similar, but if we were to hold a contest in which my five most excellent works and five of his most excellent works were chosen, and the average number of points were calculated, Dumas would surpass me by far. However, if the contest were to include 15 of our most excellent works, I would dare to say, and please forgive me if this sounds like self-flattery, but perhaps I would win. As I mentioned before, this is only because he has so few excellent works and so many second-rate ones. And the second-rate works are so genuinely poor and such absolute failures that they would greatly drag down the average.

Longing for a Revival of Literature in Modern Times

IKEDA: Mr Jin, if you and Dumas were to have a conversation about your various literary works, it would really be interesting. Unfortunately, we are not seeing the kind of great works of literature the likes of which Dumas or Victor Hugo produced, either here or in the West.

Modern literature, especially the literature of the twentieth century, certainly did produce excellent works that featured, for example, a subtle psychological style of character development and objective description as well as a well-crafted literary style.

However, the appeal of the narrative, and the irresistible magnetism and creativity it has to draw in the reader – or you might call it the power to rejuvenate and bring to life – this is the dynamism that overflows from the literature of Dumas and Hugo, and this is what is missing from more recent literary works.

Of course, we live in a different time, but when you read the work of great authors like Dumas and Hugo, you feel connected to the pulsating life force of a larger reality. I cannot help feeling that this is exactly the kind of literature that is once again sought after.

Some say that young people of today are searching for something that shakes up their world and that what we need is to borrow the power of narrative to create a world of rich and vital experience that overcomes the drab uniformity of today's society.

JIN: I agree completely.

IKEDA: The essence of the cultural and intellectual vitality that animated the

Renaissance is what we, who eagerly await the dawn of a new humanism, seek in a rebirth of literature in our own time.

My mentor used to say that if you read great literature, you will be able to understand the Buddhist teachings more deeply. The Ten Worlds as well as other elements taught in Buddhism are all illustrated in great literature. I feel strongly that in order for humanism to flourish, a rebirth of literature is essential.

JIN: Literature broadens one's horizons and enriches one's life. Buddhism offers a perspective that provides solutions to the problems of life. And both literature and Buddhist teachings explore answers to life's questions.

IKEDA: I think that in our dialogue, we are discussing our vision and the prospects for an era ushering in a revival of literature.

JIN: I think so, too. As we contemplate the nature of great literature, I think that it is very appropriate to refer to Dumas's work as such. Dumas's position in the history of world literature is firmly established. One reason for this is the vivid way he portrayed his characters. The ability to graphically depict his characters is evidence of a writer's considerable literary genius.

IKEDA: Yes. It is not just the plot of his narratives. It is also the way a writer develops his characters.

JIN: The literary value of *The Count of Monte Cristo* and *The Three Musketeers* lies, in part, in the distinct individuality of the protagonists and the striking depiction of each character.

When viewed in these terms, I think that of the two works, *The Three Musketeers* is of a much higher calibre. By this I mean that in *The Count of Monte Cristo*, good and evil are presented in such black and white terms that the characters' personalities tend to seem simplistic. It is almost as if they are typecast as the kind of actors one might see in a Peking opera; that is, they lack the ambiguity that makes for complex and intriguing literature.

IKEDA: Now that you mention it, the bad guys in *The Count of Monte Cristo* really do seem evil through and through. That is not the case with *The Three Musketeers*. The character Comte de Rochefort was d'Artagnan's archrival, but he does not seem to be such an evil man.

Mr Jin, your point is well taken. This is a perspective that I have not actually thought about very deeply.

JIN: In the context of human social relations, good and evil are intricately interrelated. It is impossible to say that someone is 100 percent good or 100 percent evil. Bad people probably have their redeeming qualities, while good people undoubtedly have their demerits. An author's concern must be the truth.

My intention in writing *The Heaven Sword and the Dragon Sabre* was to illustrate one way of perceiving life. That is, at times, distinguishing between things that are true and upright versus evil and wicked, or between good and bad, can be difficult.

Life does not always follow the saying, 'Goodness is repaid with goodness, while evil meets with retribution'. It is not always so easy to tell the good guys from the bad guys. Life is really more complex, and destiny is constantly changing.

IKEDA: Mr Jin, your view of humanity has a close affinity with the Buddhist worldview and perspective on humanity and life. The Buddhist scriptures state, 'The opposite of good we call bad, the opposite of bad we call good. Hence we know that outside of the mind there is no good and there is no bad. What is apart from this good and this bad is called the unlabelled. The good, the bad, and the unlabelled – outside of these there is no mind, and outside of the mind there are no concepts.'[4]

As the scripture teaches, good and evil are not mutually exclusive, but are part of the whole. Inherent in human life is the potential for both good and evil, and it is impossible to limit the way we think or feel to either one or the other.

Mr Jin, in light of this quote, your comments appear to be quite close to the concepts of the Buddhism.

JIN: I wonder if this means that I have had the disposition of a Buddhist adherent all along.

Dantès's Tale of Revenge

IKEDA: Personally, I like *The Count of Monte Cristo* more than *The Three Musketeers*. Forgive me for expressing a difference of opinion with such a great writer.

JIN: Oh, please! In *The Count of Monte Cristo*, the way that Dantès honours his debt of gratitude and takes revenge makes readers feel uplifted and gives them a sense of gratification. However, the most important aspects of Dantès's character are his resolve, his magnanimity, and that he carries himself like a gentleman.

IKEDA: His character portrays the depth and breadth of human personality and is not simply limited to a depiction of a vengeful devil.

JIN: When a person determines to take revenge and tries to destroy his bitter enemy, he has given himself up to a fleeting impulse. In contrast, when a person has painstakingly planned and plotted revenge, then just before exacting the revenge that anyone would agree is rightly deserved, he forgives his enemy, this reveals the depth of this person's humanity, and makes the story all the more moving.

IKEDA: I agree. I think you are right. Dantès, the 'vengeful devil', gradually becomes more forgiving. For example, after he took revenge on his archenemy Villefort by killing Villefort's wife and son, Dantès muttered, 'What have I done? Have I gone too far?' Then, finally, at the close of this tale of revenge, Dantès spares the life of Danglars.

JIN: Yes. Dantès forgives the most unscrupulous and merciless person of all.

IKEDA: In his work *The Human Revolution*, my mentor, Josei Toda named the protagonist Gan Kutsuo, a homonym for Gankutsu-Ō the Japanese translation of Count of Monte Cristo, 'Indomitable Champion'. Because of wartime oppression, both he and his mentor, Mr Makiguchi, were cast into prison. Mr Makiguchi died in prison while Mr Toda, his disciple, lived through the experience and was released.

My mentor was a bold and kindhearted person, typical of a person born in the Meiji Period (1868–1912). When the topic of Mr Makiguchi, his mentor, arose, sometimes Mr Toda's eyes would well up with tears and he would become agitated. It seemed that he was struggling to find a way to deal with his unspeakable anger. At the height of his outrage, he undoubtedly was seeking answers from the spirit of the Indomitable Champion to the questions, 'Who killed Mr Makiguchi? How can I not avenge his death!'

Vengeance does not exist in Buddhist teachings. This does not mean that Buddhism abandons the struggle with evil. But it does not advocate using violence to strike down a specific group or individual. To combat evil means to fight against the primal, diabolical force that lies hidden in each person's heart and in the far corners of every society.

This is what my mentor meant when he referred to vengeance and vendetta. It is difficult to destroy this 'invisible evil force'. This is all the more reason why a furious rage is so necessary. This is why it is so necessary to fight with all one's might.

JIN: Dantès's struggle transcends a simplistic tale of revenge that follows the principle of 'an eye for an eye, and a tooth for a tooth'. It involves redemption and illustrates the profound depth of Dumas's understanding of humanity.

The Arrogance of Sitting in Judgment

IKEDA: On the front page of Leo Tolstoy's work *Anna Karenina*, a passage from the Bible stands out. 'Vengeance is mine, and I will repay.'[5]

Vengeance is dangerous to contemplate; there is a line beyond which a person should not go. No person has the right to trample on anyone else or to take another's life. In the final analysis, one must not stoop to the arrogance of judging others, but leave the final judgment to a power transcending human capacity. I believe that this was also Tolstoy's view.

My mentor once expressed it this way: 'It is wrong to think that human beings can play God and mete out punishments. Any punishment must be determined by law. When the rule of law prevails, there is no need for human beings to take the law into their own hands and punish other human beings.'

JIN: In China, before the Early Han Dynasty (202 BCE–8), an act of vengeance was a socially accepted practice. In fact, if a man did not avenge the murder of his father, he would be labelled and cursed as a shameless and unfilial son.

In the Japanese society of the Kamakura and Muromachi periods, an ethos developed that encouraged vengeful retaliation and the support of acts of revenge by others. Acts of vengeance were viewed in a positive light.

IKEDA: Yes. Especially in the Edo Period (1603–1868), acts of revenge became an institutionalized practice, and there was a social expectation that they must be carried out. *Chūshingura* (also known as a story of Forty-Seven Ronin), based on an actual historical event in the early 1700s, depicted an act of vengeance illustrating the bonds of loyalty between a lord and his vassals, and ever since, the theme of vengeance has been repeatedly glorified in countless theatrical performances, works of literature, and images, and gained widespread popularity among the populace. It is a tale that shows how the impulse to take revenge is so deeply rooted in human passions.

In this regard, Goethe remarked that if society abolishes the death penalty, then immediately there will be a reappearance of self-defensive and retaliatory behaviour. And this will open the door to blood feuds.[6]

I believe that we must not miss this opportunity to introduce a religious perspective and sublimate; that is, redirect, this passionate energy into a more socially acceptable form, as Tolstoy suggests.

JIN: Dantès's revenge is an intensely emotionally satisfying and exhilaratingly sweet revenge. However, as you just mentioned, that is not all. Even though Dantès's plan of revenge included killing Albert, the beloved child of Fernand, an archenemy, knowing that this would cause his enemy to suffer for the rest of his life, in one scene he acceded to the supplication of his former lover, Mercédés, to forgive and spare the child.

IKEDA: Albert was Mercédés's child, and this is the scene of the duel with Albert, isn't it? The night before the duel, Dantès was so moved by Mercédés's appeal, he resolved to die at Albert's hand. However, as it turned out, after listening to his mother's explanation of all that had transpired, Albert asked Dantès for forgiveness and proposed that they call off the duel.

JIN: By emphasizing a scene such as this, the author depicts the noble character of the protagonist, who values honour and justice even more than his own life. And readers take away an unforgettable impression that will remain in their hearts forever.

IKEDA: It is a very touching scene. Mercédés risks her life by standing between Dantès and her son. Taken in by Mercédés' wholehearted determination, Dantès finally capitulates. It was, briefly stated, the majesty of motherhood; the symbol of human love, that won in the end. This all-encompassing virtue of motherhood reaches out and embraces Dantès as well as Albert. It was undoubtedly surprising that they called off the duel, because doing so was, according to the conventional wisdom of the time, an extremely dishonourable act.

JIN: My novel *Fox Volant of the Snowy Mountain* also had a somewhat ambiguous ending. Many of my readers tell me that is why they obsess about it and cannot get it out of their minds. So I am often asked, 'In the end, does Hu Fei swing his sword down upon Miao Renfeng?'

The protagonist, Hu Fei, finds himself in a dilemma because Miao Renfeng is his father's bitter enemy, but also happens to be the father of Hu Fei's sweetheart. Furthermore, he secretly looks up to Miao Renfeng as his superior in the martial arts.

Did he or did he not swing his sword down to deliver a fatal blow? This would be determined by the character of the man. How noble is he and how deep is his love for his sweetheart, Miao Ruolan? In other words, does he place more importance on his love for his sweetheart or his desire to stay alive?

This is something that each reader can evaluate and decide for him or herself. That is why I did not write a clear-cut and tidy ending. I thought that by giving the readers a kind of riddle to solve, they would exercise their creativity and experience the joy and satisfaction of making their own judgment.

IKEDA: What a great story.

Wait and Hope!

JIN: Dantès also rescues Valentine, the daughter of another archenemy, and even helps with her marriage arrangements. Here also we see Dantès's noble character showing through. What impresses people the most is not how Dantès repays a debt of kindness or takes revenge on an enemy, but rather how he relinquishes his quest for revenge and, beyond that, returns virtue for bitterness.

In the end, Dantès summarily abandons his fortune, so enormous that he could have even fought against a nation, and together with the beautiful sweet young girl, Haydee, he suddenly disappears. He leaves for distant shores. The novel's end gives readers a gentle comfort and is one reason for the success of this masterpiece.

IKEDA: At the end of Dumas's great novel are the words, 'Wait and hope!'

Wait and hope – I believe that these words are not merely a motto for living one's life. I cannot help thinking that actually, within this simple phrase lies hidden the answer to overcoming the problems of modern civilization.

JIN: Please explain.

IKEDA: Perhaps one of the major characteristics of modern civilization is that people do not wait for the truth to be revealed, but jump immediately to conclusions.

In other words, whatever the endeavour, they do not take things one step at a time, making steady progress by building upon one stage after another. The projected outcome is foremost, while little value is placed on the process and interim developments. In short, they do not know what it means to have the patience and discipline to 'wait'.

In every matter, they ask, 'So, how is it ultimately going to turn out?' and want to rush to the conclusion. They want things to go just as they have planned, and so they take out their abacus to do exact calculations, wanting everything to be as predictable as $1 + 1 = 2$. This tendency is perhaps the greatest shortcoming of our modern scientifically based civilization.

In a sense, this misplaced focus reveals human conceit. Things that are easily created may not last in the long run. Also, there is always an unpredictable element in life, so things do not always go as we would like and cannot be calculated in a numerical formula, as in $1 + 1 = 2$. A dynamic life is found right in the midst of confronting, grappling with, and making a serious and fierce effort to deal earnestly with these unpredictable events. The answers and conclusions are the results revealed at the end of this intense struggle.

Some people try to avoid expending any effort, balk at following processes, and want results as quickly as possible, but while this may seem clever, this way of life is arrogant and foolish.

To know how to wait – that is, to have patience, and to never lose hope – this wisdom that animates a healthy and optimistic life is almost totally missing in modern society.

JIN: I see. So this is what is included in the concept of waiting.

IKEDA: Yes. Previously, when we discussed Pericles, I mentioned that an important characteristic of leadership is to know the time in which one lives. 'Time' in the sense referred to by Pericles surely includes this implicit meaning.

In other words, 'time' does not refer to one specific point. It includes the process, filled with all the various struggles and difficulties experienced up to that point.

In any case, the concluding passage of *The Count of Monte Cristo* provides an opportunity to expand our imaginations in many ways.

The Unique Personalities Depicted in *The Three Musketeers*

JIN: Dumas has one more masterpiece to his name – *The Three Musketeers*. I brought this up before, but there is an excellent Chinese-language translation by Wu Guangjian entitled *Xiayinji*. The translation is absolutely superb and you will find that it is not a pale reflection of the original, but retains its force and vitality. If I were to translate the work, I certainly wouldn't be able to do as well as Wu Guangjian does.

IKEDA: Speaking of translations, the treatise on education written by Mr Makiguchi in the early twentieth century was translated and published in English in 1989 and has received a great response. Education is a worldwide concern, and Mr Makiguchi's work expounded on timeless principles that resonated with his readers.

I hesitate to mention my own work, but I hope you will indulge me for a moment. *Choose Life*, my dialogue with Dr Arnold Toynbee, was translated into 21 languages. [28 languages as of 2012] I was contacted by numerous people from all over the world, some of whom I would have least expected, who told me that they had read the book. That was when I felt a great appreciation for the work of translation.

That aside, it is clear that some works transcend language and national boundaries to become favourites all over the world. Of course, the work itself is undoubtedly masterful, but the translation bears much of the credit as well.

JIN: The translation of the sequel, *Xu Xiayinji*, unfortunately did not live up to the quality of the translation of the original. Perhaps Mr Wu, the translator, was extremely busy during the time that he was translating the sequel. And, since the prior work was such a success, it may be that he did not give as much careful attention to translating the sequel.

IKEDA: Since you thought so highly of *The Three Musketeers*, you undoubtedly also had high hopes for the sequel, so it is too bad that it did not turn out well.

JIN: The book *Xiayinji* had such a major impact on my life. It would not be an exaggeration to say that this work inspired me to begin writing martial arts novels.

When I was awarded France's National Order of Arts and Letters, in his congratulatory remarks, the French Consul General to Hong Kong paid me the highest compliment by calling me 'China's Great Dumas'. Of course, I feel that his praise was entirely undeserved. But I was truly elated, because the literary style that I adored and tried to emulate in my novels was none other than that of Dumas. Of all the writers in the entire world, the one I love the most is Dumas. This has been the case ever since I was 12 years of age.

IKEDA: When I was a child, I read the children's version of *The Three Musketeers*, which was one of the volumes from *The Complete Works of World Literature*, and was enthralled with the characters who, as I recall, were described as 'the sombre Athos', 'the red-caped Porthos', and 'the handsome Aramis'. How nostalgic this makes me feel! I remember finishing the entire book at one sitting, reading each page with bated breath.

JIN: The title in Chinese is *Xiayinji*, and if the French title had been translated directly, it would have been 'The Three Masters of the Sword'. However, besides the three main characters, d'Artagnan is another master swordsman who plays a major role. So, in actuality, the book should have been called 'The Four Master Swordsmen'. The original title used the word 'musketeers', and while it is true that the characters do use muskets, in the France of those days, swords were the primary weapon of choice. And of all the scenes in the book, swords are used in most, while muskets are used only in a small number.

IKEDA: What do you feel is the most appealing aspect of the story of *The Three Musketeers*?

JIN: I touched on this before, but I think I would have to say it is the vivid depiction of the characters. President Ikeda, which character, of the four, do you like the best? Do you like d'Artagnan or one of the others?

IKEDA: I would have to say that I am most fascinated by Athos. He is the eldest of the four men and has been described as follows. '[D'artagnan] had a marked preference for this gentleman. The noble and distinguished air of Athos – those flashes of dignity, which, from time to time, shone forth from the cloud in which he had voluntarily enveloped himself – that unalterable equanimity of temper, which made him the best companion in the world – that forced yet ironic gaiety – that courage, which would have been denominated blind, had it not been the result of the rarest coolness; – so many excellent qualities attracted more than the esteem, more even than the friendship, of d'Artagnan; they attracted his admiration.'[7]

His character combines the qualities of wisdom and courage – he is such a multifaceted and appealing character.

JIN: He definitely is. He is a great man who possesses many admirable qualities.

IKEDA: To illustrate, in one scene, Athos addresses d'Artagnan, who is anxious about the future, advising him, 'Come, gentleman, let us allow for accidents. Life is a large chaplet of little miseries, which the philosopher shakes with a laugh. Be philosophers, like me, gentleman . . .'[8]

That is truly a famous line. Here is not simply a young man who loves adventure and the sword. I sense a philosophic spirit in the way that he proceeds, head gallantly raised, while calmly dispelling anxieties about the stormy and turbulent challenges of life.

JIN: It seems to me that the literary style of *The Three Musketeers* resembles more the traditional novels of China than those of the West.

D'Artagnan is quick-witted, quick-tempered, and a most courageous man. If I were to liken him to any of the characters in *Romance of the Three Kingdoms* or *The Water Margin*, I think I would choose Zhao Yun. Porthos is a powerful giant of a man, and slightly dim-witted. I think he most resembles Zhang Fei or Li Kui (Xiao Li Guang).

Athos, as you pointed out, has a noble character and is a carefree, easy going scholarly type. You might say that his character is a blend of the qualities of Zhou Yu and Hua Rong. In short, his is a personality that elicits admiration and devotion.

Aramis strikes me as somehow mysterious and conspiratorial, and he always seems to be hatching an evil scheme. He reminds me a little of Zhi Hua (Black Fox Demon) in *Qixia Wuyi* (Seven Heroes and Five Gallants).

IKEDA: I am interested in your comment about Athos being a combination of Zhou Yu and Hua Rong. I wonder if it would be too generous to liken him to Guan Yu of *Romance of the Three Kingdoms*?

JIN: Interesting. So, when these four swordsmen get together, they have a mug of liquor in hand as they sing at the top of their lungs, and then race their horses and draw their swords. There is one more character to add to this picture. She is the beautiful Milady de Winter, a woman as lovely and charming as a peach or plum blossom, but as crafty and vile as a poisonous snake. She connives her way into the imperial court of Louis XIII. She wants to be inconspicuous, but how would that be possible?

Nurturing the Joy of Reading and a Sophisticated Understanding of History and Character Development

IKEDA: I feel that the attraction of *The Three Musketeers* is the variety of personalities thrown together and seeing how they manage as this action novel unfolds. Is it not similar in the drama of life? If our lives were populated with all of the same kinds of people, reading about it would not be any fun at all.

My mentor often said, 'In regards to appointing personnel, something magical happens when you match people together as workmates. The results are never simply a matter of 1 + 1 = 2, but sometimes it turns out to be 1 + 1 = 3, 4, or even 5. This is what is so exciting about human behaviour. It would not be very interesting at all if everyone was the same as everyone else, and it is unlikely that great things would be accomplished.'

Mr Jin, you are well known for your masterful depiction of the characters in your novels, and so I was wondering if perhaps this is an area in which you were influenced by *The Three Musketeers*.

JIN: I did not learn character development directly from reading *The Three Musketeers*. Actually, I learned this specifically from studying Chinese classical novels. Rather, *The Three Musketeers* taught me how to use historical data to best effect.

IKEDA: So, your influences were Dumas and classical Chinese novels. What other influences can you cite, for example among literary works or authors?

JIN: Another very important teacher for me was the Englishman Sir Walter

Scott. In terms of literary value, generally, Scott's works are considered to be on a much higher plane than those of Dumas. However, compared to the best of Scott's works, the best of Dumas's works are far more satisfying for the reader.

IKEDA: I have read Scott's *Ivanhoe*, and I have to admit that I think that Dumas's novels are much better. This may be my own arbitrary preference, however.

JIN: I understand that in your youth, your literary works were mostly poetry. You had not been writing novels, so when you read *The Three Musketeers*, perhaps your thoughts and observations were much different from mine. Undoubtedly, you were moved by the depiction of the four master swordsmen who, upon receiving their orders, committed their utmost to fulfilling their mission with resolution and courage.

IKEDA: They impressed me by their youth, their robust and vigorous physical presence, and their generosity. And speaking of being moved, I became very interested in the character of Cardinal Richelieu. As I am sure you know, he was the great prime minister who built the foundation for modern France. He had a rather complex nature, being a veteran politician given to stratagems and trickery, but he also had another side, which was selfless and rarely concerned with personal gain. And a trait that made him tower far above his contemporaries was his love for the people who worked for him.

In the last passage of *The Three Musketeers*, instead of punishing d'Artagnan, who had murdered Milady de Winter, Richelieu promoted him to second in command of the musketeer regiment. Richelieu had great magnanimity as an administrator, and the depth of his affection for his subordinates, whether he saw them as friend or foe, was exceptional. I feel that this aspect gives him a close resemblance to General Cao Cao of *Romance of the Three Kingdoms*.

In any case, comparing literary characters to actual historical figures is one of the great delights of reading, is it not? A good work of literature allows us to spread the wings of our imaginations and soar to great heights.

CHAPTER 6

Lu Xun, Revolutionary Humanist, Awakens the Soul of the People

Views of the People

IKEDA: Thus far, we have explored several great works of Western literature, including Plutarch's *Lives of Noble Grecians and Romans*, and Dumas's *The Count of Monte Cristo* and *The Three Musketeers*. Now, let us examine some of the literary works of your country.

JIN: Thank you. I am truly delighted to be able to discuss the literature of my homeland with you, President Ikeda.

IKEDA: The literary history of your country, China, is like the majestic flow of its great rivers – the Yellow River and the Yangtze. If we were to name all of the famous ancient as well as modern authors and their masterpieces, there would be no end to it, so let us focus on the truly great contemporary Chinese authors valued as literary giants.

In 1995, a survey was conducted to select authors representing modern China, for inclusion in the *Anthology of Masters of Twentieth Century Chinese Literature* (Wang Yichuan et al., Beijing Normal University). The author most highly recognized was Lu Xun (1881–1936). Following him were Shen Congwen (1902–88) and Ba Jin (1904–2005). And then, Mr Jin, you were selected for fourth place. Now we know how very much your literary works are beloved by the Chinese people. This is conclusive evidence.

JIN: I am humbled by your kind words. Aside from the question of whether or not my works really deserve such recognition, I was extremely honoured.

IKEDA: I am eager to discuss the themes in your work, Mr Jin, but I am reluctant to ask you. So, with the intent of retracing the flow of modern and contemporary Chinese literature, of which your work is a part, I would like to begin with a discussion of Lu Xun.

JIN: That would be excellent.

IKEDA: An old Russian proverb states, 'Find the people, and that is where you will find the truth'. What is one's view of the people? What is one's perception of the masses? I think it would be fair to say that a human being's true worth is revealed in the answer. The quality of a leader can be assessed by focusing on his or her view of the people. Then you will be able to clearly distinguish a true leader from a pretender.

JIN: That is right. Perhaps that is true also of authors.

IKEDA: In this sense, it is truly rare to discover an author such as Lu Xun, who profoundly understood the lives of ordinary people. At times he scolds and spurs the people on like a strict father, and at others he is like a tenderhearted mother, expressing fondness and affection. He resembles the surgeon, eyes filling with tears as he grasps the scalpel to operate on his seriously injured child, who is on the verge of death and crying out to him.

Lu Xun had aspired to become a physician and save the sick and afflicted, as had Sun Yat-sen. However, he later changed his mind and instead became a writer determined to transform and elevate the spirit of the people. Perhaps his real value as 'a warrior of the pen' was his continuous attention to and alliance with the people.

JIN: Master Lu Xun occupies a very prominent and exalted position in the history of modern Chinese literature. Today, when his name is brought up in conversation, he is usually referred to as 'Master Lu Xun'. In contrast, no honorific is attached to the names of other famous authors, such as Mao Dun, Ba Jin, Shen Congwen, Cao Yu, Lao She, and Xie Bingxin. A parallel may be drawn to the way we are used to referring to Sun Yat-sen as 'Master Sun Yat-sen', whereas other political figures, such as Chiang Kai-shek, Mao Zedong, Zhou Enlai, and Liu Shaoqi, are referred to with no accompanying term of respect. This does not in any way mean that the latter figures are not regarded highly, but rather that the former is singled out for special respect and reverence.

IKEDA: Perhaps this is related to the changing times. In Japan, there is no one who is referred to in that way. We do not refer to Natsume Sōseki, Mori Ōgai, or other great literary figures using the term 'master'.

Actually, it is the conventional practice to refer to historical figures without terms of respect. I feel that this is a way of assigning respect to them all. In our present discussions, I will follow the Japanese custom and omit the honorary term of reference for Lu Xun. However, this certainly does not mean that I do not hold him in the highest regard, and I hope that this is agreeable to you.

A Revolutionary Humanist with Empathy

JIN: We recognize Master Lu Xun for his literature, but we revere and respect him even more for his character, fierce patriotic spirit, intense devotion to the Chinese people, adamant and uncompromising struggle against the corruption and social decadence of feudalism; and perhaps most of all, for his scathing criticism of the lethargy, apathy, and numbness that haunted the soul of the Chinese people – in other words, their state of complete spiritual decay.

We can never imagine how much Master Lu Xun worried about this and how hard he worked to reverse this problem. He was just as you depicted earlier when you said 'it is truly rare to discover an author such as Lu Xun, who profoundly understood the lives of ordinary people. At times he scolds and spurs the people on like a strict father, and at others he is like a tenderhearted mother, expressing fondness and affection. He resembles the surgeon, eyes filling with tears as he grasps the scalpel to operate on his seriously injured child, who is on the verge of death and crying out to him.'

IKEDA: So, why did Lu Xun aspire to write literature in the first place? In a famous anecdote, Lu Xun explains that 'The people of a weak and backward country, however strong and healthy they might be, could only serve to be made examples of or witnesses of such futile spectacles; and it was not necessarily deplorable if many of them died of illness. The most important thing, therefore, is to change their spirit and since at that time I felt that literature was the best means to this end, I decided to promote a literary movement.'[1]

After the mid-nineteenth century, China was trampled by the invading world powers. Domestically, the Chinese people suffered from an oppressive regime. Even so, billions of people accepted these circumstances.

But Lu Xun could not tolerate this state of affairs. He literally was convulsed with anger and indignation. 'Countrymen, stand up and shed the darkness of your resignation! Strike down the walls of the old society!' he demanded. Every word of his vehement exhortation was a fire-breathing call to action.

JIN: The broad-based respect that Master Lu Xun received from the Chinese people was not merely because he was a distinguished author, but was also due to his very expansive character and spirit, which went far beyond the limited definition of author. If he had not written even one word in his entire life, the fact would remain that this was a great man the Chinese people produced.

A man who passionately addressed the deplorable state of the times, who courageously spearheaded a people's movement of awakening, giving no thought to his own safety, who, with sincere devotion, sacrificed himself to energize and inspire the Chinese people who faced a tragic situation – the Chinese call this kind of person a 'benevolent warrior'.

With great empathy, Master Lu Xun devoted himself selflessly and wholeheartedly to the common good of the people – in a way comparable to great men of ancient China, such as Yu the Great, who endeavoured to improve flood control infrastructure, and Confucius, who worked to expand education to the masses. These feelings of concern for the people make these men the equal of great figures such as Shakyamuni and Jesus.

IKEDA: 'Curbing the Flood', in the work *Old Tales Retold*, is a masterpiece that articulates Lu Xun's thoughts on Yu the Great, the Minister of Irrigation during the Shun period. Intellectuals who are all talk and incapable of carrying through – this kind of irresponsible and verbose type is so numerous in today's society, too. In contrast is the figure of Yu, a rustic mountain of a man with a deeply tanned face and a limp from walking so much throughout his life – a practical, action-oriented person in whom we can see the image of a benevolent warrior.

This reminded me of Shakyamuni, whose soles became leathery and hardened from walking all around the vast country of India.

Mao Dun, friend and contemporary of Lu Xun, had this to say about him: 'The ancient philosophers explained that only men of virtue (or, shall I say, revolutionary humanists) could love humanity as well as detest it. Lu Xun is this kind of humanitarian.'[2]

Lu Xun was not simply an author. The Chinese sincerely revere him as much as they do the ancient sages and holy men.

JIN: Yes. Master Lu Xun is warmly admired by the Chinese people. Yet, his only resources were his brush and ink. It is not as though he left a legacy of illustrious deeds or organized millions of people.

However, Master Lu Xun's profound love and desire to bring blessings to many people, and his heroic and tireless fighting spirit compares favourably with any of the great figures of Chinese history.

IKEDA: I once wrote an essay on Lu Xun and described him in this way. Lu Xun has two personas. One is the 'Warrior of the Pen', and the other is the face of the philosopher who peers and probes deeply into the inner consciousness of the human spirit.

It would be impossible to acknowledge only one of these aspects and do justice to Lu Xun's life and significant accomplishments.

JIN: That is exactly right. He was not only a great writer but also an impressive man.

Lu Xun's View of the Masses, Crystallised in *The True Story of Ah Q*

IKEDA: The work that most clearly articulates Lu Xun's view of the people is his masterpiece, *The True Story of Ah Q*. Ah Q is a character whose surname is unknown and who has no first name. He is literally a nameless commoner.

JIN: *The True Story of Ah Q* is a work that depicts the lot of ordinary people, and by analyzing Ah Q's interior world, Master Lu Xun tries to reveal the life of the typical Chinese person.

IKEDA: Yes. I agree. That is exactly what he does.

JIN: Ah Q, which actually means 'Mr Q', really wanted to take the surname Zhao but was told by Mr Zhao, a landlord, that 'Mr Zhao' was a name suitable for a person well beyond his station in life, and slapped Ah Q.

The narrator claims that he could not remember which of the possible Chinese characters was the correct one to write the 'Q' of Ah Q, so he simply calls him by the romanized letter 'Q.' So this figure had no name, and went only by the letter 'Q'. We do not know where he was born or where he had lived previously. His personality was nondescript and was expressed only in the routine behaviours of his everyday life.

One could say that these characteristics were like those of any Chinese person of the time, while, at the same time, they were not like those of any one Chinese person.

IKEDA: Ah Q was not meant to represent any individual person, but in a sense he depicted a broader humanity. And this is the profound and universal nature of this character.

The Chinese people who read this work when it first came out were astonished. Many people felt that Ah Q reminded them of themselves, to the extent that they wondered if they had been the model for the character.

JIN: Many commentators who analyzed Ah Q focused on how he always managed to win 'spiritual victories'. This meant that, when ridiculed by others, he would console himself with a kind of twisted superiority complex. So, I think that this trait of trying to win a so-called spiritual victory while avoiding any active effort to improve oneself is a character trait common to many Chinese.

However, more important is the sad fact that Ah Q lived his entire life being tossed about by the whims of fate, without clearly understanding anything that was happening to him. This is the point that Master Lu Xun emphasized.

IKEDA: Ah Q was foolish, vain, and always acted on the spur of the moment, living precariously from one day to the next. He interpreted everything to his advantage and was quick to retreat into his own little shell. This is why no matter how much he was ridiculed or what terrible situations he ended up in, he remained unfazed. This may sound like a wise approach to life, but what Lu Xun meant by his representation of this concept of winning a spiritual victory was to point out that it sprung from a painfully dimwitted optimism.

Lu Xun wrote satirically about the Chinese people who he felt were immersed in this spiritual victory mentality. Of Ah Q, he said, 'He was always exultant. This may be a proof of the moral supremacy of China over the rest of the world.'[3]

This is a truly memorable passage, full of painful irony.

JIN: Yes. Something that put Ah Q in a good mood was, for example, when he encountered a thief in the town and assisted him with his robbery in exchange for a share of the loot. He was always unemployed, had no opportunity to make a decent living, and was always the butt of ridicule. When he tried to take his mind off his troubles by harassing someone else, he ended up being beaten up. As a last resort, he decided to antagonize someone weaker than himself and took out his anger by tormenting a nun.

IKEDA: The passage describing Ah Q's foolishness is so realistic that it makes readers cringe and want to avert their gaze. They may even spontaneously feel like shutting the book. Ah Q's character illustrated the kind of cluelessness and ignorant darkness of which young dedicated social reformers of the time were intensely critical. Conversely, we can say that Lu Xun's penetrating insight looked through the 'basic character' of the Chinese people, the phrase which I used in my first speech at Peking University, which ordinary and usual life experiences do not make one see.

No one was harsher than Lu Xun in attacking, with scathing criticism, self-righteous wise men and fake intellectuals.

When I first spoke out about normalizing relations between China and Japan over 30 years ago [1968], one of the first people who paid attention was a Chinese literary scholar – the now deceased Yoshimi Takeuchi. He once commented that Lu Xun wielded a sharp pen, especially in regard to his opponents, of whom he was unforgiving to an extent rarely seen. Lu Xun expressed love as well as hate: two sides of the same coin, so to speak. Perhaps without the intensity and commitment revealed in this kind of emotion, a true revolutionary philosophy cannot emerge. In any case, I sensed his true power of philosophy.

JIN: In the end, Ah Q's idea of the revolution was a confused illusion, and while trying to pose as a credible revolutionary he ended up being executed for something he really did not understand. The Chinese of that period, in a similar way to Ah Q, lived desperate and lamentable lives.

In my view, Ah Q's character was defined not so much by his propensity to interpret his experience from his own 'spiritual victory' perspective, but by his apathy, insensitivity, lack of motivation, and complete ignorance.

Ah Q lived his entire life in darkness, without even one glimmer of hope. Lu Xun used his pen as a live spark to ignite millions of torches, and brought hope and promise to millions of unenlightened Chinese farmers.

Ah Q's Revolutionary Awakening and the Soka Gakkai People's Movement

IKEDA: The silent cry for help by Ah Q at his execution moved Romain Rolland to remark, 'Ah Q's suffering face will always have a place in my memory'.[4]

Ah Q's cry is itself the voiceless, unarticulated cry of the people. A revolution that was unable to awaken and enlighten Ah Q was not an authentic revolution. If the tragedy of the common people, as illustrated by someone like Ah Q, is not understood, any revolution or new government will simply be a drama in which power changes hands.

I cannot help thinking that Lu Xun was trying to say that only by descending into the inner depths of the Chinese people's psyche can the people find the strength to raise a battle cry for a true spiritual restoration.

JIN: Later on, during the birth of the new China, farmers rose up and took a stand. They made a break from a life of lethargy, hesitation, and hopeless wandering in the darkness. They took up arms and toppled the arrogant Mr Zhao and Imitation Foreign Devil who had oppressed them.

All across the vast country of China, from Jiangxi, Hunan, Shaanxi, Shanxi, Hebei, and Shandong, countless numbers of people just like Ah Q proudly stood up for themselves. Resolutely, they stood firmly on the great earth, fearing no one, becoming honoured and distinguished heroes whose fame reverberated throughout the land. It is not that they had somehow changed their physical constitution. They had changed their thinking. Something had changed in their heads.

Master Lu Xun grieved his entire life for Ah Q's thinking. He had great expectations and made great efforts to change Ah Q's mind, or rather the people's mind.

IKEDA: The goals and practices that we have pursued in Soka Gakkai resonate deeply and powerfully with Lu Xun's efforts.

We pray fervently. We battle mightily. We seek to give infinite courage and hope to those who have been battered and discouraged by crushing anguish and distress. We say, 'Restore your pride and confidence in yourself, and move forward courageously!'

This people's movement has encouraged those who had previously remained silent, to speak out for the first time. They have become able to speak out and laugh out loud with gusto.

The author Minpei Sugiura once declared, "The Soka Gakkai's greatest achievement lies in unleashing the power of people, of those at the very lowest strata of society, and in revitalizing their lives'.[5]

JIN: Indeed.

IKEDA: Apparently, in Mr Sugiura's neighbourhood there lived a family whose parents were blind, and it seemed that they single-handedly carried a heavy karma. Their lives seemed so dark and melancholy. Then, they became Soka Gakkai members. Consequently, in just a brief period of time, the sound of cheerful, lighthearted conversation could be heard coming from their house.

In another case, there was a woman who was in a difficult financial situation and who could not easily hold a conversation with others. She was a recluse, living in isolation in her village. Over time, she began to visit with all her neighbours. It became known that she had become a member of Soka Gakkai and was talking to people about the Buddhist teachings.

She began to express herself and became able to speak out in school parent-teacher association meetings. It is really very surprising. This kind of behaviour cannot be dictated from above. It is not possible without a faith and conviction that is voluntary in nature. And people with conscience are noticing.

Mr Jin, I am sure that you understand that I am not simply trying to make Soka Gakkai look good. It is just so rare in Japanese history for a wave of spiritual transformation to occur in the lives of the common people. In this sense, I can confidently declare that our forward movement is bringing about a kind of cultural revolution in the history of the Japanese spirit.

It seems that Soka Gakkai had attracted the attention of Premier Zhou Enlai as early as the 1960s, and when I asked what was especially notable about it, he said, 'It is an organization that has arisen from the people, the grassroots'. I was impressed with his keen insight and felt that he was indeed a great prime minister. We really appreciated his esteem towards us.

JIN: I understand. I am quite familiar with the complexity and the power of that process of empowering people. These days, even if you were to search all the agricultural villages in China, you would not find anyone who reminds you of Ah Q. You will encounter only energetic and active men and women. If you speak of China and international issues, they will, undoubtedly, discuss the return of Hong Kong as well as numerous other current global issues.

I am sure that most Chinese, whether they be farmers, employees of township enterprises, or retailers of small local businesses, know how to use a handheld calculator and have newspapers, magazines, radios, and televisions in their homes. China has been truly transformed.

When the People Become the Masters

IKEDA: China's growth in the recent past has been truly remarkable. I came to this realization over the course of just ten visits to China. When I visited Shanghai in May 1997, its many skyscrapers seemed to pierce the heavens with an unmistakable dynamism and vitality.

At one point during his tenure, Premier Zhou Enlai is said to have remarked that China is plagued by traffic congestion and they needed to research highway construction in Japan. In retrospect, we see that China has developed with even greater momentum than the Prime Minister predicted. Nothing would make me happier than to see China continue to flourish and prosper in the twenty-first century.

JIN: I appreciate your kind thoughts. China's progress that we see today is due to the strong foundation that was built by many predecessors like Master Lu Xun.

IKEDA: Lu Xun stated that there are only two periods in the history of the Chinese people. Speaking frankly, he said they are the period in which people could not become slaves, even if they wanted to, and the period in which they could be safe for a time as slaves.

He said that his long-held hope was for the creation of a completely new third period that would sever the karma of this unfortunate history. In short, this third period, he felt, should be the period in which the people become the masters.

JIN: Just as Master Lu Xun fervently wished, Ah Q, and the people of China, whom he represented, experienced a fundamental shift in their thinking. This was not due completely to the efforts of Master Lu Xun, but it is certain that the many young people who were inspired and spurred to action by his advocacy and calls for reform responded to his direction and succeeded in many arduous endeavours.

As time passed, more and more young people valiantly joined the fight against the forces of corruption. This movement grew even larger as intellectuals adopted revolutionary ideas from abroad.

And as a result, a majority of the people, including labourers, farmers, soldiers, and others, experienced a change in thinking and stepped up to the fight.

IKEDA: This new vitality that animated the birth and building of the new China is depicted in great detail in Edgar Snow's commemorative reportage *Red Star Over China*.

Snow documented the efforts of the young revolutionaries who taught the farmers and who attempted to convince them to join their mission. They made the case that people must fight for the sake of freedom, peace, and justice, as well as the dignity of the people. And so the farmers were stirred to action, and their consciousness and strength helped to awaken China from 2,000 years of slumber. This brought about a period of wrenching change to this earth.

JIN: In addition to the character Ah Q, Master Lu Xun also created an indifferent and apathetic character type, represented by Mr Zhao and the Imitation Foreign Devil, as well as, for example, the characters Xiang Linsao in *Well Wishes*, Kong Yiji in a work of the same name, Hua Laoshuan in *Medicine*, and Si Ming in *Soap*.

Not all of these characters are farmers, but they are all decadent and degenerate members of the old Chinese society, devoid of vitality and living their lives in a fog. If human beings are in a state of decay and decline, the society made up of them will disintegrate from the inside out and dissipate.

IKEDA: Mr Jin, I believe that the common thread between the characters to which you have just referred is Lu Xun's thorough approach, through these characters, to the negative aspects in the essential nature of the people.

Call it 'revolution' or 'social reform' – whatever it is, it all begins with human beings who seek revolutionary change. There can be no transformation of society without a transformation of people. Lu Xun's revolutionary humanism resonates closely with the 'human revolution' that we advocate.

JIN: Master Lu Xun observed, after reflecting on several thousand years of Chinese history, that the people never had a firm foundation on which to build their everyday lives. He maintained that they never had even one real opportunity to experience life as full human beings. As you pointed out previously, President Ikeda, he lamented that at best, they could become slaves, and at worst, slavery itself was not even a possibility.

When war broke out, the people had no idea which side they were on. When the insurgents came, of course, they murdered the people. When the government troops came, it was the same. They plundered and brutally massacred the people.

Finally, when peace was restored to their lives, the people had to serve as labourers and pay land tax, but they thereby could avoid being killed. In other words, the time had come when they were finally able to become slaves and live in peace.

IKEDA: Mr Jin, in your three-volume novel *Sword Stained with Royal Blood*, which was published in Japanese, you also wrote about the endless vicissitudes of the lives of the people. In every age, it seems that those who suffer the most are the common people.

The people's lives in Japan may not have been as harsh as the people's lives in China, but in Japan also, crushing taxes were imposed on the populace. Expressions such as 'Do not allow farmers to live, but also do not let them die' and 'Farmers are the same as oil crops – the more you squeeze, the more they produce' reveal the kind of conditions that continued for a long period in Japanese history.

Perhaps because the people were brought to heel, at a certain point an attitude of resignation and acceptance of authority became firmly rooted in the Japanese psyche.

Fukuzawa Yukichi, the great Japanese philosopher, astutely observed in his work *An Outline of a Theory of Civilization*, 'The ups and downs of the warriors meant no more to them than the daily changes of weather. All they did was silently watch to see what happened.'[6] So the reality of the situation was that the people became resigned to being the servants of the powerful.

We are resolute in our challenge to overcome the impoverished spiritual mindset of the Japanese, but unfortunately, this seems to be very far in the future.

Lu Xun and Gandhi Struggle for the Hearts and Minds of the People

JIN: The two periods of history – one in which people could not become slaves even if they wanted to, and the other in which they were able to be slaves and live in safety for a little while – basically describe the state of a world alternating between peace and turbulent times.

When the land was under the control of a powerful ruler, the people were safe from indiscriminate slaughter by government troops and rebels. Alternately, when the country was in a state of turmoil, people would be murdered by both government troops and the rebels. In short, the only two options people had were living like a dog during peacetime and, during conflict, fearing recognition as a full person. In other words, during a time of conflict a person's life was worse than a dog's.

Of course, conditions such as these must be ameliorated. Lu Xun dedicated his entire life to this struggle – a struggle to forge a path toward reform in the society of his time.

IKEDA: The significance of Lu Xun to China can perhaps be compared to that of Gandhi to India. Jawaharlal Nehru, Gandhi's ally and close friend, said Gandhi's greatest gift to India was his admonition to fear nothing. He removed the dark cloak of terror from the people's hearts and gave them a completely different outlook.

As you pointed out, Lu Xun struggled to change the hearts and minds of the people. And just as in Gandhi's struggle, through his efforts Lu Xun radiated an eternal light. Through the life of Lu Xun – one human being – the people of China became aware of their own potential and discovered their true selves that had remained hidden until then.

JIN: Just as Gandhi's life ended in tragedy, the prominent writers and intellectuals of China during the Cultural Revolution faced misfortune and tragedy. Someone asked the question, 'If Lu Xun had been alive at the time, would he have been criticized and struck as a target?'

This question was asked in Hong Kong. And the opinion of everyone who participated in the discussion was unanimous: without a doubt Lu Xun would have been targeted for annihilation.

IKEDA: I think so, too. As you so keenly observed, the truth about the Cultural Revolution was that it was a power struggle, and Lu Xun would not have overlooked this. Also, he probably would not have succumbed to the crude and violent attacks of the Red Guards.

Lu Xun's discerning and penetrating gaze directed toward people as well as history resulted in a view that transcended the prevailing outlook of the times. It strikes me that he had the presence of a seer or prophet.

Being proudly independent, Lu Xun firmly refused to accept the status quo, and one has the sense that arising from deep inside his spiritual being was a subtle and uncanny glow. If he had experienced the Cultural Revolution, I don't think that it would have been a pleasant experience for him.

JIN: I am sure you are right. Master Lu Xun's historical perspective was essentially his view of the people. He recognized that history is basically created by people.

The two periods of history that we discussed just a moment ago represent a macro view of Chinese history. Sima Qian's *Records of the Grand Historian* truly depicts this macro view. On the other hand, the characters Ah Q, Kong Yiji, Xiang Linsao, and Run Tu portray a micro perspective of Chinese history. The diaries of people such as Emperor Gaozu of the Han, Xiang Yu, and Shi Huang of the Qin Dynasty (221–202 BCE) present another micro perspective of Chinese history.

Yet Master Lu Xun thought that real history was created by ordinary people such as Ah Q, Kong Yiji, and Xiang Linsao, not by the powerful Emperor Shi Huang of the Qin Dynasty, Xiang Yu, or Emperor Gaozu of the Han Dynasty. Nevertheless, the implications for the people were still the same; that is, the people's experience alternated between periods of governmental control and periods of conflict and social disorganization.

IKEDA: The question is this: Do heroes create history? Or do the people create history? We are starting to see a trend in the field of history as historians give greater recognition to the role that common people have played in the creation of history.

JIN: In the West also, historians have gradually begun to place greater importance on disciplines such as sociological history, cultural history, and the history of manners and customs. And now, unlike before, political history is not viewed as the only kind of history. Also, in recent years, even more books on people's history have been published.

Among relatively early works, some of the most illustrious are *The Making of the English Working Class* by Edward Palmer Thompson (1963) and *Hard Times: An Oral History of the Great Depression* by Studs Terkel (1970). However, these present history from a social science perspective. They differ from the people's history that Master Lu Xun revived in our hearts through literature.

Lu Xun's Internal Desolation and his Hopes for Youth

IKEDA: Incidentally, when we look back through the writings of Lu Xun, ever since his earliest commentaries, we repeatedly encounter the word 'desolation'. Desolation – the sense that no matter how loud he shouted, not a single reverberation, not a single echo returned. During his entire life, Lu Xun always felt that he was talking to a bottomless swamp whose only response was a deafening silence. However, this feeling was different from a sense of meaninglessness or despair.

Lu Xun described this loneliness and desolation as the wellspring of his creativity. He thought that 'When a man feels lonely, he can create; when his loneliness is dispelled, he cannot create any more, for he no longer feels any love'.[7]

JIN: Yes. 'Desolation' is a very important and indispensable word for understanding Master Lu Xun's literary career.

IKEDA: Lu Xun once said that all he was doing was wrestling with the darkness. As he looked back over his literary career, he was plunged into a deep sense of desolation and darkness, lamenting the future of China and the Chinese people. It was a complex feeling.

Perhaps we can say that his anguish was like a medal of honour representing his role as 'a warrior of the pen'. Lu Xun's goal was to bring about a revitalization of the hidden spirit of the people; and I dare to say that no one has yet scaled that peak. Only those who have ascended the steep mountain face know the intensity of the biting wind that blows at the summit. I believe that his anguish is a testament to the story of his heroic struggle. Those who try to achieve great deeds must come face-to-face at least once with the lonely trials of pursuing their goals. The word 'desolation' describes the profound emotions that Lu Xun undoubtedly felt.

JIN: President Ikeda, you have focused on Master Lu Xun's commentary, *On the Power of Mara Poetry*. I am impressed with your unique insight. By this I mean to say that, although there are many scholars studying Lu Xun's work in China, very few of them make any mention of this work.

On the Power of Mara Poetry was written 14 years before *The True Story of Ah Q*. Many of the works he wrote during this period introduced the knowledge and philosophy of the West, and this work falls into this category.

The word 'Mara' originated in India and means 'demon'. It is the equivalent of Satan in Western thought. By using this word, Master Lu Xun expressed his desire to destroy China's vehement reactionary philosophy and existing social system. Satan is the figure who turned his back on heaven and rebelled against God. In this case, Master Lu Xun expands this concept of rebellion to include his own fierce opposition to feudal values and concepts and his rejection of the established system and its principles, which he fought unrelentingly with all his might.

IKEDA: That is undoubtedly why Lu Xun so loved young people. Youth are fundamentally oriented toward the future. And, they have an innovative and reformist perspective. They do not become complacent with the way things are, but are always challenged by the possibilities of the unknown.

We have just discussed Lu Xun's sense of 'desolation', but he still embraced the light of hope, which reflected his love for young people. Great writers sometimes are plunged into despair by the rash and thoughtless criticisms and attacks from earnest young literary enthusiasts, but they still believe tenaciously in the potential of youth.

Once, feeling in his hand the warmth of the coins with which a youth had paid for one of his books, Lu Xun worried whether his book might be harmful to the future prospects of that youth. On another occasion, he shed tears of anguish for the youths whose lives were snuffed out by ruthless authoritarian power, and took up his pen to compose a eulogy. And as we might have expected, in the last photograph taken of him, he is pictured talking to young people.

He mused, 'It is a joy to nurture others, even though one knows doing so means growing weaker and frailer, one drop of blood at a time'.[8]

Youth represent hope. A person who loves the young and seeks to nurture them can never truly fall into despair. This is what I believe.

Life Force and the Commentary *On the Power of Mara Poetry*

JIN: Let us explain a little bit more about Lu Xun's *On the Power of Mara Poetry* for the youth. Through this work, Master Lu Xun aimed to deepen a sense of patriotism as well as advocate war to liberate the homeland, secure freedom, and resist oppression.

At the beginning of this work, he pointed out that ever since ancient times, many civilized countries have fallen into decline, their cultures never again to flourish. He pointed to ancient countries such as India, Israel, Egypt, and Iran which fell quietly into ruin.

Master Lu Xun also pointed out, however, that even if a country fails militarily or politically, if later a great poet produces an inspiring work that awakens the souls of its people, then there is sufficient opportunity for a cultural revival, as happened in Prussia and England. He called a person of such inspiration a poet of the 'Mara School'.

IKEDA: These are patriotic poets who are fiercely passionate about their country and its people.

JIN: The so-called virtuous gentlemen view these poets as completely evil and treat them as traitors. Actually, the writings of these rebels express the conscience of society and the vitality of the people.

Master Lu Xun was especially taken with the work of Lord George Gordon Byron, the great English poet, and praised him highly. In his essay, he introduced Byron's work and his sensational exploits, which had taken the public by surprise.

IKEDA: In order to realize his ideal of achieving freedom, Byron plunged himself into the Greek war of liberation. And ultimately, he sacrificed his life for his beliefs.

I feel a strong affinity with this revolutionary soul, who was never complacent, but continually pursued the new and creative.

JIN: Master Lu Xun's essay then moves to an introduction of the work of Percy Bysshe Shelley, who similarly extolled the virtues of freedom in his poems entitled 'Prometheus Unbound' and 'The Cenci'.

In 'The Cenci', the father of the Cenci family was a cruel and tyrannical man who indiscriminately committed murders and atrocities against the people. His young daughter sympathized with the people, killing her own father to protect them from his murderous ways. Patricide has always been considered a serious crime, but in his poem, Shelley applauds and praises the young girl.

Master Lu Xun also introduces the work of Alexander Pushkin and Mikhail Lermontov of Russia, Adam Bernard Mickiewicz of Poland, and Sándor Petöfi of Hungary.

Sándor Petöfi was a magnificent patriotic poet and author of this famous verse: 'Liberty, love! These two I need. / For love I'll sacrifice my life, / For liberty I'll sacrifice my love.'[9] He died in battle, struggling against the oppressive rule of the Russian Czars.

IKEDA: Ever since I was young, I have enjoyed reading the works of poets such as Byron, Pushkin, and Shelley. I could very much identify with them. Unfortunately, some of the poets that Lu Xun introduced are not very well known in Japan.

That aside, the poets to whom Lu Xun drew attention lived their ideals and their convictions and radiated a life force created by being true to themselves. Their world was one of unlimited adventure.

There is an expression about living life that says 'If you renew yourself daily, then day after day you will be renewed, and yet once again will you be renewed'.[10]

This is one of my favourite sayings, and from each of these poets I cannot help sensing this same fresh and invigorating inspiration in my soul.

Where are the Japanese Authors of Lu Xun's Stature?

JIN: Lu Xun concluded his essay with the following words, 'The character, words, deeds, and ideas of all these men – despite the many differences produced by the variety of nationality and background – are united in one school: each was a vigorous, unflinching defender of truth; none turned conformist to please the crowd; they spoke with strength to stir new life in their countrymen and make their country a great one. Who on Chinese soil compare?'[11]

IKEDA: Lu Xun undoubtedly saw these poets as pioneers on the same path that he pursued – that is, a path toward the awakening of the public consciousness. This passage reveals the intensity of conviction beating in his heart.

JIN: This text was written in classical form, and perhaps because it is somewhat difficult, it did not attract the attention of the youth of the day.

Nevertheless, in those words are revealed Master Lu Xun's philosophy regarding his love of country and desire for its development, his passionate concern for the awakening of the people, his opposition to the customs and traditions that shackled the people, and his efforts to clear away the ruinous practices and ideas of the old China. All of Master Lu Xun's words and deeds were completely consistent with his philosophy, throughout his entire life.

Master Lu Xun's question, 'Who on Chinese soil compare?' truly shows, as you said, President Ikeda, that he had already clearly determined his path in life.[12] He posed this question to himself, as if he were giving himself words of encouragement.

IKEDA: I would like to ask, 'Were there literary figures equal to Lu Xun, in Japan in those days?' If I were to answer this question, I would have to say that among the major literary figures of early modern Japan, there was probably no one of Lu Xun's stature who directly confronted the ills of society.

Of course, the circumstances and background of the times were undoubtedly different in China compared to Japan.

Within the current of nineteenth-century imperialism, Japan was a relative latecomer to the club of imperialist world powers. As a consequence, Japan's rate of modernization was fast in comparison. And so Japanese popular sentiment was in accord with the drive to rush ahead to catch up and overtake the early imperialist powers.

It is a fact that literary people keenly understood the deceptiveness and ugliness of modernization.

In the beginning of his famous book *Kusamakura* (literally 'The Grass Pillow'), Natsume Sōseki writes, 'However you look at it, the human world is not an easy place to live. . . . when you understand at last that difficulties will dog you wherever you may live, this is when poetry and art are born'.[13] Just as Sōseki observes, it is a fact that the world of literature and art forms the basis for a critique of society.

However, the basis for determining the extent of livability, in the sense expressed by Sōseki, is quite different in China compared to Japan. Consequently, in Japan, writers' awareness of the issues was not such that they could, as Lu Xun did, turn their gaze on the evils and contradictions of society and stand up to tackle these issues directly. Rather, they turned their focus inward to the self, and some, in diametric opposition to Lu Xun's vocal disassociation from the Chinese classics, retreated into the world of classical literature.

Depending on your perspective, classical literature could be viewed as a relaxing pastime or, conversely, a kind of escape. Whichever the case, the fact is that Japanese society and the soil of its intellectual environment did not give rise to a fierce activist writer such as Lu Xun. In comparing Japanese and Chinese modern history, we must take a serious and much longer-range view in order to accurately judge the relative merits of each approach. In any case, I do believe that we must keep asking the question: Has a writer of Lu Xun's stature ever emerged in our respective societies?

It is often said that Japan has never had a revolution. Whether we point to democratization after the Pacific War or to the Meiji Restoration, both instances of societal change are said to have occurred as a result of foreign pressure, rather than through the will of the people. Generally speaking, they say that the Japanese people did not, of their own accord, deliberately seek to change society.

The society based on this kind of spiritual firmament did not produce even one writer such as Lu Xun. I cannot help thinking that this is a serious commentary on the spiritual development of the Japanese psyche.

The Power of the Pen: *From* On Establishing the Correct Teaching for the Peace of the Land *to Ba Jin*

Concise and to the Point – Lu Xun's Commentary and Nichiren's Four Dictums

IKEDA: In the previous chapter we discussed Lu Xun and his work. I would like to add another point that we did not mention.

In 1974, on my first trip to China, I visited the former residence of Lu Xun in Shanghai. Everything remained just as it was when he was alive. On display were the desk where he wielded his pen to write, oblivious to the passage of time, battling the 'enemies of the people' both day and night; and the bed where he lay down, like a warrior resting between bouts of fierce fighting.

During his Shanghai period, Lu Xun stopped publishing novels and instead used most of his energy writing commentary that he called 'miscellaneous essays'. In this fierce battle of the pen, as the saying goes, 'Words cut deeper than a sword that draws blood'.

JIN: He was indeed wielding his pen in a great struggle.

IKEDA: In the history of Japanese literature, it is rare that authors battled with words. The literary critic Shuichi Kato points to our founder Nichiren as one of just a few exceptions. Kato wrote, 'Nichiren had a kind of a genius as a prose writer, his work displaying a fiery nature and spirit. In Nichiren's writing, particularly his letters, Japanese prose as a polemical medium reached standards seldom surpassed.'[1]

JIN: I sincerely regret that I do not read Japanese and cannot read the original writings of Nichiren in Japanese. I do, however, know 'The Four Dictums', which describe Nichiren's view of four major Buddhists sects – the Nembutsu sect (Jōdo or Pure Land sect), the Zen sect, the True Word (Shingon), and the Precepts (Ritsu): (1) 'Nembutsu leads to the hell of incessant suffering', (2) 'Zen is the teaching of the heavenly devil', (3) 'True Word will ruin the nation', and (4) 'Precepts is traitorous.'[2]

IKEDA: One of the characteristics of the so-called Kamakura New Buddhism was the concept of *Senchaku*, which followed a certain standard for sorting through the teachings of Shakyamuni and systematizing them.

What was the standard used for this task? Many different standards were advanced, but the one chosen by Nichiren was called 'the four teachers of the three countries'. The three countries referred to were India, China, and Japan. The four teachers originated from these three countries, and they all proclaimed the Lotus Sutra as the foundation of their teachings. Following this lineage – Shakyamuni, Tiantai, Dengyo, and Nichiren – Nichiren carried on Tiantai's comparative classification, categorizing all the sutras according to the Buddha's will as clearly revealed in the Lotus Sutra.

Based on the evidence of the sutras themselves, there were many reasons for identifying Nichiren as a Tiantai Buddhism revivalist, and it appears that the four dictums also were established within that classification system.

JIN: Nichiren's profound conviction in the truth of the Lotus Sutra was the reason for his vehement attacks on other sects. His brazenness and ferocious hate for his bitter enemies are expressed fully in these four dictums.

In Japan, calamities befell the nation one after another: a great earthquake in the first year of the Shōka period (1257), a violent storm in the second year, a great famine in the first year of the Shōgen period (1259), and an epidemic of a contagious disease in that same year and the year after. The death toll throughout the entire country was incalculable. Politicians were frantic and many different Buddhist prayers and incantations were tried, but none of them had the slightest effect.

During the Bun-ō period (1260–61), Nichiren wrote *On Establishing the*

Correct Teaching for the Peace of the Land, in which he argued that Japan was originally a Buddhist country that adhered to the Lotus Sutra, and that because of this, the nation was at peace and the people were able to live stable lives. However, over time various sects emerged, such as the Pure Land, Zen, True Word, Flower Garland, and Precepts schools and the Lotus Sutra was neglected. As a consequence, Nichiren maintained, every year a major disaster struck the nation. In short, he believed that the true teachings had been abandoned and erronious teachings flourished and that this was the fundamental cause of the misfortunes that had befallen the nation.

IKEDA: That is correct. My mentor, Mr Toda, often mentioned that it is essential to know how to distinguish the causal factors precipitating historical events. He said there are remote, or underlying, causes, and immediate causes.

Nichiren focused his attention on the underlying, fundamental cause of the disasters, referred to as 'the three calamities and seven disasters', that were creating misery and distress among the people during that period. He asserted that 'When a nation becomes disordered, it is the spirits that first show signs of rampancy. Because the spirits become rampant, all the people of the nation become disordered.'[3] According to Nichiren, the fundamental cause of the repeatedly occurring disasters was the religious and philosophical confusion among the people.

On Establishing the Correct Teaching for the Peace of the Land: A Revolutionary Strand in the History of Buddhism

JIN: In one passage in the text of *On Establishing the Correct Teaching for the Peace of the Land*, Nichiren claimed that people were being taught to believe in false interpretations of the sutras and, specifically regarding true sutras such as the Lotus Sutra, a priest named Hōnen was urging them to:

> 'discard, close, ignore, and abandon' them. With these four injunctions, he leads all people astray. On top of that, he groups together all the sage monks of the three countries [of India, China, and Japan] as well as the students of Buddhism of the ten directions, and calls them a 'band of robbers', causing the people to insult them.
>
> In doing so, he turns his back on the passage in the three Pure Land sutras, the sutras of his own school, which contains Amida's

vow to save the people 'excepting only those who commit the five cardinal sins and those who slander the correct teaching'. More fundamentally, he shows that he fails to understand the warning contained in the second volume of the Lotus Sutra, the heart and core of the entire body of teachings the Buddha expounded in the five periods of his preaching life, which reads, 'If a person fails to have faith but instead slanders this sutra. . . . When his life comes to an end he will enter the Avichi hell.'

Now we have come to this latter age, when people are no longer sages. Each enters his own dark road, and all alike forget the direct way. How pitiful that no one cures them of their blindness! How painful to see them taking up these false beliefs in vain![4]

IKEDA: I am impressed by your erudition. The focus of *On Establishing the Correct Teaching for the Peace of the Land* is the desecration of the Nembutsu. Why were their prayers to be abandoned? One reason, according to Nichiren, was the sound of lamentation. In the work of Han Feizi (c. 233 BCE), there is a story about the fall of a country, and it was thought that the chanting of the lament Namu-Amida-Butsu would weaken a person's motivation to keep on living. There was an uneasy concern that it carried with it an indescribably sorrowful quality that would steal away a person's life force.

In fact, in the Pure Land school, people single-mindedly pray for rebirth in the Pure Land when they die. They dismiss this world as impure and corrupt, viewing any efforts made in this world as secondary in importance. This kind of thinking ultimately urges people to evade reality.

We must not overlook the spiritual history of Japan and the major impact the Jōdo sect has had on the Japanese psyche – namely encouraging an aversion to reality. This perspective is illustrated in the proverbs 'If bound by long twine, it's better not to resist', and 'If you have to take shelter, choose a big tree'. Both of these proverbs suggest a psychological ethos in which people readily ingratiate themselves and defer to the powerful.

When I say this, I am not referring to the past. Lately in Japan, we hear the phrase 'Peace Nembutsu Ideology', and for the moment let us set aside the issue of defining peace as the absence of conflict, which is not really peace in the true sense. Japanese today think that simply by paying lip service to peace and by chanting Nembutsu, as if humming a tune to themselves, somehow this will make the world better. But this is a complacent attitude and an abdication of responsibility. You might say that this is a prime example of Japan's so-called 'Nembutsu mentality'.

JIN: I understand what you mean. Nichiren relied on the sutras, and after making predictions of disasters, pestilence, and famine, he also prophesied that Japan would be attacked by foreign enemies and have frequent domestic rebellions. In other words, he said that conflict and warfare were certain to occur. He was deeply concerned about the many woes facing the nation and expressed this as follows:

> Emperors and kings have their foundation in the state and bring peace and order to the age; ministers and commoners hold possession of their fields and gardens and supply the needs of the world. But if marauders come from other regions to invade the nation, or if revolt breaks out within the domain and people's lands are seized and plundered, how can there be anything but terror and confusion? If the nation is destroyed and people's homes are wiped out, then where can one flee for safety? If you care anything about your personal security, you should first of all pray for order and tranquillity throughout the four quarters of the land, should you not?[5]

IKEDA: The concept 'establishing correct teaching for the peace of the land' truly expresses the essence of a peace philosophy. The significance that I assign to this concept is this: while without correct teachings a peaceful country is not possible, establishing correct teaching completes with the peace of the land achieved. If 'correct teachings' are interpreted as the religious mission, then 'peaceful country' could be considered the humanistic and social mission. The mission of religion is not constrained to the religious sphere. Nichiren's assertion was that only by achieving the objectives of a broad humanistic and socially oriented mission can the religious mission be achieved.

JIN: I see.

IKEDA: In an analysis of the political orientation of various Japanese Buddhist sects, Masao Maruyama, a political scientist who passed away in 1996, called the teachings of Nichiren a confrontation against secular authority.

What Maruyama meant by the term 'secular authority' was, frankly, the political system. He did not say to avoid or sever relations with secular authority. Neither did he teach that one must be servile to it. He taught his followers to take on secular authority directly, engage it in a positive way, and at times confront it without hesitation.

As I am sure you are well aware, it has been pointed out that Buddhism is known to be somewhat lacking in communality and that it does not promote active engagement in the issues of the real world. In China, this is a point on which Confucianists often criticize Buddhism.

However, the guidance of 'establishing the correct teachings for the peace of the land' broke completely out of the framework of conventional Buddhist thought. I believe that it is this aspect of his teaching that distinguishes Nichiren, not only in Japanese history, but also in the 3,000-year history of Buddhism.

JIN: After writing his work *On Establishing the Correct Teaching for the Peace of the Land*, Nichiren presented it to Hōjō Tokiyori, the supreme authority of the time, and due to the intensity of the resulting argument, Nichiren became the target of a full-scale offensive by all of the major Buddhist sects. At the same time, the shogunate viewed him with enmity and condemned him to exile, expelling him from Kamakura, the seat of government at the time. Later, Nichiren was pardoned and he returned home, but his position had deteriorated, and powerful adversaries had surrounded and attacked his organization, dispersing all his disciples. Nevertheless, Nichiren would not succumb to hardship, and his indefatigable faith sustained him through this ordeal.

In the fifth year of the Bun'ei reign (1268), news came of a vast Mongolian military force that was preparing an imminent attack on Japan – news that seemed to substantiate the prescience of Nichiren's work *On Establishing the Correct Teaching for the Peace of the Land*. Nichiren continued to cry out with all his might: 'Revere only the Lotus school, and save the country from destruction!'

Nichiren's assertion advocating the Hokke sect, meaning those revering the Lotus Sutra, was grounded in an entirely religious and doctrinal perspective. However, it was the welfare of the country and the people that Nichiren had foremost in his mind, and he constructed his argument with no thought to his own safety and without bending to public opinion. His compassion and courage are truly reminiscent of Lu Xun's.

IKEDA: That is a very apt comparison. Nichiren once said, 'It has been twenty or more years now since I found myself in that situation and began the great battle. Not once have I thought of retreat.'[6] Nichiren's relentless offensive against evil and his uncompromising fighting stance resonate profoundly with Lu Xun's spirit of determination to fight mightily using the power of his pen.

The Competition to Produce Global Citizens to Manifest Genuine Peace

JIN: After some time had passed, the Nichiren sect led the common folk as well as samurai of lower rank and urban tradesmen, all struggling and unhappy with their lot, in the struggle against their oppressors. This was the so-called Hokke Uprising. The noble ethos of the Nichiren sect had created a steadfast and unwavering tradition emphasizing love of country and equality of all beings as well as sympathy for the hardships of the poor.

IKEDA: Those are certainly distinguishing characteristics of the Nichiren sect. However, its struggle against the powers was often intermittent and intense, like a geyser suddenly bursting forth into the sky. The intent was to fight to the death, and so this approach did not reflect the spirit of the times or capture the hearts and minds of the people. Perhaps for this reason, in modern times this aspect of the Nichiren's teachings has been taken out of context and misinterpreted as an extremist kind of patriotism and nationalism. I think that this is extremely unfortunate.

JIN: My understanding of Nichiren and the Nichiren sect is exceedingly limited and may be inaccurate at times. President Ikeda, I hope that you set me straight, if necessary.

In the preface of the Chinese language edition of *The Complete Writings of Nichiren Daishonin*, you wrote that *On the Establishing Correct Teaching for the Peace of the Land* was written to establish a peaceful world and show a way to radically transform humankind's destiny away from that of inevitable war. You also maintained that this was the source of SGI's (Soka Gakkai International) peace philosophy. I interpreted this as saying that if more people around the world were to believe in true Buddhist teachings, the entire world would become a Land of Eternally Tranquil Light and, naturally, there would be no more war.

In other words, this fundamental journey to realize world peace is, as the saying goes, a matter of removing the kindling from under the rice pot – that is, we must remove the causes of war if we are to achieve a true peace. This is no common, ordinary task, and we must firmly resolve to carry this heavy burden down the still long road. And with each step forward, the power of peace grows decidedly stronger.

IKEDA: The proverb you mentioned about removing the kindling from the hearth underneath the rice pot, truly describes the thrust of our movement. Based on Nichiren's teachings, we are seeking to build a system of internal values that is open and receptive to the world – this is what I have called 'the competition to produce global citizens'. In order to give substance to this concept of global citizenship, an important point to consider is the extent to which a spiritual foundation should be created. And also, how will this spiritual foundation be built? I believe that it is here that religion has a role to play.

In order to build a peaceful world, of course, cooperation between the political, economic, cultural, and educational sectors of society is necessary. But, in 'removing the kindling', so to speak, a major focus will be the extent to which religion will be able to produce people who are motivated by a deep underlying sense of spirituality.

In this sense, I firmly believe that religion will make a major contribution to building a peaceful world, and also that, in order for it to do so, it must be the kind of religion that can respond to the needs of the times.

JIN: Yes. Among the religions that heed this call, I think that the illuminating spiritual values of Buddhism will shine ever more brightly in the world.

IKEDA: Here I would like to mention the Belgian sociologist and religious scholar Dr Jan Swyngedouw, who is fluent in Japanese and deeply knowledgeable about the Japanese religious landscape. He observed that Soka Gakkai members appear to have a firm belief in their faith. He also noted that the Soka Gakkai's strong religious core has a philosophy that differs greatly from conventional Japanese religion, which tends to encompass almost every religious belief as if it were a *furoshiki* (cloth used for wrapping) carelessly wrapped around everything.

Dr Swyngedouw also stated, 'Japanese society is said to value "harmony" (Jpn. *wa*), but this harmony cannot be limited only to Japan. The harmony toward which President Ikeda and the members of the Soka Gakkai are working has as its object the peace of the entire world, and this I believe represents an important change in Japanese religious attitudes.'[7]

Dr Swyngedouw considers Soka Gakkai to have a spiritual energy and global consciousness that transcends the conventional Japanese religious framework. We are resolved to continue our struggle in order to meet the high expectations of many, including you, Mr Jin.

The Enduring and Ever-Dynamic Creativity of Ba Jin

IKEDA: Speaking of 'a warrior of the pen', I cannot help but recall Ba Jin, the chairman of the Chinese Writers Association. I had the pleasure of meeting with him on four occasions in both Japan and China. At our first meeting in April 1980, he was accompanied by authors Xie Bingxin and Lin Lin. Our young women's junior high school group sang their favourite song to welcome him and his entire group, and he was so pleased. He declared, 'I am so thrilled when I see young people who are developing themselves. . . . Youth are the hope of humankind.' He was filled with feelings of fondness for the youth, and I sensed that he held some of the same strong convictions as Lu Xun.

JIN: I see.

IKEDA: At the time, almost a year had passed since I had voluntarily relinquished my position as president of Soka Gakkai, and I, personally, as well as the organization had become targets of arrogant and domineering clergy, who vilified and slandered us with groundless accusations.

Ba Jin had to endure 'The Ten-Year Great Calamity' that was the Cultural Revolution. He had come through the storm with an unyielding faith that could be threatened by no one and, despite these experiences, he radiated an infinite human warmth toward others. As soon as we met, we were able to establish a warm rapport. At 76 years of age, he was already advanced in years.

JIN: Not long ago, I received an invitation, as a Hong Kong-based writer, to attend the Fifth National Delegate Conference of the Chinese Writers Association, held in Beijing. I also participated as a guest in the Sixth National Delegate Conference of the China Federation of Literary and Arts Circles.

Mr Ba Jin was the head of the Writers Association and Mr Cao Yu was chairman of the Federation of Literary and Arts Circles. I had long held these two gentlemen in the highest esteem for their immense talent and admirable character. I had not had the opportunity to meet them before, so

I went to Beijing filled with anticipation and excitement at the prospect of seeing them.

However, unfortunately, on the evening before the conference, Cao Yu, who had been suffering from a protracted illness, passed away. And Ba Jin was unable to attend because of his advanced age and illness.

Even so, the Writers Association members voted for Ba Jin to continue as chairman, and he accepted and remained in office for another term. This gave me reason to presume that even though his health might not be very good, his spirit was vigorous and his mind was sharp.

IKEDA: When I met with Ba Jin, he told me, 'I have made a five-year plan for what I would like to have done by the time I become 80 years of age. One of my goals is to write two full-length novels. Another is to write a retrospective of my work. Also, I would like to produce five volumes of essays and complete my translation of *My Past Thoughts: The Memoirs of Alexander Herzen*.' I recall marvelling at Ba Jin's unflagging vigour and abundant creative energy.

JIN: I grow nostalgic looking back on my junior high school days and remembering two of the most widely read authors, popular among both female and male students. One was Ba Jin and the other was Ivan Turgenev (1818–83).

Ba Jin was the only Chinese author of the period who was loved and respected by the young people of my generation.

At the time, my peers and I felt that Lu Xun's writing was a little too severe. He had a tendency to be too strident in expounding his strict social consciousness.

Among other authors of that period, Zhou Zuoren's literary style seemed detached and esoteric in implication, which was not an approach that readily resonated with the youth. Lao She struck readers as being insincere and nasty, as if he were laughing with a smirk on his face. Shen Congwen's writing was unmatched in its beauty, but his depiction of western Hunan Province made it seem like an exotic world to those of us from Jiangnan. And the passion for revolution in the works of Mao Dun was not well understood.

The Easily Accessible Literature of Ba Jin and Turgenev

IKEDA: I think I understand what you mean. The literature of Ba Jin and

Turgenev has a certain accessible quality, and it appeals directly to youth who feel a rage toward society.

When Tolstoy, in his later years, began denigrating all of his own creative works, it is well known that Turgenev, from his deathbed, pleaded with him to refrain from doing so. In contrast, I think that Turgenev's work was easily comprehensible and well received.

Tolstoy had a certain thoroughness in everything he did, and so his philosophy and way of life could not be emulated by others. This is somewhat similar to Lu Xun's seriousness and the quality of his work which, as we discussed in the previous chapter, seemed to glow with an eerie darkness about it. This was perhaps a slightly heavy and burdensome dimension that did not match with the impatient and social reformist zeal of the youth.

This reminds me of a story that I read during a side trip I made to Bulgaria, on my third visit to the then Soviet Union. It was 1981, and I remember that at the Japanese Embassy in Bulgaria I was introduced to Turgenev's book *On the Eve*. As I recall, this work depicted the period around the Bulgarian revolution and was the story of a young Bulgarian man and a young Russian woman.

Turgenev's work conveys a motif similar to that of the one in Ba Jin's *The Family*, in the sense that it depicts the passion of the youthful yearning for independence and freedom for their homeland.

JIN: Growing up in Jiangnan with its temperate climate, blessed natural surroundings, and abundance of regional products, my peers and I had a blissful and contented youth, oblivious to the concerns of the world. If we had not experienced eight hard years of the Anti-Japanese War period, I probably would have lived my entire life in a foggy, dreamlike state completely uninformed and oblivious to the outside world.

Ba Jin's works *The Family*, *Spring*, and *Autumn* closely resembled our own lives, philosophy, and feelings, and so the warmth, romance and sympathy that flowed from his pen directly touched something deep inside of me.

IKEDA: *The Family*, which is Ba Jin's most important work, has been read widely in Japan.

JIN: My family owned land and my father worked in the banking industry, and so our family was approximately of the same social status as the Gao family that appears in *The Family*. The only difference was that Jiangnan was a country town and the Gao family lived in Chengdu, a large metropolis.

Perhaps because the country town of Jiangnan was close to Shanghai, a free and open-minded atmosphere developed there more quickly than in Chengdu. And so my family did not have the intensely heavy feudal character that weighed upon the Gao family.

Also, my family did have quite a few female servants, but I do not think that we ever had anyone as beautiful and intelligent as Ming Feng.

This is probably because I left my family home at the age of 13, and I was too young to really pay much attention to whether the girls were good-looking or not. In retrospect, I remember that the girls were very ordinary in their looks. But they were all gentle and kind and took very good care of me.

When I read in *The Family* about the romance between Jue Hui, the Gao family's youngest son, who was passionate about overthrowing the feudal system, and Ming Feng, I understood what was happening. This was because the feelings I had reading *The Family* were not that different from how I felt when I read *Dream of the Red Chamber*. For example, my feelings of sympathy for Ming Feng, who committed suicide by drowning herself in a pond, were identical to the sympathy I felt for Qingwen and Fang Guan, both servants in *Dream of the Red Chamber*.

IKEDA: Compared to the tenaciously feudalistic household in *The Family*, your household it seems had an open and free atmosphere.

JIN: Ba Jin declared that he viewed anything that destroyed love as an enemy and that he was determined to fight against the outdated feudal system. I think we can say that he was able to wage this battle through his novels.

He depicts the character Jue Xin, the eldest son of the Gao family, as a spiritless and tragic figure, clearly representing the influence of the decaying feudal system. At the time, I was just a child, but I was profoundly impressed and struck by the realization that I shared the same sentiments as the author.

IKEDA: *The Family* is a work that has a subtle charm. At the end of this masterpiece, Ba Jin creates a scene in which Jue Hui, who has left home and is on a boat heading toward Shanghai, where the fomenting revolutionary movement is at its height, casts his gaze on the expansive flow of the river. 'Before his eyes is the boundless emerald water. This water surges forward unceasingly. It was carrying him to a major metropolis completely unknown to him. There, everything new is evolving. There, a new movement is coming into existence.'[8]

I will never forget Ba Jin's response to my question about this one passage. He said, 'When I mention "water", I am referring to young people. I am referring to the potential they hold for the future.'

Vehement Denunciation of Social Contradictions

JIN: When I read Ba Jin's works *Destruction* and *New Life*, in which Ba Jin portrayed the philosophical and emotional life of revolutionary youth, I did not really understand his message. I was mostly drawn to the dramatic unfolding of the story, and that was the extent of my understanding.

The two works that I was profoundly impressed by were the two medium-length novels, *Autumn in Spring* and *Spring in Autumn*. The first is his original work and the second is a translation. They are the stories of a young person whose heart is aflutter with love. I was most deeply moved by the fact that the thoughts of the youth were exactly the kinds of things that I had been thinking. I was also especially touched by his anguish at failing to win his true love.

IKEDA: The works you just mentioned are, unfortunately, ones with which I am unfamiliar. Ba Jin kindly presented me with the complete collection of his works, but the fact is that most of them are not yet translated into Japanese.

JIN: The novels *Cold Nights* and *The Garden of Repose*, which he wrote relatively late in his career, are imbued with profound sentiments rich in nuance, and so require greater discernment on the part of the reader than do his earlier novels. And because these works are of a superior aesthetic quality, fewer readers are able to appreciate them. Just as in music, if a piece of music is too elegant, fewer people will enjoy it.

Let me cite Beethoven as an example. The piano piece 'Für Elise' has a lilting and lively melody beloved by many. However, Beethoven's 'Ninth Symphony', a tour de force both profound in concept and imposing in structure, is difficult to appreciate, and so, naturally, a drastically smaller audience is able to enjoy it.

IKEDA: I see. The work *Cold Nights* has, shall we say, a kind of darkness or bleakness that is found in Lu Xun, in its fundamental denunciation of society. The protagonist is a man who is well-intentioned, but faint of heart, and sees no escape from his circumstances. He becomes entangled in the ugly conflict between his wife and mother, and becomes afflicted by a grave illness. His wife feels pushed to breaking point and, though she loves her husband, decides to leave him.

The protagonist and his adoring mother are reduced to extreme poverty and can only struggle hopelessly as the man's incurable disease progresses. The man suffers anger and indignation as, ultimately, his illness robs him even of his voice.

Ba Jin writes, 'No one could hear from him. He demanded justice, but where could he find it? He could not even shout out his grievances; he must die in silence.'[9]

The man asked himself, 'Why me?' He wanted to know why he alone had to suffer this tragedy. Call it fate, or divine will. Was this ultimately a good or an evil phenomenon?

This question brings to mind the story of Sima Qian, who was castrated as punishment for a crime he did not commit, as a consequence of groundless accusations, and was left to suffer disgrace and humiliation. He famously asked, 'Is this so-called Way of Heaven right or wrong?'[10]

Just as we see in the Old Testament figure of Job, who continues desperately trying to understand the nature of divine will, though buffeted by one disaster after another, the anguished quest of the character in Ba Jin's novel is synonymous with this eternal pursuit of meaning in the religious sense.

However, in Ba Jin's novel, whether for good or bad, he makes no attempt to spring toward a religious perspective. Rather, he vehemently denounces society's contradictions. On this point, it can be surmised that the literature of Ba Jin inspired revolution, and gave courage to the enthusiastically receptive young activists who helped birth the new socialist China.

Forerunners who Devoted their Lives to China–Japan Relations

JIN: President Ikeda, you and Ba Jin met for the first time in 1980. In his *Random Thoughts*, which was written one year before that, Ba Jin wrote a passage in remembrance of his Japanese friend, Kenzō Nakajima (1903–79). He also mentions many other Japanese friends, including Zenmaro Toki (1885–1980), Yasushi Inoue (1907–91), and Tsutomu Mizukami (1919–2004).

Ba Jin writes the following about Kenzō Nakajima:

Kenzō loved his sake, and in fact was a heavy drinker. On a number of occasions, I threw a party for him and always cautioned him to moderate his liquor consumption. My admonitions had no effect, however. I knew that he used the power of liquor as a way to banish his depression. During that time, Kenzō worked tirelessly and fought fiercely to advance friendly relations between China and Japan, but he endured much harassment, which included his receiving threatening mail, being denied venues to present his writings, and having his books rejected by publishing companies. Consequently, his means of making a living were obstructed and he had to sell his car. He lived a life of great adversity. Kenzō, nonetheless, refused to succumb to these hardships and never wavered in his firm commitment to the enormous undertaking of furthering cultural relations between China and Japan.[11]

IKEDA: From what I have heard, Mr Nakajima was fearless. I heard an anecdote about his meeting with Yao Wenyuan, one of the Gang of Four, who was then at the height of his power. Apparently, Mr Nakajima lost his patience with Yao Wenyuan's overbearing and arrogant manner which caused him to raise his voice. The flustered interpreter tried as much as possible to soften his language, but Nakajima's severe tone and facial expression made Yao Wenyuan's face change colour. After that episode, the Japan–China Cultural Exchange Association, of which Nakajima was general director of the Board, experienced even more annoying and aggravating incidents than before.

JIN: During his life, Mr Nakajima held a central position in the Japan–China Cultural Exchange Association. Ba Jin wrote:

> On one occasion when I was having a casual conversation with Mr Nakajima, he shared that he thought that his activities to promote friendly relations between China and Japan would likely be his last major work, and he added that he had no worries and nothing to fear. He said, 'I chose this work and have followed this path to the present with absolutely no regrets'.
>
> Next, Mr Nakajima began relating his experience in Singapore. In 1942, Mr Nakajima went to Singapore as a war correspondent. There, he witnessed the Japanese military's arbitrary arrest and execution by firing squad of many overseas Chinese. Afterward,

a number of victims' mothers came to him carrying photographs to inquire about their sons. From that time on, Mr Nakajima felt great anguish over these events. He often thought about Japan's future. This famous literary critic and scholar of French literature finally discovered his major life's work, which was to devote himself to encouraging friendly relations between the peoples of China and Japan, for the sake of their children, grandchildren, and all future generations.[12]

IKEDA: I understand his motivation exactly. As I mentioned before, for almost 30 years, I, too, have worked earnestly to advance goodwill between China and Japan. One source of my motivation was the observation expressed by my eldest brother when he returned home after fighting on the front lines during World War II. He stated that the Japanese military was brutal toward the local people. He died on the battlefield in Burma (now called Myanmar). So, deep in my heart I feel the same kind of anguish and heartache that Mr Nakajima must have felt.

Incidentally, while the members of the Japan–China Cultural Exchange Association became disheartened and discouraged by harassment from remnants of Yao Wenyuan's faction, Mr Nakajima brushed it off saying, 'Don't expect that when death comes, it will be on the glorious path to victory. It is more honourable to die like a dog in a ditch by the roadside. You have to keep going, even when you feel like you are about to be crushed.'

What striking words! They seem like they could be the famous lines uttered by a Kabuki star as he cuts a striking pose on the stage. Mr Nakajima really had backbone.

Subsequently, after hearing about this situation, Premier Zhou Enlai bowed in apology saying, 'It seems that we have caused you much trouble. Please forgive me because this is all my responsibility.' I can only say that this is what I would have expected from Premier Zhou Enlai. It takes an exceptional person to say what he did.

JIN: President Ikeda, you endured hostile and slanderous attacks for your support of friendly ties between China and Japan, just as Mr Nakajima did – attacks based on fabricated, groundless rumours aimed at destroying your honourable name. Yet you simply have paid no attention, and continued to assert that Japan should apologize for the crimes Japan committed during its invasion of China during World War II.

I believe that this is perhaps the most patriotic action that a Japanese person can take. It is only by acknowledging the crimes committed during the invasion and by swearing to never make the same mistake again, that Japan can become a nation of peace and tranquillity and begin to walk in righteousness toward a bright future. This is exactly the goal to which a true patriot should aspire.

IKEDA: The first time I visited China and the former Soviet Union, I encountered numerous obstacles, which I cannot discuss here in detail. I was also the target of much criticism and many defamatory comments.

From a historical perspective, it is nothing but ambient noise, unworthy of attention. The mirror of time will clearly reflect who is right and who is a fool. In the meantime, I humbly take it all in and continue on my way.

Those who Suffer the Most Deserve the Most Happiness

JIN: I may be straying from the topic, President Ikeda, but this year Jilin University in China broached the subject of awarding you and me honorary professorships. I would like to extend my appreciation to the people from the university for their kindness and good wishes.

Personally speaking, I need to focus my time and energy on writing my historical works and novels and am trying to limit outside engagements so as to avoid diverting my attention away from my work. Therefore, because of this, I had to decline the university's kind suggestion.

President Ikeda, you responded to the university by recalling that the Japanese began their invasion of China in the three eastern provinces: Liaoning, Jilin, and Heilongjiang provinces. You continued by noting that the capital of Manchuria was Changchun in Jilin province, and that of all the damage that Japan inflicted on China, the attack on Jilin province was the longest and caused the most civilian suffering.

IKEDA: I believe that those who suffer the most have the right to become the happiest. This is a belief based on my religious faith. The only people who experienced war on Japanese soil were the Okinawans, and this was in a conflict that saw so many civilian fatalities and in which the very topography of the land was transformed by a windstorm of steel from the artillery bombardment of Okinawa. This is the reason that I began my novel *The Human Revolution* in Okinawa. I have the same hope for happiness for the people of Okinawa as for the people of Jilin province.

JIN: President Ikeda, please let me continue with your comments regarding Jilin University. You mentioned that you sincerely hoped that by establishing a cooperative agreement with Jilin University, you would be able to contribute to the development of the university. You acknowledged that this would not expiate the crimes committed against the people of Jilin, but that you at least, as one Japanese person, wanted to make a statement of conscience and regret.

I was very impressed with your statement. It was open and honest and a commendable action to take. I am convinced that if Ba Jin, who was on his deathbed, had known about it, he surely would have been pleased to have such a friend as you.

IKEDA: You are very generous. I remember that in my third discussion with Ba Jin, the subject of Tolstoy's death came up. Ba Jin asserted, 'I don't think that Tolstoy would ever have contemplated suicide'. Though perhaps it was rude of me, I felt that I had to respond to his resolute tone by inquiring, 'In the midst of the raging fury of the Cultural Revolution and the worst suffering that you experienced, did you give a thought to death?'

He answered firmly, 'No, not one thought'. Ba Jin's eyes gleamed with a penetrating light. 'I endured many hardships, but the thought foremost in my mind was to "keep fighting, fighting, fighting to overcome and survive!"'

Of course, amid the unprecedented madness of the Cultural Revolution, which, like a bad dream, ensnared many men of letters – in the face of this agonizingly twisted situation his faith was like steel and his character like a massive rock, and this gives us a glimpse of the substance of this man, Ba Jin.

The Courageous Confession in *Random Thoughts*

JIN: Ba Jin authored five volumes in total of *Random Thoughts* during the period from 1979 to 1986. He devoted quite a bit of space to reproaching himself for being unable to maintain a firm will and remain steadfast in his beliefs during the Cultural Revolution.

Specifically, Ba Jin summarized and criticized the way that he yielded to political pressure and turned his back on his conscience, and even while grasping the irrationality of doing so, he had denounced himself and also many of his friends and other writers.

For a writer to expose his flaws and be so critical of himself was surprising and undoubtedly unnerved his readers. Coming from a person of Ba Jin's stature, this kind of sharp self-rebuke and reproach for such despicable and shameful behaviour was completely unprecedented in all of Chinese history.

IKEDA: In one of the volumes of his *Random Thoughts*, entitled *Collection of Explorations*, he writes, 'I cannot blame everything on the Gang of Four. I myself accepted the authority of the Gang of Four, docilely submitting with bowed head and bended knee, entrusting to them the power to do anything they wanted to do. Therefore, how on earth can I say that I have no culpability! And surely, we cannot say that the majority of people do not bear some responsibility!'[13]

This fiery outpouring of feeling clearly reveals the greatness of Ba Jin's character.

JIN: During the Cultural Revolution, many people wrote humiliating self-criticisms after being intimidated by threats of harm to their families and being beaten and enduring brutal, barbarous treatment at the hands of the authorities.

However, when Ba Jin wrote his *Random Thoughts*, he was free from any pressure. This is why this work was a pure and sincere expression of contrition by an honest, virtuous human being. I also think that perhaps Ba Jin was motivated by his lifelong admiration and respect for France's Jean-Jacques Rousseau.

IKEDA: Yes. Rousseau's *The Confessions* immediately comes to mind.

JIN: After reading *Random Thoughts*, my regard for Ba Jin grew immensely, and I thought ashamedly to myself, 'If I were him, I probably couldn't have done that'. If I had found myself in similar circumstances, I doubt that I could have done even half of what he did.

IKEDA: But your statement itself is a sincere and courageous admission. It might seem like an easy thing for a person to be honest, but I think that it can actually be very difficult. I understood your admission to be honest in the truest sense of the word.

It is at this point that Ba Jin contemplated the internal evil and the 'internal Gang of Four' in himself. He suggests that his comprehension of this 'internal Gang of Four' was inadequate and therefore he succumbed too easily, even if briefly, to the threats and intimidation of the external Gang of Four. So, in a sense, he accepted their perverse and unjust authority. He did not claim that other people were responsible but took ownership of it as his own problem. This is the most important point.

In this regard, T. S. Eliot (1888–1965) pointed out that 'one reason why the lot of the secular reformer or revolutionist seems to me to be the easier is this: that for the most part he conceives of the evils of the world as something external to himself. They are thought of either as completely impersonal, so that there is nothing to alter but machinery; or if there is evil incarnate, it is always incarnate in the other people.'[14]

While evil exists externally, at the same time it is also internal within ourselves. As long as this reality is not acknowledged, every social reform and revolutionary action will simply be limited to substituting one powerful regime for another.

JIN: As soon as the Cultural Revolution began, I immediately wrote an editorial in the newspaper severely condemning the irresponsible ways of the Chinese Communist Party authorities. Furthermore, the *Ming Pao Monthly* was launched, and we brought to light the numerous irrational things that happened during the Cultural Revolution.

We were opposed to Jiang Qing, Lin Biao, Kang Sheng, Chen Boda, Ke Qingshi, Zhang Chunqiao, Yao Wenyuan, Guo Moruo, and Mao Zedong. People we commended and supported were Peng Dehuai, Deng Ta, Wu Han, Liao Mosha, Deng Xiaoping, Zhou Enlai, Li Xiannian, Liu Pocheng, Chen Yi, Ba Jin, Cao Yu, and Lao She. And we also supported artists such as Huang Zhou and Huang Yongyu.

IKEDA: I am very familiar with all of them. And I know why your legendary sharp-tongued editorials in the *Ming Pao* are, even now, well known.

JIN: I do not intend to say that I was in any way bolder, inspired by a stronger sense of justice, or looking at things from a more correct perspective. The fact of the matter is, simply, that I lived in Hong Kong. In other words, I lived in a place in which it was safe to speak my mind. At one point, the ultra-left wing of the Chinese Communist Party discussed plans to assassinate me, but soon afterwards Zhou Enlai handed down a ruling prohibiting the ultra-left factions from committing any violent actions in Hong Kong. And so we were able to continue without incident.

The intelligentsia living in Hong Kong were unafraid to boldly speak our minds and were able to avoid any serious problems of political persecution only because we were relatively lucky. It is simply not the case that we were any more courageous or correct about things as compared to our fellow reporters in the media on the mainland. On this point, I feel that we must have the wisdom of self-knowledge to accurately discern the reality of our situation in those days.

Literature Builds Spirit

IKEDA: That is what you say, but at that time in Japan there were also many who were caught up by the hysteria over the Cultural Revolution. There were people who adorned this blatant power struggle with an appealing philosophy, and while heightening people's expectations for a cultural revolution unprecedented in human history, they merely repeated hollow, bankrupt ideals.

In the middle of this, Mr Jin, you were able to see what was really happening and clearly stated, 'This is a power struggle'. It was indeed a keen insight.

Incidentally, I once asked Ba Jin about politics and literature. He answered, 'Literature cannot separate itself from politics. However, politics can absolutely never take the place of literature. This is because literature elevates the human spirit.' He made this statement after experiencing the ordeals of the 'Great Misfortune' – that is, the persecution of the Cultural Revolution. Given all that he went through, it would not have been surprising if he had shunned any political involvement and determined to remain indifferent to everything. It would have been perfectly understandable if he had displayed animosity and bitterness. Yet, he was able to make this positive statement.

There is a Chinese saying, 'Literary works are the supreme achievement in the business of state, a splendour that does not decay'.[15] I sense that this truly expresses a pure resolve to completely embrace the written word.

JIN: Ba Jin expresses his approach to writing in these terms. He wrote, 'The reason that I write is to battle the enemy. In other words, I write to strike down outdated traditions, all irrational systems that hinders humanity's progress and thwart the enhancement of our humanity, and everything that destroys the precious love that uplifts humankind.'

Ba Jin always continued to embrace one lofty objective. Of course, he also said, 'I write literature only to sustain myself and not because I want to make a name for myself'.

IKEDA: He had a youthfulness about him – a youthfulness of spirit. When Ba Jin came to Japan, I understand that he gave a lecture on his view of himself as a writer in which he said: 'With every new day and night it is as if my soul is spurred on, and deep inside myself, the flames of passion burn brightly. The suffering and hardships of so many people, myself included, compel me to take up my pen and write without a moment's rest. My hand is possessed by an unstoppable force that moves it across the paper. It is as if the spirits of the masses yearn to tell the story of their anguish and have engaged the pen in my hand to that end.

'When that happens, I lose myself and become oblivious to my surroundings, becoming a writing machine intent on doing their bidding. Sometimes, I crouch on the chair or rest my head on the desktop, and at other times I stand up and walk to the sofa, and then immediately sit down again, my heart racing as I dispatch my pen to do its work.'

This image of Ba Jin's daily struggle hovers before our eyes, revealing how this 'Warrior of the Pen' plunged himself into the heat of battle.

JIN: Ba Jin's work brims with intensity. He has said that his creativity is defined by the motto 'to offer my heart to my readers'. Without a doubt, Ba Jin's writings make us feel as if we have seen into his heart and have a sense of the depth of his feelings. From a classical perspective, his work may lack nuance and have a tendency to seem too strident in opinion. Personally, I prefer writing that is tranquil in tone and elegant in its simplicity, and in my work, I put my whole heart into writing that way.

However, when I have read Ba Jin's works, I have wept. When I was a child, I cried when I read that, in *The Family*, Ming Feng had committed suicide and that Rui Yu died from complications in childbirth, and more recently I shed tears when I read Ba Jin's depiction of the death of Mr Xiao He.

Authors never let themselves be carried away by their emotions, but rather hold back their tears while etching a profound sense of grief and anguish deep into their hearts. When they are engaged in the creative process, they make sure to refrain from shedding tears, but I cannot help being moved to tears when I read their works.

CHAPTER 8

A Literature of Hope

Long Live Hong Kong, the People's Realm!

JIN: I received a letter recently from a Soka Gakkai member living in Hokkaido. The letter read, 'Our youth group meets regularly once a month to read and discuss your dialogue series in the *Ushio* magazine, and we are benefiting so much from it, so I am writing to thank you'.

IKEDA: I am glad to hear that. I also receive quite a few letters expressing the same sentiment. I am especially happy to know that many young people are reading the dialogue.

JIN: I really admire the young people in your organization for their passion for knowledge and the great efforts they put into advancing their learning. I am also impressed by all the leaders of the area groups for the way they are managing their organizations and for the achievements they have realized. All the SGI members have a lively interest in pursuing learning. I imagine that this is a direct result of your spiritual influence.

IKEDA: I believe that youth is a time for learning. Young people must have a voracious appetite for learning at all times. And I would hope that they would open their eyes widely to the world to greatly expand their horizons. This is my hope and prayer.

JIN: In their letters, the members have expressed their concern and prayers for the future of Hong Kong. They express the same thoughtfulness that you have.

The then SGI of Hong Kong General Director Lee Kong Sau conveyed to me your message, President Ikeda, wishing for Hong Kong's peaceful return to China. Thank you so much for your kindness.

In your message, the friendship and goodwill that you have had all these years for the people of China and Hong Kong shines through. I am sure that anyone from China or Hong Kong who encounters your goodwill cannot help being moved by your warmheartedness.

IKEDA: You mentioned the return of Hong Kong to China. Some time has passed since this historical drama occurred, and so I would like to depart for a moment from our literary discussion and touch once again upon the significance of Hong Kong's return.

I have mentioned before that I am convinced the key to the direction of civilization in the twenty-first century lies in China. The story of the world in the twenty-first century cannot be told without including the role of China. Also, I consider Hong Kong's return to the immense Chinese 'family' as another defining event in the flow of world history.

I am sure that you were extremely busy around the time of the transition.

JIN: Yes. During that time, a total of 6,000 foreign reporters and commentators visited Hong Kong to report on the event. Among them were some Japanese reporters from the *Yomiuri Shimbun* and a news gathering team from NHK, who came to our place to do interviews.

IKEDA: I read the article in which you were interviewed. What was your impression of the interview?

JIN: My friends in the Japanese mass media sometimes have a somewhat brazen attitude, but they did not publicly express any hostility or ill will regarding the return. In contrast, the majority of the Western correspondents hurled biased and blatantly hostile questions at me.

IKEDA: Really? For example?

JIN: I had the following exchange with a certain British reporter.

REPORTER: If China limits freedom of expression in Hong Kong after the return, what will you do?

JIN: What would YOU do if the British government revokes your freedom of speech in two or three months?

REPORTER: That would never happen because the British Constitution guarantees the freedom of expression for its citizens.

JIN: Well, you know, the Basic Law of the Hong Kong Special Administrative Region of the People's Republic of China guarantees freedom of expression in Hong Kong.

REPORTER: Do you believe it?

JIN: Believe what?

REPORTER: Do you believe in the Basic Law?

JIN: Of course I believe in it. I was a member of the Basic Law Drafting Committee, and I helped write it.

IKEDA: That reporter was at a disadvantage. He was up against Jin Yong, a giant in the press world of Hong Kong. No reporter would be a match for you.

JIN: No, no, no. I sincerely doubt that! This is how our conversation continued.

> REPORTER: I trust in the British Constitution, but I have no confidence in the Basic Law of the Hong Kong Special Administrative Region.
>
> JIN: Ever since the Chinese Communist Party came into power, it has not once violated any international agreements. I am firmly convinced of it. However, Governor Christopher Patten, who was dispatched to Hong Kong by the British government, publicly violated an agreement about the election of the Legislative Council of Hong Kong at a 1995 Sino–British Conference. The British government upheld the governor's infringement. Based on the facts, I think that it is clear in whom we should have more confidence.

Needless to say, this interview ended in a somewhat strained mood, without our resolving this issue.

IKEDA: In September 1968, I advocated for a restoration of diplomatic ties between China and Japan, and in my discussion I pointed out that China had said that it would not export revolution through military might. I believed that as long as China honoured its word, it deserved our trust. China has not betrayed this trust. The Chinese government has said that it will comply with the Basic Law of the Hong Kong Special Administrative Region. I agree with you, Mr Jin, that China will keep its promise.

JIN: Thank you. How have things been going since the return? I hope that as many of my foreign friends as possible come to see the reality for themselves. If they do, President Ikeda, I am sure that they will immediately see what you have portrayed so splendidly in your beautiful poem.

> Hong Kong!
> It is home to a people of unflagging spirit.
> Here you will find the enthusiasm and the pulse of a vivacious existence.
> The bustle of the city of full of vitality,
> And the cheerful clamor of voices upon voices
> Echoes through groves of high-rise apartments.

The Historical Wisdom Underlying China's Multifaceted Thinking

IKEDA: That's very nice of you to say. To that I would add my fervent hope: Long live Hong Kong, the people's realm!

The reason that I am optimistic about the future of Hong Kong is because, first of all, China's way of thinking and making decisions is flexible, pragmatic, and reasonable.

The Chinese government has agreed that Hong Kong will be governed under the 'one country, two systems' policy and has announced that Hong Kong will be a capitalist society under the jurisdiction of communist China. This means that China will place Hong Kong's prosperity and stability first and, for the time being, set aside national causes and concern about 'face'.

Not every country would be capable of taking this kind of approach. Rather, it is often the case that when a new national or foreign policy goes into effect, friction and confusion arise when it is pushed or rushed through.

China does not view matters from a one-dimensional perspective. It considers, first of all, the degree of dissension and disorientation that may arise from a hasty approach. This is because the application of policy and law must be in alignment with reality. The most reasonable course of action is considered by looking at both the ideal and the reality and by creating a skilful balance of the two. In brief, the perspective is multifaceted, not one-dimensional.

JIN: It is just as you say. China's Hong Kong policy is both moderate and realistic.

IKEDA: What interests me is that this multifaceted way of thinking is supported by a time-honoured historical wisdom.

I once heard this Chinese tale. It is about a distinguished judge named Teng Dayin. The Japanese equivalent is the story *Ōoka Sabaki*.

A man took a scroll to Judge Teng Dayin, according to the instructions in his father's will. Teng Dayin took the scroll in his hands, and noticing a disguised hidden message, he tore off the paper to find the words, 'Five pots of gold are sealed within the earthen walls on the left side of the store-house, and five pots of silver are in the walls on the right side'. The father had been worried that, after his death, his greedy eldest son would deprive his younger sons of his rightful inheritance, and so he devised the arrangement indicated in the message.

Upon reading the message, Judge Dayin called the brothers to come before him and said, 'Your father's ghost appeared to me and revealed that within the walls of your family storehouse are sealed five pots each of treasures. Your father instructed that the eldest son will take the pots sealed in the right wall and the youngest will take the pots in the left wall, and I, Teng Dayin, will take one of the pots from the share of the youngest.' The youngest son did not protest this decision. The greedy older brother was satisfied because he believed his father had left him with a larger inheritance than his younger brother. Judge Dayin gained one pot of gold, and thus all three benefited.

JIN: That is a well-known story. This kind of story is called a *gongan*, or court tale.

IKEDA: In Japan, people would reject a story about a judge who is supposed to be one of the 'good guys' but profits from his position on the bench. In contrast, in a Japanese story such as *Ōoka Sabaki*, the principle of *Sanpō ichiryō zon*, or 'sharing a burden split three ways', is illustrated by the judge who ends up contributing money from his own pocket. Whatever the reality, the Japanese seek honesty and integrity in a judge. They are pleased by simplicity and transparency in all matters.

On the contrary, the Chinese understand and accept the very human qualities of Teng Dayin. Rather than thinking in the unambiguous terms of integrity and fairness, they say 'Human beings are not such perfect creatures – and judges are no exception'.

In short, the Chinese tend to accept the reality that every matter has a variety of different aspects to it. If there is a front, there is a back. Virtue coexists with evil. This principle is emphasized in the worlds that you create in your novels, Mr Jin. It is an understanding of human nature that views a person's sense of morality as composed of a fusion of diverse values and influences.

This way of thinking is not one-dimensional or myopic. It is multi-dimensional and multifaceted. It certainly is not an unprincipled kind of ideology. One example of this is China's diplomatic relations after World War II. China's return to the United Nations was based on very clear-cut principles and these were never abandoned. This approach allowed for the flexibility of a realistic response.

The late Shigeki Kaizuka was an eminent researcher of Chinese history who claimed, 'when dealing with performance-oriented peoples such as the Chinese, one must not immediately think of winning on the diplomatic front. It is all right to lose. Just make sure to lose in the best possible way.'[1] Of course, he must be talking about 'performance' in a positive sense, I think.

JIN: I have a sense that you may be a little too complimentary, but you do have a deep understanding of the Chinese character.

IKEDA: Hong Kong's 'one country, two systems' policy is another example that shows the Chinese did not take a superficial and haphazard approach to this matter. I believe that this traditional Chinese multifaceted thinking is deeply rooted in the historical wisdom of the Chinese people. This is why the Chinese people are so firmly grounded. They have confidence. And this is why I am very optimistic about the future of Hong Kong.

The Objective of the SGI Movement: To Become Good Citizens

JIN: On the evening of 17 July 1997, SGI of Hong Kong held an event called 'An Evening Blessing the Return'. I spoke at the event on behalf of the assembled guests. As I mentioned at the time, that kind of event itself showed how SGI of Hong Kong had become one with the people of Hong Kong.

SGI is an international organization with groups all over the world, and wherever it is located, its members connect intimately with the local people and share their lives.

In the West, when a couple wed, they pledge to become one forever, for better or for worse. In China, it is thought that taking an oath of friendship establishes one of the most important relationships in a person's life. By their vows, friends pledge to share in their blessings as well as in their misfortunes.

IKEDA: In your novel *Sword Stained with Royal Blood*, this is illustrated in a scene in which blood brothers swear to 'share our blessings as well as misfortunes'.[2]

JIN: Yes. Life is not made up of infinitely continuing good times. When people have decided to share the same destiny, they share the joy of the happy times. When hardships are encountered, they also share in trying to overcome these difficulties. This is what the two aspects of the pledge mean.

IKEDA: On the day that my mentor, Josei Toda, became the second president of Soka Gakkai, he composed the following *waka* verse.

> Sharing our destiny
> Of joys and sorrows
> In the present and the future,
> How Marvelous!

The karmic destiny of like-minded companions and friends is profound. I sense that the pledges of the heroes who appear in your novels, Mr Jin, resonate with a deep and powerful affection that binds kindred spirits.

JIN: I think that these pledges of friendship are a testament to the humanness of the heroes. In any case, the return of Hong Kong to the homeland was a truly auspicious event that had long been the ardent wish of Hong Kong's six million people. This is the sentiment underlying the pride and self-respect felt by every single citizen of Hong Kong.

Under the guidance of the leaders of SGI of Hong Kong, including the former General Director Lee Kong Sau, the members joined with us, the people of Hong Kong, in celebrating this joyous occasion. This truly expressed their pledge to share in the good times as well as the bad and to receive the blessings as well as face the hardships together.

Our feeling is that the people of SGI of Hong Kong are like family to us. Whether Hong Kong's tomorrows will be better, and even if they are not, I believe that our friends at SGI of Hong Kong will do their part to help Hong Kong fulfil the role it is meant to play.

IKEDA: The objective of the SGI movement is for SGI members to become good citizens in whatever country the organization is located. In the words of Nichiren: 'One should have a correct understanding of the country. People's minds differ according to their land. For example, a mandarin orange tree south of the Yangtze River becomes a triple-leaved orange tree when it is transplanted to the north of the Huai River. Even plants and trees, which have no mind, change with their location. How much more, then, must beings with minds differ according to the place!'[3]

Broadly defined, 'mind' can be interpreted to include culture, customs, traditions, and social convention. In this sense, each country has its own 'mind' or cognitive framework for its social and cultural life. Through contact with that consciousness, good citizens are nurtured. And by producing good citizens, a country's objective of creating a prosperous and thriving society is achieved. This is the essence of the SGI movement. Buddhist teachings do not cast the human personality into any specific mould.

JIN: President Ikeda, you have consistently maintained your watchful concern over Hong Kong for many years. I know this because you have written numerous poems extolling the spirit of Hong Kong's working people, who spare no effort to continually better themselves.

In our discussions as well, you have bestowed your sincere blessings and hopes on Hong Kong, while at the same time you have pointed out the pessimistic tone expressed by certain critics in the Japanese media and have taken them to task for their error.

You declared that there was no basis for this pessimism, and expressed your belief that, even after its return, Hong Kong would continue its excellent progress and contribute even more to bringing about peace and prosperity, especially in the Asia and Pacific region.

I would like to once again sincerely thank you, President Ikeda, for your kindness. My hope is that under your leadership, with each passing day, SGI of Hong Kong will develop and move forward in step with Hong Kong, and we will all celebrate these joyous developments.

Courtesy Animates Human Character and Expresses one's Humanity

IKEDA: I have long heralded the coming of the era of Asian and Pacific civilization. Over ten years ago, I called for the establishment of an Asia-Pacific Organization for Peace and Culture.

In the sense of this kind of Asia-Pacific community, we will see China become even more predominant. And henceforth, the relationship between China and the US will become especially important. If these two countries establish truly friendly relations, there is no doubt that together they will become a major pillar supporting world peace. Of course, Japan will have to do its best to work toward this objective of peace as well.

JIN: This is why I have great expectations for SGI. In February 1996, I participated in the World Peace Youth Culture Festival with you, President Ikeda, and was blessed to be able to enjoy a programme of many magnificent performances.

We were able to see the exciting spectacle of young men and women from many different countries and races joining together to sing and dance, and they sang with all their hearts about the beautiful world that we live in and the beautiful future that they hope to build. The youth differed from each other in the colour of their skin and the languages they spoke, and I could see that, as they took each other by the hand, passionately seeking peace and cultural understanding, there was nothing that could stop them.

IKEDA: Thank you. Professor Bryan Wilson gave his impression of our festival and touched on the concept presented by philosopher William James in his 'The Moral Equivalent of War'. He observed:

> All over the world, a typical pattern of the so-called peace movement has developed, which includes demonstration marches, and other events. The objective is a good one. However, the events often tend to elicit too much emotion, invite confusion and disorder, and give others a negative or antagonistic impression.

In contrast, the Soka Gakkai peace festival concept places importance on self-discipline. A peace festival event brings together the energies of many different kinds of people and provides a way to release these energies in a disciplined form. An event such as this is, in a sense, a 'moral equivalent' and, I believe, differs greatly from the demonstration march, which runs counter to the objective of peace, provokes antipathy, and creates a negative effect.

JIN: I think that Dr Wilson was exactly right. Soka Gakkai's motto is to create a civilization that embodies lofty spiritual values and enhances the spiritual development of the inner self. At the same time, Soka Gakkai also strives to pursue these objectives throughout the world, promote peace, and oppose war and all manner of injustice.

Reflecting back on the twentieth century, we can see that humankind evolved in its respect for spiritual values and, as a result, hitherto colonial states have won their independence or been returned to their original suzerain states. Moreover, the majority of these transactions were accomplished in a peaceful manner.

In the ceremony in which the sovereignty of Hong Kong was transferred, both the Chinese and the British conducted themselves with decorum and grace in their remarks.

In China's Spring and Autumn Period (770–403 BCE), diplomatic relations with other countries were conducted amid banquets at which poems were composed and exchanged. I think we ought to revive the practice of this kind of peaceful deportment and civilized etiquette today.

I believe that this spirit of diplomacy, which the two great countries of China and the United Kingdom have demonstrated by their relations in the international community, is in precise alignment with the ideals upheld by Soka Gakkai.

IKEDA: The words 'courtesy' and 'etiquette' may seem like old-fashioned words, but the spirit that they represent could also be described as 'having the grace and generosity to be considerate of the other person's situation'. In essence, this is a kind of 'performance', in the sense of social etiquette.

Let me illustrate. Before diplomatic relations between Japan and China had been restored, a former general from the old Japanese military visited China and met with Premier Zhou Enlai. He asked the premier if there were any Japanese people that he just could not bring himself to forgive. Zhou Enlai responded, 'Since you asked, I will answer. There are three.' The general continued, 'Who are they?' The answer was, 'One of them is the former Prime Minister Tōjō Hideki. He was somewhat of a representative figure, so of course, it cannot be helped that I would choose him.'

The general persisted in asking, 'Who are the other two'? The premier answered: 'We will not forgive these two. However, they have left behind family members. These family members are innocent. If, for example, I, the Premier of China, accused someone's father or husband of being a war criminal, and they somehow found out about it, those family members would be deeply saddened. That is why I will not divulge the names of the other two.'

The Chinese people, including Premier Zhou Enlai, must have hated these individuals beyond measure. However, though the prime minister may have struggled to hold back tears of pain and anguish, he never divulged those names. His reason was that he did not want the family members of those people to suffer.

It is in this sense, I believe, that Shigeki Kaizuka, the Chinese history specialist I mentioned before, praised Zhou Enlai as one of history's great performers.

JIN: What a great story about a noble man.

IKEDA: Originally, the meanings of 'courtesy' and 'etiquette' probably did not imply external pressure restraining and dictating human behaviour and customs.

Sometimes we must overcome our desire to push our own opinion, our desire to bring our own grievances or point of view to the fore, and instead stand in the other person's shoes and carefully consider his or her concerns. This noble spirit of restraint is what is meant by the true practice of 'courtesy' and 'etiquette'.

The definition of 'etiquette', which was debated continuously in ancient China, is something that is not to be found outside the self. Rather, I believe that it must be sought within the self.

'Etiquette' animates human character and expresses one's humanity. In today's world, human relationships are suffering, and nothing is more necessary and in demand than that kind of noble spirit.

This is why we seek to nurture this sense of 'spiritual etiquette'. I want to emulate the character of Zhou Enlai by viewing the broad picture, but not overlooking the details; by concealing the severest conviction in my heart, while putting on a smile as fresh as a spring breeze; by putting others first rather than being self-centred; by becoming an outstanding Chinese person as well as a cosmopolitan world citizen; and by always gazing upon the people, the great terra firma of consciousness, with kindness and equanimity. I want to train myself to be like that.

I believe that the peaceful attitude and civilized etiquette that you mentioned, Mr Jin, will blossom precisely because of that kind of 'character training'.

The Fundamental Purpose of Literature and Reading Between the Lines

IKEDA: Well then, we have digressed a little, so let us return to the topic of literature. I would like to revisit Ba Jin's thoughts about writing, which he shared when he spoke in Japan. He explained: 'The reason that I write my books is not to earn a living and not to be famous, but to fight against enemies. What is an enemy, you may ask? It is all kinds of old traditional views, all irrational systems that hinder the progress of society and the cultivation of our humanity, and all things that destroy love, affection, and all tender feelings. All of these are my greatest enemies, and I have attacked these foes many times.'

This perspective is not limited to literature. In general, in every human endeavour, there must be a fundamental aspiration; that is, a reason. In this sense, Ba Jin's passionate writings deeply touched my heart.

Why do we write? In our youth, one view held that literature was to be written for the sake of literature. In other words, it was art for art's sake. The opposing view was that literature was to be written to illuminate ideology. This view heralded the cause of literature for the people and prioritized the duty to write for the sake of ideology. Paradoxically, however, when literature is written for ideology, the very life that animates it withers away.

This may be a somewhat difficult question, Mr Jin, but what do you think is the fundamental purpose of literature?

JIN: It certainly is a difficult question. If my beginning to write novels falls within the bounds of writing literature, my objective at the time I began was, in any case, to do some kind of work of my own.

In those days I was editing an arts column in *The New Evening Post* newspaper. Someone mentioned that the arts column made no mention of martial arts novels, and my colleagues strongly encouraged me to accept the challenge of writing one. And so this is how I began writing my first martial arts novel, which was entitled *The Book and the Sword*.

As soon as the book was published, it was so well received by readers that I continued writing martial arts novels. Writing novels was a means of income generation and a tool to support myself. I cannot say that I held the lofty aim of contributing to society. I had no desire to educate the young or enhance the national honour by repaying my debt of gratitude to the country.

Whatever the case, I simply enjoyed writing novels. When I write, I can let my imagination roam. I know how fun it is to, with just one pen, make many chivalrous knights do as I command.

However, I think that in a capitalist society, a vast majority of creative writers and artists have this same experience. A composer writes a piano piece, an artist with pencil in hand draws a picture, a movie director and a scriptwriter make a movie. Probably, most creative artists and writers started their careers with the intent of making money.

IKEDA: You have made a very frank statement. On that point, Dostoevsky produced so many masterpieces, being pursued relentlessly by debt collectors.

Aside from the reality of the economic motive, Goethe intently maintained that the gifted writer is always driven by a demonic force hidden within, and when it is aroused, a work of art manifests itself. This force is something that cannot be diminished or trivialized. The greater the work of art, the greater the force.

When an author tries to write something and only writes what he intended, this is an indication that the writer is a limited vehicle. However, once a gifted writer takes up his pen, there is an additional element – a demonic force at work inside of him – that naturally shines through and he is able to create a work of art that far exceeds his own original objective and expectations. The writer's hidden genius is revealed in between the lines.

In regard to financial difficulties as a driving force, some of the great authors, such as Goethe, had wealthy sponsors. Sponsorship was not unique to literature. For example, the incredibly talented Leonardo da Vinci and Michelangelo both had patrons. Yet this in no way diminishes the value of their works of art. As they say, gold, no matter where you find it, is still gold.

Recently, it was suggested that the creation of great works of art was made possible precisely because their creators had financial security, and so from this perspective, the presence of a sponsor or a patron has come to be viewed positively.

JIN: When writing political commentary or analyses of social problems, I of course take care to observe the ideals of fairness, justice, and morality. However, when creating a work of literature, I have never approached my writing with the intention of articulating these concepts in my work.

Even so, within my martial arts novels, I place great emphasis on the concepts of justice and fairness. Virtue and evil must be clearly differentiated, and it is always necessary for the virtuous character to utterly vanquish the evil character.

The heroes appearing in these works must never tell a lie, forget their debt of gratitude to their benefactors, or turn their backs on justice. Nor must they ever behave inexcusably toward a friend, but always take great care in their relationships. And they must never commit heinous acts or be cruel, underhanded, or unscrupulous.

Therefore, I unconsciously end up articulating in bold relief the most traditional virtues of Chinese culture throughout the story. These ideals may be expressed through specific individuals, events, or behaviour, and I do not simply delineate ideas in a sermon-like manner or hold forth on moral concepts.

IKEDA: Yes. A writer must not give in to excessive sermonizing. These concepts must be made to come alive, embodied in the behaviour of the characters in the work. For example, in your novel *Sword Stained with Royal Blood*, the hero is admonished by his teacher, who says, 'In some cases, it's difficult to judge between right and wrong. The world is full of deception, and it is difficult to gauge a person's heart. In some cases, a virtuous person may actually be evil, or an evil person may be virtuous. However, if you never mislead others and always treat others with generosity and goodwill, you will not mistakenly harm a virtuous person.'[4]

Here we have a passage that reveals the philosophy and ideals that you artfully express in your martial arts novels. I have a sense that we can hear your own voice coming through and that we are catching a glimpse of your character in those words.

The Traditional Chinese View of Literature and Sense of Exquisite Balance

JIN: Thank you. Personally speaking, I think that the primary aim of literature is to elicit a sense of empathy from the reader, which the writer does by articulating feelings and emotions. In other words, the writer aims to make a powerful impact on the reader through intense and profound emotions. The main content of literature, including poetry, novels, and drama, is emotion. This is the traditional Chinese view also.

Of course, it is also the traditional Chinese view that one of the most important objectives of literature is to express philosophical ideas. At the beginning of a notable interpretive text of *The Book of Songs*, which is the oldest Chinese literary compilation, the preface provides the main point of the entire book. It says, 'Poetry is an expression of aspiration'. This is a line from 'The Canon of Shun', which is found in the *Classic of History*. It is said that Yu Shun, an ancient and legendary Chinese ruler, wrote these words, although there is some uncertainty about his authorship.

IKEDA: This line expresses the Chinese traditional view of literature. At a meeting of *Suiko-kai* (Water Margin Group), a young men's study group of Soka Gakkai, our mentor Josei Toda gave us tips on reading. He told us, 'The ideas contained within a literary work are clearly presented in the preface and in the afterword'.

JIN: The meaning of the word 'aspiration' includes emotion and sentiment as well as the nuance of heartfelt ambition, thought, and will. Or to express this somewhat differently, one could say that one aspect is sentiment and the other is intellect.

The great Confucian scholar of the late Han dynasty (25–220), Zheng Kangcheng, appears in *Romance of the Three Kingdoms*. Apparently, in his household, even the servant girls could quote verses from *The Book of Songs* at will. According to his interpretation, in ancient times the relationship between a ruler and his vassals was very close, and so when a vassal wanted to communicate an opinion or some kind of message to the ruler, he simply approached the ruler and spoke to him directly. However, as time passed and rulers gradually ascended to greater stature, power, and authority, vassals were required to show more deference and hesitated to speak directly to the ruler.

IKEDA: This increase in the power and authority of the ruler is one characteristic of Chinese history, isn't it? It was said that in the Han and Tang (618–907) dynasties, the rulers and the vassals were able to sit down and talk together. In the Song dynasty (960–1276), vassals were forbidden to sit, and had to stand to speak to the ruler. Then in the Ming (1368–1644) and Qing (1644–1912) dynasties, vassals were not even permitted to stand, but had to kneel in front of the ruler.

JIN: And so this is how vassals began to quote from *The Book of Songs* to indirectly offer advice and suggestions to the ruler. This is called 'insinuative exhortation'.

During the Spring and Autumn Period of Chinese history, when the diplomats of each kingdom met with their counterparts from another country, they always made a preliminary statement before any diplomatic discussions were held, drawing from *The Book of Songs*.

In recent times, when the representatives of China and Great Britain met to discuss issues related to Hong Kong, the Chinese representatives, as if following ancient Chinese tradition, were given to mixing in ancient poetic verse into their statements.

Also recently, the Chinese Vice Premier of the State Council (1993–2003) and Foreign Minister, Qian Qichen, quoted a poem by Li Bai in a speech about the future of Hong Kong. It was at a time when the inevitability of the return of Hong Kong had been accepted, but the fast pace of developments made it clear that there was no turning back. This poem expressed some of the apprehension and anticipation of that moment.

> The screams of the monkeys on either bank
> Had scarcely ceased echoing in my ear
> When my skiff had left behind it
> Ten thousand ranges of hills.[5]

By referring to this poem, Vice Premier Qian Qichen meant to urge those opposed to the return of Hong Kong to express their concerns and anxieties completely at that time and forego any plans for subversive mischief later.

IKEDA: This story gives me a real sense of the deep and rich traditions of Chinese culture. It has a kind of sophistication to it.

There is a saying, 'Borrow from the past to explain the present', and indeed, in your country in ancient times, in literature as well as in politics, people often quoted from the classics. By doing so, people wanted to emphasize that their own opinions and assertions were not just their own self-centred views, but had a universality and legitimacy to them.

To put this differently, no matter how correct a person might think his own opinions are, he would stop and look carefully at them before speaking out. If he were to spontaneously utter his thoughts without reflection, people might privately think that he is vain and presumptuous. And so a means to keep vanity in check, something that was universal was sought. And that was classical literature and philosophy.

JIN: I see. That is an astute observation.

IKEDA: So, people felt that they should not use themselves as the only standard. Rather, it was thought that there should be a standard larger than the self. They understood that as long as human beings were without self-awareness, they would be vulnerable to the diabolical influences of self-righteousness and self-indulgence. This is consistent with the teachings of Buddhism.

In one of his last sermons, the Shakyamuni Buddha said, 'Whoso, Ānanda, either now or when I have passed away, shall abide grounded on self, self-refuged, taking refuge in none other; grounded on the Norm, with the Norm for refuge, taking refuge in none other – they, Ānanda, shall be my monks, they shall be atop of the gloom.'[6]

To paraphrase, the Buddha taught that in order to develop self-discipline and self-governance, one must find strength in the inner core of one's own self and build a calm and stable mind that is not distracted or misled by other people or external events. To create this 'immovable self', he explained that one must reject the attitude of conceit, which underlies self-righteousness, dogmatism, and arrogance, and instead make the universal law one's source of support and authority.

The term 'written evidence' refers to Buddhist teachings that have been written down and preserved carefully over the ages. In Chinese culture, the teachings of the classics and sages of the past are held in the highest esteem, and I believe that this attitude of sincere reverence and appreciation has helped maintain an exquisite sense of balance that prevents people from falling into self-righteousness.

We Need Revolutionaries not Revolutionary Literature

JIN: By the way, I heard that in your conversation with Ba Jin, you touched on the theme of literature and politics. In his short work entitled 'Things to Never Forget', Ba Jin wrote, 'Throughout my ordeal, I never abandoned my sense of patriotism. The reason is that I am Chinese, and even though I had grievances from the constant abuses, cruel treatment, and discrimination I suffered, I always felt that my destiny was indivisibly tied to my homeland.'[7]

Long before I was born, China had been under pressure from the imperialist world powers. I myself was never personally discriminated against or scorned by a foreigner, but the oppression and outrages suffered by my country were deeply inscribed in my mind ever since childhood. Shortly after the war of resistance against the Japanese began, our house was burned completely to the ground by the Japanese military. Although indirectly, my beloved younger brother and mother were killed by the Japanese military.

IKEDA: I again offer my deepest condolences for your loss.

JIN: When I was a boy, China and its people faced a critical point in their existence – it was a matter of life and death. The entire country united, and risking extinction as a people, we plunged ourselves into the violent struggle. Therefore, I think that it was natural that all literary activity dealt with attacking the enemy and focused on protecting the country.

After the war against the Japanese, the bitter fight between the Chinese Nationalist Party and the Communist Party of China evolved into a civil war. Nearly the entire literary world was wholeheartedly supportive of the Communist Party.

After the establishment of the People's Republic of China, a series of movements began to unfold. They were the Three Anti-Campaigns, the Five Anti-Campaigns, and the Anti-Rightist Movement; and the Three Red Banners policy, which included The Great Leap Forward, the Great Cultural Revolution, and so on. This series of political movements continued to develop until the Great Cultural Revolution was finally over. The political movement formed the core of the literary movement, just as activities in all other fields were centred on the political movement. Everyone was forced to support unquestioningly the political movement; and everything revolved around it.

IKEDA: One aspect of Chinese history is that politics took precedence over culture. We can say that this traditional pattern continued even after the establishment of the new China.

JIN: Yes. The question, 'What is the fundamental purpose of literature?' would not have been posed in the new China. It was not even considered an issue. It was believed without question that literature existed to serve the purposes of the revolution, the people, and the then-unfolding political movement.

If anyone had expressed even the slightest doubt, they would have been immediately labelled as an 'anti-revolutionary', been made to wear a dunce cap, and been widely condemned.

IKEDA: Ba Jin's friend, Lao She, became a victim of that revolutionary fervour. Ba Jin wrote this description recalling the situation.

'I felt as if I saw an old man wrapped up in a silk cloth, lying silently on the ground. Blood covered his head and neck. A myriad of thoughts was surely going through his mind – thoughts that he wanted to express. He must not be allowed to die in this pitiful way. There are so many wonderful things that he must share with future generations before passing on! However, one day after the conference, his body was found lying on the west bank of a Taiping lake, covered by a tattered straw mat. Lao She had closed his eyes for the last time, his thoughts filled with regret, never to share all the treasures in his heart. This is how we imagine Lao She drew his last breath.'[8]

'Everyone, please lend your ear to Chinese intellectuals, those to whom Lao She's screams give voice. They cry out, "I have loved my country. But who, I ask, has shown me love?"'[9]

Ba Jin lost many of his friends, including Lao She, in the Cultural Revolution. Even his wife, the greatest love of his life, was stolen from him. This sorrow and regret comes through in his words.

JIN: When the entire country unites to combat the enemy and save the country from destruction, every single person must do their utmost. Even if it means sacrificing one's life for the country, of course this is what one must do.

However, must literature serve only the political sphere, even after peace is re-established? Shouldn't we put our primary focus on creating works of literature which deal with subject matter that is worthwhile and uplifting to the country and the people, while at the same time a benefit to all of human society?

IKEDA: I feel the same way. A quotation by Ba Jin, which I referenced previously, states, 'Literature cannot separate itself from politics. However, politics absolutely cannot take the place of literature. This is because literature helps shape the human soul.' Literature deals with the human soul and universal human themes.

Therein lie the fundamental principles found in the literary perspective of Lu Xun, whom Ba Jin looked up to as his teacher. There cannot be a 'literature for the sake of art' or a 'literature for the sake of literature', just as there could never be a 'literature for the sake of politics'. Ultimately, we must have a 'literature for life' and a 'literature for human beings'. At the time that Lu Xun was active, proletarian literature, or revolutionary literature, which espoused the superiority of politics over literature, was the mainstream trend in literature. However, Lu Xun loudly asserted that what was necessary were revolutionaries, not revolutionary literature.

He meant that the times awaited revolutionary persons. If that was the case, then no matter how many hundreds of thousands of volumes of revolutionary literature were created, if they were not excellent and of high quality, then there would be no hope that they would nurture revolutionary people.

If literature strays from the fundamental principle of shaping people and building souls, then no matter how many volumes of revolutionary literature are written, these will be nothing more than hollow propaganda.

Hope for Life: A Message to Stir the Masses

JIN: Yes. In considering the special characteristics of literature, we must recognize that the function of literature is qualitatively different from that of an advertising catchphrase or a reasoned explication. The purpose of a reasoned exposition is to clearly explain the nature of a matter or a circumstance in a coherent and rigorous logical analysis so that the reader is thoroughly convinced and accepts the author's opinions.

If one wants to heighten the people's resistance to an enemy, one must depict the actual nature of the hated enemy in great detail. It is imperative that the people recognize that if they do not come forward and resist the enemy, the nation will soon be destroyed and the people will be annihilated.

If one wants to inspire revolution in the people, one must make them aware of the numerous ways that the current government and system are causing considerable harm. Also, they must know that if they do not reverse this situation and promote the power of the people, the destiny of the nation and the people will be at risk.

Literature is a vehicle for resistance to the enemy and can rouse the passions of the people for revolution. But it is different from sermonizing. And it does not do to make the characters preach the message. The writer's feelings must be internalized by means of a gripping story that excites and inspires through dramatic scenes that capture the imagination and a lyricism that strikes deep into the heart of the readers or audience.

In order for literature of this kind to be truly effective, it must make readers not simply accept and agree with the author's message, but also be roused to a fiery zeal and be brought to tears of passion.

IKEDA: Yes. It is not just principles or noble causes that sway people's hearts. Rather, it is the author's expression of his own feelings that well up inside and then come bursting forth. A good case in point is the pamphlet *Revolutionary Army*, written in 1903 by a young Chinese revolutionary named Zou Rong, which whipped up the passions of hot-blooded patriotic youth on the eve of the Xinhai Revolution of 1911.

We see in Ba Jin's work *Cold Nights* the gut-wrenching rage at the evils and absurdity of society, articulated in compelling and irrepressible emotion. Advertising and propaganda cannot even touch this kind of powerful writing.

JIN: When I wrote my martial arts novels, I never intended to glorify any kind of concept or topic. Even if I occasionally highlighted or satirized a scandalous event or a repulsive character that appeared in the news, it was nothing more than a passing interest that I explored casually.

My primary objective was to affirm the superb quality and noble concepts of traditional Chinese aesthetics and to inspire an appreciation and respect toward them in the hearts of the readers – and to have readers understand that because they have been given life in this world, they of course should appreciate these things.

Perhaps the majority of readers cannot express this appreciation readily in their daily lives – and I have the same problem – but I believe that if I can elicit a respect for these virtues, then I have achieved my objective.

IKEDA: You are far too humble. The fact that millions of readers love your writings is evidence that your writing is successful and that you have achieved your goal.

JIN: Thank you. Speaking from a relatively broad perspective, the aim of literature is to use language to create characters, a story, and passion – with the exception that Chinese poems usually do not include characters or a story – and to express aesthetic, virtuous, and pure emotion and sincere values.

These emotions and values are inherent in the fabric of people's lives. The artist epitomizes and organizes them in a way that moves and inspires, and at the same time, enables readers to discover those values from a new perspective.

At times, a writer will depict a character or write a story that has no obvious aesthetic or moral aspects. Even so, I believe that the essence of what the writer attempted to express was none other than an affirmation of aesthetic and moral values. As examples, we can point to Lu Xun's *The True Story of Ah Q*, *Diary of a Madman*, and *Medicine*, Nikolai Gogol's *Overcoat* (1942), and Fyodor Dostoevsky's *Crime and Punishment* (1866) and *The Gambler* (1867).

These questions of why and how a writer writes are ones that have been debated by many philosophers and scholars in the past. Each has his or her own particular view. I do not claim to have the correct or perfect answer myself.

IKEDA: For a sincere soul the act of living – in and of itself – is a journey toward hope. It is a constant, never-ending march forward toward hope.

One engages in the bitter struggle when one throws oneself into the chaos of reality, and it is at this point that one begins to forge one's path in life. In this sense, all human endeavours, including daily life and the act of living itself, are part of the struggle to create value.

For a writer, the act of taking up a pen to write is no exception. Johan Huizinga, a Dutch historian, wrote, 'Life is struggle', and 'All the terminology related to human spiritual life functions within this domain'.[10]

Huizinga felt that life and language were struggles that enabled people to live better and to discover the meaning of life.

Of course, there are plenty of entertaining works as well as those that try throwing the realities and contradictions of life, as is, directly in front of the reader. However, literature that is able to touch a wide readership, even if that literature is paradoxical in nature, contains in some form a discussion of hope for one's life.

Illuminate the World with the Light of Humanity: The Essence of Victor Hugo's Literature

Discussions on Victor Hugo's *Les Misérables* and *Ninety-Three*

IKEDA: In our youth, we both shared a love for the works of Victor Hugo, one of our favourite authors. Hugo – the great author who illuminated the world with the light of humanity, the unyielding and fearless warrior for human rights. He is one author who must play a central role on the stage of our discussion of literature. Don't you agree, Mr Jin?

JIN: Absolutely! We must definitely discuss Hugo's work.

IKEDA: Located in the southern outskirts of Paris, France, in the city of Bièvres, is the Victor Hugo House of Literature. It opened in June 1991, thanks to the efforts of SGI-France and friends. The chateau, which Hugo often visited, is in a natural setting where the changing seasons may be enjoyed in all their beauty. It is a beacon of light revitalizing the great author's 'light of humanity' in current times, and fortunately it has been fondly embraced and utilized as a place that nurtures the creation of new art and literature.

JIN: It is magnificent what you have done. I am sure that the opening of the Victor Hugo House of Literature surprised and delighted the people of France.

IKEDA: I was first introduced to the works of Victor Hugo in my mid-teens. It was during World War II and four of my older brothers had been sent, one after another, to fight in the war. I suffered from tubercular lung disease and was unable to study as I had hoped.

It was during that time that Hugo's masterpiece *Les Misérables* taught me that the strength and grace of the human spirit are deeper than the ocean and as boundless as the sky. I was profoundly impressed by this work. I felt as if I had discovered a ray of hope breaking through the dark clouds that were casting a shadow over my life and times.

My mentor, Josei Toda, was also deeply drawn to Hugo's work. Under his guidance in our reading group we read Hugo's *Ninety-Three*, which taught us about the tragedy of violence and the importance of having respect for humanity and empathy for those in distress.

JIN: I have a small apartment in Paris. When I was travelling through Europe, I just happened upon it. Thinking that it was the perfect place for me to study French and become more familiar with French culture, I stayed there for several weeks. It was in the Sixteenth Ward of Paris on Raffaello Boulevard – a street named after Raphael, the great painter of the Italian Renaissance.

Just near this street, which runs by a park, is the great impressionist painter Monet's house (now the Monet Commemorative Museum). In order to get to Raffaello Boulevard from the Arc de Triomphe, you must go down a long street. This street is called Victor Hugo Boulevard. The French value their culture highly, and so many of the streets you come across in Paris are named for famous artists.

IKEDA: In Europe and the US, many of the public parks and streets carry the names of people who have long been recognized and honoured by the people. I personally have gone many times to the Michelangelo Public Square, which commands a magnificent view of the city of Florence, and taken pictures there.

Similarly, in the Americas, there is now in Brazil a Makiguchi Boulevard, a Makiguchi Park, and a Toda Park named after our first and second presidents. As their disciple, nothing could give me more joy and satisfaction.

JIN: Mr Makiguchi and Mr Toda have parks named after them, and I have heard that soon there will also be an Ikeda Park. I am delighted for you.

Victor Hugo was someone who made an enormous contribution to French culture. His contribution was so highly valued that at the peak of his fame, some even advocated that Paris be renamed Hugo City. This proposal was not adopted, but even so, I think that only in France, a country that places such great value on culture and the arts, could one writer have had such enormous influence.

IKEDA: France definitely has, shall I say, a sophistication and depth conducive to the appreciation of culture.

In my dialogue (entitled *Human Revolution vs. Human Condition* for the Japanese edition) with André Malraux, we discussed his well-known relationship with Charles de Gaulle. Malraux was a dominant figure in French as well as European politics and culture. De Gaulle was an unabashedly opinionated and proudly independent politician who once said, 'I am France'. He was a Machiavellian, a no-holds-barred unconventional diplomat, and an astute politician. Decades after his death, conflicting views about the legacy of this military man and politician still persist. Coming from such different perspectives – right wing versus left wing – the two men did not always see eye to eye.

Even so, Malraux, an intellectual and man of culture, had great esteem for de Gaulle, and an intimate friendship developed between the two men. Their friendship was one of perfect harmony, and Malraux continued throughout his life to be of service to de Gaulle. The profound friendship between these two great individuals was extraordinary in and of itself, but perhaps only in France, in the context of the depth and refinement of French culture, could it have developed and flourished.

Felled Oaks, a part of a poem by Victor Hugo, is the title of the book documenting Malraux's last conversation with de Gaulle. After reading this record of their dialogue, one can clearly feel the sympathetic resonance between these two great minds.

During a meeting I had at the Kremlin with then President Gorbachev, we talked about the concept of perestroika. President Gorbachev called it 'a marriage between politics and culture'. This grand experiment did not achieve the results that he had envisioned, yet in his brief description of it, the man's enlightened attitude was revealed.

Speaking of enlightened influences, Malraux once said to de Gaulle, 'Your predecessor, in France if not in Iran, is not a politician – not even Clemenceau: it is Victor Hugo'.[1]

The Model Cleric of *Les Misérables*

JIN: Whatever the field of endeavour, great people always return to the past, looking back for sources of inspiration, and in the case of France, this source is often Victor Hugo.

President Ikeda, you recalled that during the war, a period in which you experienced many hardships, you read Hugo's full-length novel *Les Misérables*. I see that the Japanese translation carries the original French title. The title for the Chinese translation is, rendered in English, 'Tragic World'.

The Chinese translation was by Su Manshu, the famous intellectual and priest who had studied in Japan. Translated directly from the French, the title would have been *Pitiful People*, but it was thought that 'Tragic World' would more closely approximate the meaning of the original French title.

Recently, an English composer and theatre group created the English-language musical of *Les Misérables*. I understand that the English version of the musical was a highly successful collaboration and was performed in both Singapore and Hong Kong, where I went to watch it. It was an incredible performance of captivating music, acting, and singing. The street-fighting scene in the streets of Paris, I am sure, took a lot of sophisticated design planning and was especially well done.

IKEDA: The musical, which also played in Japan, was well received and had quite a long run. Incidentally, Kaho Shimada, one of our members, received high acclaim for her magnificent performance in the role of Eponine Thenardier.

JIN: Is that so? It is not surprising that you have attracted talented people from all walks of life.

The original work of Hugo, on which the musical is based, is grand and profound. So I never entertained the hope that the captivating power of the novel could ever be done justice in a two- or three-hour musical. In comparison, the production of 'Phantom of the Opera', which I saw in London, was much more impressive. The difference, I think, is due to the fact that the novel on which it is based was an ordinary, popular novel. No matter how you produced it, no one would be disappointed with the production, because it would not be that different from the original.

IKEDA: I agree. A young person once told me, 'We probably just have to accept the fact that a play or movie is going to be different from the novel'.

For example, a person may see a movie before reading the novel and be impressed with it. After that person reads the book, it perhaps cannot be helped if images of the actors keep coming to his or her mind. For example, after you saw the movie *War and Peace* starring Audrey Hepburn, you then read the book, and you could not help picturing Audrey Hepburn's face when reading about Natasha. I guess this kind of thing cannot be avoided to a certain extent.

JIN: Yes, I know. I first read *Les Misérables* when I was about 15. It was part of the *Complete Works of Su Manshu*; that is, the Chinese translations of Su Manshu. However, the translation only covers the first part of the story. In brief, the translation ends after the protagonist, Jean Valjean, steals the bishop's silverware, is caught by the police, and is then protected by the bishop who conceals the facts of the case from the police.

IKEDA: The character of Bishop Myriel is depicted the way a man of the cloth should be. This quotation provides a glimpse of his character: 'The soul of an unfortunate who thanks God for consolation, he said, "is the best of all altars".'[2]

He was a man who led a simple life and was hard on himself, but infinitely compassionate with others. He referred to the less fortunate as 'patients' and 'the sick', and, regardless of their religion or denomination, devoted himself to serving them as their 'physician'. His service to others made him a model man of the cloth. Unfortunately, the reality is that many clerics may fall into corruption and decadence.

JIN: Yes. President Ikeda, I have heard that you have had to struggle against such kinds of shameless clerics.

In any case, even though I read only a small part of *Les Misérables*, I was deeply moved. Reading that small portion had a much more powerful impact on me than reading any other work by any other author. I could clearly see that in terms of literary value, it was on a higher plane than the works of the great Dumas and another of my favourite French novelists, Prosper Mérimée (1803–70).

Literary style and genuine value are intriguing phenomena. I believe that even young people, with an as yet undeveloped sense of discernment, can clearly grasp differences in quality.

In Hugo There is Poetry

IKEDA: 'In Hugo there is poetry. There is boundless love and compassion for the oppressed. There is a spirit vaster than the ocean, broader than the sky. And his anger toward falsehood and injustice, as well as his thirst for truth and justice, rage fierce like a blustery storm. Hugo is a comrade in spirit of my youth – no, of my entire life.' This is what I once wrote about Hugo's work.

The light of Hugo's humanity brought into focus one human being faced with suffering and distress. While striking out at the society that would give birth to such tragedy, he envisioned an ideal world where all people could coexist in peace. Furthermore, this vision encompassed the universe – nature, the great earth, the cradle of life.

A special characteristic of Hugo's work is his powerful gaze, which unceasingly observes, envelops, and nurtures the full spectrum of experience, from the microcosmic to the macrocosmic.

JIN: Exactly.

IKEDA: In the preface to *Les Misérables* are the following words. 'While ignorance and poverty persist on earth, books such as this cannot fail to be of value.'[3]

Hugo's literary passions never ceased to focus empathy and concern for the poor and starving masses suffering in this world. He did not close himself off in his own world, amusing himself with esoteric and abstruse monologues as do the highbrow authors of today.

Hugo's social consciousness extended, as you know, even so far as to envision the ideal of a united Europe. In a century in which bloody rivalries had flared up between world powers sharing national boundaries, it is amazing and admirable that Hugo brought a grand vision anticipating a bold new era.

JIN: I did not grasp the meaning of Hugo's 'light of humanity' from his poetry, but rather from his novels. Generally speaking, it is very difficult to translate foreign poetry into Chinese in a way that fully expresses the meaning and is moving to the Chinese reader. Hugo's romanticist dramas, for example *Hernani*, were translated into Chinese relatively early. I was struck by his intense passion and the anguished cry from his soul, expressed in the electrifying lines of the script.

IKEDA: Perhaps you are referring to lines such as this: 'But they who bleed remember far better. Th' evil that the wrong-doer thus so senselessly forgets, forever stirs within the outraged heart.'[4]

All his life, Hugo fought those who oppressed others, and it is almost as if we can hear him crying out in these words.

JIN: Hugo and Dumas are similar in that they were both influenced by Shakespeare and Sir Walter Scott, and both began to write adventure novels based on historical material in the Romantic tradition. This is the reason that the preeminent Scottish novelist Robert Louis Stevenson loved Dumas.

In the spring of 1993, I was invited to the University of Edinburgh to give a lecture on novels. In a preface to my talk, I spoke briefly about the inspiration for my work.

IKEDA: If you don't mind, please share with us what you said.

JIN: It is a little long, but it went something like this:

> Yesterday, my wife and I took a walk around the city of Edinburgh. I lingered for a while in front of the statue of Sir Walter Scott, thoughts of the heroes and heroines depicted in his novels running through my mind.
>
> I recalled another great novelist of Edinburgh – Robert Louis Stevenson – whose work also stirred my heart. I have heard that each time Alexandre Dumas met a British man, he always greeted him excitedly with a warm and enthusiastic welcome. He did this to wholeheartedly express his gratitude to the British for the lessons he learned from the works of Sir Walter Scott.
>
> I have come to Edinburgh today to discuss novels, but frankly I have only one thing to say. And that is that I attribute my ability to write novels to the lessons and enlightenment I have received from two great writers from Edinburgh. They are Sir Walter Scott and Robert Louis Stevenson. Therefore, I have come not to discuss the understandings that I have gained or my opinions; rather, I have come here today to pay my respects and express my gratitude to these two great men from your city.

IKEDA: You speak with such humility. I am sure that the people of Edinburgh were moved by your tribute. Victor Hugo wrote an essay entitled 'On Sir Walter Scott'. In this work, he explored the mission of the poet and, like the fearless general of the Romanticists that he was, spoke with conviction of the energy of poetry and the power of words to cultivate and guide people.

To confront society directly, rather than turn one's back and withdraw inside oneself, to struggle against the tragedies and contradictions of the world – this articulation of the poet's mission is an exact description of the work of Victor Hugo. In this sense, Hugo undoubtedly felt a great resonance with the works of Sir Walter Scott.

The Archetype of the Witch Hunt in *Notre-Dame de Paris*

JIN: Besides *Les Misérables*, another very memorable full-length novel by Hugo is *Notre-Dame de Paris*. The Chinese translation is entitled *Chivalrous Hunchback of the Bell Tower*. The Chinese character depicting the term 'chivalrous' may impart a very striking impression, but it is the same character used in the titles adopted for the movie and animated versions.

As you well know, Notre Dame is the cathedral of the Catholic archdiocese of Paris, located in the heart of Paris. The cathedral, with its distinctive twin towers and magnificent French Gothic architecture, is the setting for the novel.

IKEDA: In the chapter entitled 'Notre Dame', Hugo goes into great detail about the design, architectural style, and history of Notre Dame cathedral. It seems that Hugo had a powerful emotional attachment to the cathedral as a symbol of French history.

JIN: President Ikeda, you are very familiar with the novel, but it is not as well known as *Les Misérables*. Let us give our readers a brief overview of the story-line.

The character Quasimodo, whose task it is to ring the great cathedral bell, is depicted as a central figure holding an important key to the story. He is portrayed as a large and powerful man who is repulsively ugly. His back is bowed and he stands with a slouch. His teeth protrude and his eyes emit a frightful gleam. And his droopy nose and contorted face add to this an even more unpleasant impression. He seems almost alien in appearance.

IKEDA: The setting for the novel is the Middle Ages, isn't it? And the novel itself was written in the nineteenth century. It is important to consider that it reflects the sense of the times in which it was written.

JIN: Yes, that's right. The story takes place in the Middle Ages, and so it was a time in which people believed in superstitions. So, Quasimodo was abhorred and treated like a bogeyman. He was placed on top of a platform, where he was bound, beaten, and left to die in the scorching sun. However, Esmeralda, a young gypsy girl, took pity on Quasimodo and scrambled up to the top of the platform to give him water. She saved his life.

Esmeralda was a stunningly beautiful young woman. When she danced, she never failed to take people's breath away with her captivating charm. Because of this, the people began to believe that Esmeralda was a witch, and before long, they captured her, tied her up, and sent her to the gallows to be hanged.

IKEDA: Witch hunting is a concept that exists even today. False rumours and hearsay are a familiar ploy used by those in authority to frame a person as evil. The persecution of Esmeralda brings this practice, in its original form, into bold relief.

One more central character is Phoebus, the captain of the King's Archers. Like Quasimodo, Phoebus is madly in love with Esmeralda. However, his egotistical and foul nature greatly distinguishes him from Quasimodo.

At the end of his book, Hugo juxtaposes two scenarios: 'The Marriage of Phoebus' and 'The Marriage of Quasimodo'. To briefly summarize, the first is depicted as a marriage resulting from ego and self-interest and the other is a marriage radiating faithfulness and integrity and filled with eternal love. These two personalities create an excellent contrast.

JIN: Phoebus is a sophisticated young man, blessed with talent and presence. However, when he sees that Esmeralda has been captured by the now violent crowd, he is afraid and pretends to not know her, feigning an air of indifference and passing quickly by on his horse. The one who struggles mightily to rescue Esmeralda from this desperate situation is Quasimodo. The two escape to Notre Dame. There, Archdeacon Claude Frollo becomes captivated by Esmeralda's beauty and tries to use his authority to compel Esmeralda to become his. She firmly rejects him. The mob attempts to storm the cathedral to capture Esmeralda, and from the top of the bell tower, Quasimodo hurls down large rocks, holding back the mob ascending the ladder.

Taking advantage of the chaos, the archdeacon slips out of the cathedral and flees to the forest with Esmeralda, all the while threatening and intimidating her. He continues to try to force himself on her, but Esmeralda resists. Finally, the archdeacon, insanely outraged at her rejection, hands her over to the mob.

The Depth of Hugo's Understanding of Humanity

IKEDA: The character Claude Frollo is the exact opposite of Bishop Myriel in *Les Misérables*. Both virtuous and wicked clerics appear often in Hugo's works. This is an indication of how deeply, for better or worse, Christianity had become rooted in the spiritual history of Europe.

Virtuous clerics such as Bishop Myriel appear, but it seems that the depictions of the wicked scoundrels come alive more vividly.

Johann Wolfgang von Goethe once commented that 'everything that the church touches becomes weakened'.[5]

In this passage, we see an expression of the belief that, generally speaking, ministers engage in evil deeds. This perspective exists also in Japan and perhaps can be considered a kind of historical empirical rule. Ever since the Edo period (1603–1868), it has been said that at the top of the list of things that ordinary people hate most are priests, samurai warriors, and beasts.

JIN: In China, this has been also more or less the case.

In Hugo's book, when Quasimodo learned that Esmeralda was in danger, he raced to the scene to rescue her, with no thought to his own safety. However, Esmeralda was destined to die by the hangman's noose. Quasimodo was enraged by Esmeralda's death and first went directly to Archdeacon Frollo, pushing him from the heights of the cathedral to his death. Then he went to find Esmeralda's dead body and took it away with him.

Several years later, the sun-bleached bones of Quasimodo and Esmeralda were discovered in a desolate public cemetery. Quasimodo was firmly embracing the gypsy dancer. Their whitened bones had already become weathered and had partly returned to dust.

IKEDA: This is a beautiful depiction of unconditional love. Both Jean Valjean and Quasimodo were nearly illiterate, and though their burdens were heavier than anyone could be expected to bear, they struggled desperately to live life fully. A pure love resides in innocent and pure souls – souls yet to be tainted by the embellishments of pedantry and sophistication. I view Quasimodo's love and death as a statement about pure love. I sense that it is here that we can see the way that Hugo viewed humankind.

JIN: I agree completely. Hugo's novels teach us that no matter what a person looks like, a beautiful and elegant soul may reside inside, and that someone like the Archdeacon of Notre Dame, who has the bearing of a monarch, or someone like the suave young captain of the King's Archers may have the most revolting and abominable personalities imaginable.

By highlighting the ignorance of the crowd turned mob and the superstition and merciless brutality that drove it, Hugo was also sounding the alarm about these dangers.

IKEDA: Yes. Hugo did not joyously and unreservedly welcome revolution. In *Les Misérables* he writes: 'Multitudes are inclined to accept the existing master; their very mass creates apathy. Crowds lapse readily into compliance.'[6]

He did not overlook the failings of mass psychology. His was an accurate and realistic picture of the populace, which he viewed as wise with a tendency toward foolishness, but at times foolish with flashes of wisdom.

Besides the works of Hugo, other excellent novels that took their material from, for example, the French Revolution, to some extent depicted that kind of modern revolution and the dark and somewhat fatalistic side it drags along with it. In other words, these works portrayed despotism and terror and how they were supported by the senseless masses mired in their deep-seated grievances, resentments, and twisted fanaticism. Among these are Charles Dickens' (1812–1870) *A Tale of Two Cities* and Anatole France's (1844–1924) *Les Dieux ont Soif*.

Honesty: The Greatest Human Quality

JIN: As you pointed out before, President Ikeda, the character of Bishop Myriel in *Les Misérables* depicts a true man of faith. The protagonist, Jean Valjean, steals the bishop's silverware and is caught by the police and taken back to the bishop's house. Yet the bishop is concerned about the young man and not only conceals the theft from the police but also gives him silver candlesticks. The bishop's kindness has a powerful impact on Jean Valjean – it is something that he never forgets for as long as he lives – and he goes on to wholeheartedly devote himself to doing good deeds. This novel is truly filled with a spirit of humanism.

IKEDA: In a way, this story illustrates the triumph of virtue. Moreover, in this work we see two triumphant events – a double victory. The first is the victory of Bishop Myriel in regard to his relationship with Jean Valjean.

And the other is Jean Valjean's victory over Javert, his relentless and callous pursuer.

A very Hugo-esque image is that of the owl. Hugo uses the image of an owl to represent people who have never experienced the generosity of a heart of compassion or the light of virtue. And so, Hugo uses the owl symbol to refer to both Jean Valjean before his change of heart through Bishop Myriel's influence, and to Javert, who struggled with the contradictions between his commitment to his police duties and the humanistic feelings he had after Jean Valjean saved his life. The meaning of this image is a profound revelation of Hugo's view of humankind.

Hugo writes: 'The true division of humanity is between those who live in light and those who live in darkness. Our aim must be to diminish the number of the latter and increase the number of the former. That is why we demand education and knowledge. To learn to read is to light a fire; every syllable that is spelled out is a spark.'[7]

This is Hugo's perspective on humankind. And referring to those who live in darkness as owls is one manifestation of this view.

JIN: I think you have grasped his perspective accurately. Jean Valjean struggled in grinding poverty during his youth and stole a loaf of bread to help his family, which was suffering from hunger. But he was caught and thrown into prison. He was sentenced to five years in prison, but because he could not bear the horrible abuse he suffered, he escaped again and again. Each time he was caught, years were added to his sentence, so altogether he had to serve 19 years of prison time.

After he was released, he was required to return to the prison periodically to report on his activities. His identification documents clearly indicated that he was an ex-convict. Therefore, there was no one who would look out for him and no way for him to find a job.

Jean Valjean changed his name, and amid numerous hardships and privations, he overcame each one with diligence and thrift. Finally, he was able to demonstrate his ability as a manager and make a success of his glass factory. He treated his workers well and voluntarily engaged in charitable work, donating to many institutions. As a result of these activities, he earned the respect and affection of the community and was appointed mayor.

IKEDA: At this point, Valjean's name was Monsieur Pére Madeleine, and he is described as a man who 'demanded goodwill from the men, pure morals from the women, and honesty from all'.[8] What a concise statement of principle! The favourite motto of Jean Valjean, now calling himself Madeleine, was 'honesty'.

Certainly, honesty is one of humankind's greatest qualities. There are a variety of human virtues, but based on all my life experience, I believe that the greatest source of radiance in the human character is honesty. No matter one's social standing or outward appearance, the quality of the human being is determined by honesty. Honesty is the fundamental characteristic that humanizes human society.

Jean Valjean's Honesty Triumphs over Persistent Evil

JIN: President Ikeda, as you mentioned previously, at this point in the story the tenacious police captain, Javert, appears. Javert had previously worked in the prison, and he had had a nagging suspicion that the mayor was actually Jean Valjean.

One day, when Javert had become excited about evidence that seemed almost within his grasp, he happened upon an accident in which a cargo wagon had overturned, pinning an old man underneath. The old man's life was in danger, and there was not a moment to spare. At that moment, Jean Valjean appeared and, with his extraordinary physical strength, lifted the cargo wagon, freeing the old man and saving his life.

The police captain saw this superhuman feat before his very eyes and was immediately confident that this was Jean Valjean, the man who had been imprisoned. And so he reported this to his superior.

IKEDA: That Javert surely was persistent. He has the spitefulness and dark slimy character of a poisonous snake. And the pitiful part of it is that he thought that he was carrying out justice. In any case, he is a classic example of evil itself, and reading about him elicits a very unpleasant feeling.

As a clear representation of evil, this character demonstrates how deeply rooted, tenacious, and unforgiving evil tends to be. Our first president, Tsunesaburo Makiguchi, proclaimed that virtue, if it fails to battle evil, is made synonymous with evil. To battle evil, virtue must have the same degree of persistence and perseverance. If not, evil will win out.

JIN: That is exactly right. One of the female workers at Jean Valjean's factory paid a couple to care for her only daughter as a foster child, and the foster parents continually tried to extract more money from her. She was unable to pay the child care expenses, so she resorted to prostitution to earn enough money. The factory manager is about to fire her, but Jean Valjean, knowing her circumstances, has her admitted to a hospital, where she can focus on recovering her health. He also takes in the woman's daughter, Cosette, and makes plans for mother and daughter to live together.

In the meantime, police captain Javert pretends that his suspicions about Jean Valjean were unfounded and says they were a mistake. At the same time, he reports that Jean Valjean, the prisoner, had been arrested and imprisoned.

IKEDA: This part of the story really targets Jean Valjean's vulnerability; that is, his commitment to be true to his conscience. And it truly illustrates Hugo's masterful craft of dramatic storytelling.

JIN: The honest Jean Valjean knows that someone else has been charged with his crime and is serving prison time in his place. He feels very conflicted about the situation, and after agonizing over it, he voluntarily goes to the court to confess his true identity. He is committed to go to prison to save the person falsely accused of his own crime.

Around the time that Jean Valjean is released from prison, the female factory worker who had prostituted herself dies from her illness. He finds the woman's daughter, Cosette, now an orphan, and takes her to Paris, where he raises her.

Cosette grows up and falls in love with Marius, the boy next door. Soon after, Marius is in a Paris crowd that turns into a riotous mob. There is a confrontation with the military police and the situation becomes violent.

During this clash, Javert is captured by the rioters and is about to be put to death. Jean Valjean realizes that the captured person is Javert, and at the height of the pandemonium, he rescues Javert and allows him to escape. Then, using the underground sewer system, he also rescues Marius from the conflagration.

Even though Javert knows that the person who saved his life was Jean Valjean, his sense of duty as a police officer continues to compel in him the desire to arrest him and put him on trial. Unable to reconcile this with his conscience, he ends his life by throwing himself into the Seine.

IKEDA: The process that led to Javert's suicide can be understood in the following terms: 'He could no longer live by his lifelong principles; he had entered a new strange world of humanity, mercy, gratitude and justice other than that of the law. He contemplated with horror the rising of a new sun – an owl required to see with eagle's eyes.'[9]

This passage powerfully highlights Jean Valjean's triumph of virtue.

JIN: Javert's suicide is the most dramatic scene of any musical I know, and I am sure that directors tax their creative ingenuity to come up with the most dramatic effects.

In due course, Marius and Cosette get married. It is then that Marius learns that Jean Valjean is an ex-convict and, after that, becomes very cool towards him. Later, when he finds out that Jean Valjean had saved his life, he realizes how wrong he has been and rushes with Cosette to Jean Valjean's side. At that point, however, Jean Valjean is in a critical condition and near death.

IKEDA: Just as in *Notre-Dame de Paris*, the nobility of unconditional love is a central theme. This is a scene that cannot be read without shedding tears.

JIN: How true. It is a very moving scene. This novel is very long and depicts many serious social problems of the time. Through the process of contrasting the relative goodness of individual characters, the reader is able to clearly see the brutality and merciless nature of the social system.

In the capitalist system, there are various ruthless means to secure wealth, and people in the lower classes are oppressed. Unfortunately, opportunities to reform this system are not so easily come by.

A prime example of this oppression is the implementation of police powers. In terms of the cold and indifferent enforcement of the law, it is almost as if it is considered a noble or lofty cause, and compassion and humanity are completely disregarded.

IKEDA: Hugo spent his whole life fighting against this oppression. In June of 1981, I had the opportunity to go to the French Senate to visit with the Speaker of the House, the Honourable Alain Poher (1909–96). On that occasion, I viewed the chair in which Victor Hugo sat when he served in the Senate.

It was from that spot that Victor Hugo, my favourite author ever since my youth, delivered impassioned speeches advocating justice. I once again recall with deep emotion the life of this great man who launched piercing words, as if they were arrows, to protect ordinary people.

Sacrificing Oneself for Love: Dickens' *A Tale of Two Cities*

JIN: In China, the literary works of Romanticist authors are highly regarded, and love stories are widely read. Most of these are tragic love stories depicting a young man and woman who are deeply in love but, because of external factors such as family or social norms, are prevented from uniting. Works such as *Butterfly Lovers* are typical examples. Similarities can be found in works of Western literature such as *Romeo and Juliet*.

IKEDA: In 1997, at the World Peace and Culture Festival sponsored by SGI in Hong Kong, the Chinese singer Mao Amin performed a beautiful song based on the theme of *Butterfly Lovers*.

JIN: Yes. It was a magnificent performance. It symbolized the cultural festival's theme, 'Encounter between East and West', and featured guitar, the *erhu*, which is the Chinese violin, and the Chinese flute, harp, and drums.

With the beginning of the modern period, Western love stories came to depict self-sacrifice by one character, either the man or the woman, out of a deep love for the other. For example, let us take a look at *A Tale of Two Cities* by Dickens, the English novelist.

Charles and Lucie, two young people living in the time of the French Revolution, were in love. Sydney, another young man who closely resembled Charles, was also madly in love with Lucie, but Lucie would have nothing to do with him. Later on, Lucie and Charles married.

Though innocent of any wrongdoing or involvement in the revolution, Charles is arrested and sentenced to death. Upon hearing about Charles's sentence, Sydney decides to take Charles's place – all for the sake of his beloved Lucie. After stealthily entering the prison and trading places with Charles, Sydney's short life ends abruptly, vanishing like the evanescent morning dew, at the guillotine.

IKEDA: I sense that a religious belief may underlie Sydney's act of self-sacrifice. One passage includes a biblical verse which reads, 'I am the resurrection and the life, saith the Lord; he that believeth in me, though he were dead, yet shall he live and whosoever liveth and believeth in me, shall never die'.[10] Sydney must have believed that by sacrificing his life, he would live in eternal love.

Another theme, which is related to a point I mentioned previously and which we must not overlook in *A Tale of Two Cities*, is the dreadfulness of labelling people. According to the novel, there was a banner used in the French Revolution which carried the declaration, 'National Property. Republic One and Indivisible. Liberty, Equality, Fraternity, or Death!'

This admonishes that one must clearly distinguish one's enemies from one's allies, and cast one's lot with one side or the other. By labelling people so starkly, this exhortation whips up the flames of sinister human passions. It provokes a kind of warped combativeness – as if portraying a design to promote fanaticism. If a revolution yields to that kind of sentiment, no matter how noble the cause or lofty the founding principles, the initial spirit is already dead. Further, this revolutionary effort will be doomed to failure.

A World Filled with the Light of Humanity

JIN: Hugo's full-length novel *The Toilers of the Sea* is another work that exalts unconditional love and elicits the same powerful emotion. A young man by the name of Gilliatt is in love with the young woman Déruchette, who loves another man. Gilliatt forfeits his right of marriage with Déruchette, yielding to the man she loves, and arranges their marriage. Afterwards, Gilliatt goes to the ocean, where he calmly sits down on a huge boulder and gives himself to the approaching high tide, which swallows him up in a watery grave.

IKEDA: It is unfortunate that this work is not as well known in Japan as *Les Misérables*.

JIN: In China, translations of foreign works of literature were done in rapid succession, reaching a peak during the 1920s and 1930s. The majority of the translated works were full-length novels with serious themes. For example, many of the works were by Tolstoy, Dostoevsky, Turgenev, and Romain Rolland.

Thus far, the works of Hugo that we have discussed have been romance novels filled with the pathos and sorrow of the Romantic tradition. Romance novels did not attract the interest of progressive and patriotic translators, who preferred novels about revolution. And even if someone had put much time and energy into translating a love story, they would surely have been harshly attacked by the critics.

IKEDA: Really? But that is such a distorted interpretation of those novels. I believe that very few authors had as true and pure a perspective on revolution and progress as Hugo had. In other words, he thought about issues through the lens of humanism rather than ideology.

In a passage from *Les Misérables*, Hugo writes: 'Citizens, no matter what happens today, in defeat no less than victory, we shall be making a revolution. Just as a great fire lights up all the town, so a revolution lights up all mankind. And what is the revolution that we shall make? I have already told you: it is the revolution of Truth. In terms of policy there is only one principle, the sovereignty of man over himself.'[11]

His assertion seems to be that if a revolution ushers in a world that is not filled with the light of humanity, then that revolution is not worthy of its name.

When the former Soviet Union collapsed, it was said that the Russians had brought the French Revolution to a close. In other words, from a left-wing ideological perspective, the Russian Revolution was an extension of the French Revolution. Accordingly, this meant that the breakdown of the Russian Revolution put closure on issues raised in the French Revolution.

However, the more that this ideological stance loses its lustre, the ever more luminous the humanistic perspective grows. The extent to which the twentieth century was a century of war, characterized by repeated episodes of misery and carnage, is perhaps the extent to which people lost sight of the light of humanity that shines on all of mankind.

In this sense, I firmly believe that many more people should read, and reread, the works of Victor Hugo.

The Noble Path to the New Century: Adventure in Romance of the Three Kingdoms *and* The Water Margin

Yoshikawa's *Romance of the Three Kingdoms:* A Favourite in our Youth

IKEDA: What do you say to wrapping up our literary discussion with a look at *Romance of the Three Kingdoms* and *The Water Margin* – works that fired up our youthful imaginations.

JIN: That would be delightful. These two works are the most beloved among what are called the four great classical novels of Chinese literature – *Romance of the Three Kingdoms*, *The Water Margin*, *Journey to the West*, and *Jing Ping Mei*.

IKEDA: *Romance of the Three Kingdoms* is a particularly bright star in the vast universe of Chinese literature. I remember reading it many a time in my youth. I found it incredibly irresistible.

Romance of the Three Kingdoms defies simple description because it exists not only as a historical text but also as a popular historical novel, which itself has a number of variations. So, for this discussion, I would like for us to consider Eiji Yoshikawa's novel *Romance of the Three Kingdoms*.

A Japanese scholar of Chinese literature had this to say about Yoshikawa's work: 'This is a work that brings out the most interesting aspects of the

Chinese historical classic *Romance of the Three Kingdoms* and makes it compelling and accessible for people today.' A Chinese-born literary critic added: 'Mr Yoshikawa has completely mastered the genre, and both *Romance of the Three Kingdoms* and *The Water Margin* are superb successes. I think we can safely say that Mr Yoshikawa masterfully demonstrates his ability to portray a truly defiant as well as chivalrous spirit, producing characters that achieve a superior degree of self-development as compared to Zhuge Kongming or the 108 stars of destiny.'[1]

In Japan, Yoshikawa's depiction of *Romance of the Three Kingdoms* has been so well received that when the title *Romance of the Three Kingdoms* is mentioned, it usually refers to Yoshikawa's work. In the youth reading group formed by my mentor, Josei Toda, *Romance of the Three Kingdoms* was used as study material.

Also, as you may know, Yoshikawa has been hailed as one of the best historical novelists in Japan, just as you have similarly been lauded in China. So when you have been introduced in Japan, you have even been called 'the Eiji Yoshikawa of China'.

JIN: I am very pleased by that title. I have read several of Yoshikawa's novels. He has rendered both *Romance of the Three Kingdoms* and *The Water Margin* into modern historical novels. And thanks to his brilliant prose, these two works have continued to enjoy great popularity among Japanese readers.

I have also read your dialogue in which you discuss Yoshikawa and his life [*Yoshikawa Eiji: Hito to Sekai* (Eiji Yoshikawa: The Person and His World), Rokko Shuppan]. After a cursory reading of the book, I sensed the deep affection you have for his works.

IKEDA: Thank you. I did not have the opportunity to meet Eiji Yoshikawa before he died. However, I visited the Yoshikawa Eiji House & Museum in Oume, Tokyo, in the mid-1980s and was able to speak with his wife, Mrs Fumiko Yoshikawa.

It was an unforgettable experience to hear Mrs Yoshikawa's recollections of her husband and to recall the bygone days of this great writer's life. I was moved to compose a poem, 'Like Mount Fuji', at that time.

JIN: I read your poem and could sense your familiarity with and affection for Yoshikawa.

Poetry and Adventure:
A Tapestry of Numerous Great Heroes

IKEDA: I am happy to hear that. Now let us focus on why *Romance of the Three Kingdoms* has such appeal. I think we can say that people are attracted to the immense scale of it, but most of all, to the multidimensional personalities in the novel. Memorable literature brings characters to life as individuals with names, faces, and vivid personalities, imprinting them upon the reader's heart. This is what Chinese literature has done traditionally, and I believe it is a very special feature. And *Romance of the Three Kingdoms* is especially representative of this distinctive quality.

For example, take the following real-life characters: Zhuge Liang (also called Kongming) of the Noble Way; the benevolent Liu Bei; the military ruler, Cao Cao; and the courageous and decisive Sun Quan. We can also point to the loyal hero, Guan Yu; the great man, Zhang Fei; and the courageous General Zhao Yun. Only the Chinese mainland could have produced such extraordinary and magnanimous people. Each of their stories conveys a sense of poetry and adventure.

The long-term popularity of these works in Japan and on the Korean peninsula is certainly due to the way that the many great heroic characters are interwoven into this romantic tapestry of poetry and action adventure.

JIN: I agree. Eiji Yoshikawa himself also said that *Romance of the Three Kingdoms* conveys a poetic sentiment, and I think it does so quite skilfully.

IKEDA: Perhaps the Chinese had the same kind of amusements as in Japan. They say that especially after the Ming period, one could observe scenes here and there of storytellers on street corners recounting the story of *Romance of the Three Kingdoms*, as adults and children listened intently with bated breath.

In these traditional storytelling events, when Liu Bei or Zhuge Liang were victorious, everyone clapped enthusiastically. Conversely, when Cao Cao won, the listeners stamped their feet in chagrin. I am sure that the listeners were influenced by the doctrines of Zhu Xi, in which good is rewarded and evil is punished, but also, deep within their hearts, they loved the drama and adventure of the story.

JIN: Among all the novels of Chinese classical literature, no other has attained such high prestige as *Romance of the Three Kingdoms*. Works of its equal simply do not come to mind. For over 300 years, *Romance of the Three Kingdoms* has continued to be the most recommended book for sophisticated readers and the most popular literary classic.

From the standpoint of 'pure literature', however, modern literary critics attribute higher value to the work *Dream of the Red Chamber*. This is also my view. Mao Zedong thought that *Dream of the Red Chamber* expressed a revolutionary sentiment that sought to conquer feudal consciousness. This gave unprecedented recognition to *Dream of the Red Chamber* as a work with a class-consciousness perspective. Mao even went so far as to tell General Xu Shiyou, well known for his boldness, military exploits, and lack of patience with trivialities, to read *Dream of the Red Chamber* carefully.

IKEDA: As we have mentioned already in this dialogue, *Dream of the Red Chamber* is a novel representing the Qing period. It is a story of a young aristocrat and the women who surround him, set against the backdrop of the rise and fall of the aristocracy. It would be somewhat comparable to the Japanese novel *The Tale of Genji*.

The author Minpei Sugiura compared and contrasted *Dream of the Red Chamber*, which does not have as broad a readership in Japan, and *The Tale of Genji* on such points as skilful depiction of everyday life and degree of realism, and he declared *Dream of the Red Chamber* as the better novel.

JIN: It is not as if this novel is a favourite of all Chinese. When General Xu Shiyou picked up the book because Mao Zedong had urged him to read it, what was his reaction? He might not be able to be patient with the lines with its flowery imagery and esoteric meaning such as 'Earnest sentiments, on a clear and peaceful evening, flowers discern meaning, wafting continuously and quietly, fragrant orbs'.

In contrast, we can easily imagine General Xu Shiyou's heart beating with excitement at scenes from *Romance of the Three Kingdoms*, such as the Battle of Hu Lao Gate between Lu Bu and the three heroes – Liu Bei, Guan Yu, and Zhang Fei – as well as the Battle of Red Cliffs, where Commander Zhou Yu destroyed the enemy forces.

IKEDA: Actually, Mr Sugiura, in response to a comment by Kōda Rohan, argues for the exact opposite point: that is, that there is value in realism and in the depiction of everyday life. He said, 'Rohan criticizes *Dream of the Red Chamber* because, he says, the characters in the novel are always eating.

Having gone to all the trouble to translate the novel, he probably appreciates it, so I wonder why he would say something like that. Personally, I really like the fact that the characters are always eating.'

Putting aside the literary criticisms for the moment, it is a fact that *Romance of the Three Kingdoms* transcends history and continues to capture the imaginations of many people.

JIN: Yes, it does. The influence that *Romance of the Three Kingdoms* has had on society goes far above and beyond its literary significance.

That said, this does not mean that the work is of inferior literary quality. Even when considering the work in terms of pure, serious literature, the character development is certainly first rate. In China, generations of novelists have gained inspiration and nourishment from this work.

IKEDA: What do you think is the source of this success in character depiction?

JIN: It undoubtedly is the exceptional skill in creating the setting and mood of the novel's scenes.

Take for example the famous 'Three Visits' passage. Here, as Zhuge Liang, one of the main characters, appears, a dramatic stage effect is created with the beating drums and gongs resonating everywhere as he gradually comes into view.

Following this entry, Zhuge Liang's activity is depicted in soft focus that becomes clearer incrementally, and he gradually comes into bold relief.

For example, in the 'borrowing the enemy's arrows using thatch-covered boats' scene, how exactly did he secure the enemy's arrows? Or in the 'borrowing the west wind' scene, how did he use the wind to win a major victory?

IKEDA: I see. So, dramatic effects are used liberally and achieved through the use of devices of meticulous detail.

JIN: Yes. Foreign novels, at least the more well-known works, do not make use of these kinds of techniques. The protagonists of foreign novels often appear suddenly as full-blown characters, or alternatively, their true identities are hidden so that they are not clearly depicted until the very end of the story.

In contrast, the characters appearing in *Romance of the Three Kingdoms* have very distinct personalities. The loyal characters are fiercely loyal.

Wicked characters have a coldheartedness and mercilessness rarely seen and commit the most unimaginably brutal atrocities. As soon as readers start reading the book, they are able to immediately distinguish each character from the others and know clearly which ones they most like and most dislike.

The Idealism of Zhuge Liang and Liu Bei and the Pragmatism of Cao Cao

IKEDA: I see. Your perspective is one I would expect only from a great writer who has painstakingly created his own literary works. Whenever possible, my mentor used *Romance of the Three Kingdoms* to stimulate thought and instruct us in areas such as leadership theory, human nature, and historical viewpoints – and each lesson is an irreplaceable treasure of my youth.

I will never forget what he said about the conflict between the Noble Path, as exemplified in the characters of Zhuge Liang and Liu Bei, and the military rule of Cao Cao: 'Zhuge Liang Kongming and Liu Bei Xuande in *Romance of the Three Kingdoms* were idealists, and sadly, the pragmatists such as Cao Cao conquered the idealists.'

Idealism and pragmatism. Ideals that are not firmly based on reality are merely fantasy. Cold, hard reality without ideals is too odious. But above all, the result is that people are forced to make an enormous sacrifice. How is this contradiction to be overcome? To put this thought in different terms, what we seek in a leader is the ability to wield a combination of 'justice and power'.

JIN: A great work of literature abundantly stimulates the reader's imagination. And as you mentioned, centuries after it was written *Romance of the Three Kingdoms* provides us with much to contemplate.

IKEDA: One point to note regarding the Noble Way and military rule in *Romance of the Three Kingdoms* is the slightly different positions taken in the fifteenth-century novel by Luo Guanzhong and Yoshikawa's modern version. In the fifteenth-century novel, the great General Cao Cao is portrayed as the embodiment of evil. In Yoshikawa's *Romance of the Three Kingdoms*, he is a man who is highly regarded as a beloved hero. As is symbolized in Cao Cao's almost obsessive adoration of Guan Yu, one facet of Cao Cao's personality is his warmhearted and charming character.

Also, he and his two sons, Cao Pi and Cao Zhi, were among the most distinguished poets of the time. In actuality, if they had simply been crude and cunning egotists, it probably would have been impossible for them to assemble that many talented people around them.

The tendency to sympathize with a tragic hero or the underdog exists in every culture, but the fifteenth-century version of *Romance of the Three Kingdoms* is harsh in its judgment of Cao Cao.

JIN: When I read *Romance of the Three Kingdoms* in my youth, I was firmly supportive of Liu Bei of the Shu Han. I absolutely refused to acknowledge that the kingdom of Shu Han had fallen before the states of Wu or Jin.

My eldest brother and I spent many an hour of intense debate on this point. Finally, he pulled out his junior high school history textbook, which he was studying at the time, and pointed to the passage clearly explaining that the state of Shu Han was overthrown by Deng Ai and Zhong Hui.

And so, I was forced to accept the defeat. But even so, I could not contain my disappointment and frustration, and my tears flowed unrestrained.

In one part of the fifteenth-century version of *Romance of the Three Kingdoms*, Deng Ai and Zhong Hui overthrow the Shu Han state and kill Jiang Wei of Shu Han. This scene is depicted with great skill. However, after reading it, I lost all interest in reading about Zhuge Liang's death on the Wuzhang Plains and in reading the rest of the book.

IKEDA: In the scene in which Zhuge Liang stepped forth at the first great assembly of officers at court and presented a memorial to Liu Shan, the eldest son of Liu Bei, on the expedition he contemplated, he earnestly indicated his intention to advance his cavalry to fight a decisive battle with the Wei on the Wuzhang Plains. This is the campaign during which he would fall sick and die. No one can read this scene without shedding tears. The thoughts of those who gathered around Zhuge Liang were the eternal hopes of all humankind. In Yoshikawa's version of *Romance of the Three Kingdoms*, the death of Zhuge Liang is actually the end of the book.

On a New Year's Day some time ago I sang 'Hoshi Otsu Shūfū Gojōgen' ('A Star Falls in the Autumn Wind on Wuzhang Plains', lyrics by Bansui Doi), a lament of Zhuge Liang's death, and my mentor was so taken with the song that he urged me to sing it again and again. He kept saying, 'One more time, one more time!' And as I sang, he listened intently, tears streaming down his face. He seemed to empathize completely with Zhuge Liang's fierce loyalty and commitment to carry out his lonely duty.

Incidentally, Mr Jin, you have written many martial arts novels in which you have depicted numerous fascinating characters. When you consider, from your own experience, the painstaking writing process such characters require, to which of the characters in *Romance of the Three Kingdoms* do you feel drawn?

The Striking Hero, Zhao Yun, or the Illustrious Characters, Zhou Yu and Lu Xun

JIN: My favourite character is Zhao Yun. I have long felt that even the likes of characters such as Guan Yu and Zhang Fei don't come close to this great hero.

Zhao Yun ferociously battled Cao Cao's overwhelming force in the Battle of Chang Ban Po. This was a far more difficult exploit than when Guan Yu killed his enemies, Yan Liang and Wen Chou, or when he succeeded in crossing five passes and slaying six generals. Moreover, Zhao Yun was a much more vibrant and vigorous man. He also had a virtuous and noble personality, was diligent in his attention to detail, and was a resourceful and ingenious strategist.

IKEDA: In addition to the military dimension, I am interested in the fact that Zhao Yun lived a long life, and as is befitting one who has lived long, he died a calm and peaceful death, which was rare for a character in *Romance of the Three Kingdoms*. It was so peaceful that we do not know when he actually died. In regard to Guan Yu and Zhang Fei, these characters were quite different in that they both met with a dramatic and violent death. It is said that people die as they have lived, and in this sense, Guan Yu and Zhang Fei met an appropriate fate. In Zhang Fei's case, it may seem at a glance that he died an ordinary, unheroic death, but that in itself is striking.

In a broader sense, when a person lives a long life, their way of life, maturity of perspective, and influence on future generations can be quite significant. As Nichiren once said, 'It is better to live a single day with honour than to live to 120 and die in disgrace'.[2] It would be meaningless to live a life without purpose.

In contrast, a long life of living each moment to the fullest with every ounce of one's being displays the genius of an outstanding person. And as historical examples reveal, often we see that such outstanding people conducted their lives this way at a surprisingly young age, and so the nature of their maturational process was undoubtedly a decisive factor.

For example, it is said that the Shakyamuni Buddha's long life had a major impact on the nature of Buddhism. If I may be permitted historical licence to speculate, I imagine that if Jesus Christ had lived as long as the Shakyamuni Buddha, Christianity would have a much different character than it does today.

JIN: That's a very intriguing thought. In terms of *Romance of the Three Kingdoms*, if Providence had granted Zhuge Liang a long life, Chinese history would have been very different.

IKEDA: In Japan, how different the course of history might have been if Toyotomi Hideyoshi had lived as long as Tokugawa Ieyasu.

Returning to your prior point; that is, that Zhao Yun is your favourite character, do you have any other favourites?

JIN: My next favourite characters are Ma Chao and Lu Bu. When I was a child, I was enthralled with the military prowess of the generals, and I was less concerned about major character flaws, such as Ma Chao's impatience and Lu Bu's simplemindedness.

Also, these two characters are so handsome on stage that they get points from me for leaving such a refreshing and bright impression in my heart.

IKEDA: There is an expression, 'As a boy, so the man'. So, perhaps the experiences you had as a boy were like sprouts that grew into the foundation for the master novelist that you became. In my case, I read *Romance of the Three Kingdoms* when I was a youth, and while I recognized Lu Bu's talent, he left me with the impression that he lacked discretion and was rather egotistical although he is certainly strong. I must say, however, that I am a little surprised at your evaluation of him.

JIN: Once an image becomes fixed in one's mind, it is hard to erase it. Whether we are talking about the story of *Romance of the Three Kingdoms*, the versions told by street corner storytellers, or the compilation by Luo Guanzhong – based on a mixture of historical fact and oral tradition – all of these have completely crossed the line to reveal an extreme partiality toward the Shu Han.

Luo Guanzhong is from Taiyuan, Shanxi province – although previously it was thought that he was from Hangzhou, which is where I am from. Recently, however, Professor Zhou Zhaoxin of Peking University presented historical evidence for Luo Guanzhong's birthplace as being in Taiyuan, Shanxi province, and that has become widely accepted. Luo Guanzhong seems to have a special favour for Guan Yu, who was also from Taiyuan, Shanxi province.

Iᴋᴇᴅᴀ: Are you suggesting that Chinese writers are partial to those originating from their own region of the country, and that this sense of geographical identity is reflected subtly in their literary works?

Jɪɴ: Yes. Exactly. So, it cannot be helped that Cao Cao is portrayed as a completely evil figure. Since growing up, I have always felt unhappy about how negatively people from the southern part of the lower Yangtze River are uniformly portrayed.

For example, Sun Jian, Sun Ce, and Sun Quan are people from Fuyang, in my home province of Zhejiang Province. Fuyang was called Fuchun Province during the Han period and was the birthplace of Yu Dafu.

Therefore, I have been very eager to write my own version of *Romance of the Three Kingdoms*, set mainly in the eastern part of Changjiang. Of course, the main characters would be Zhou Yu and Lu Xun. Sun Ce and Sun Quan would be the supporting cast. The great statesman and politician would be Gu Yong. The beautiful women would be the elder Qiao and the younger Qiao. However, since this would be incompatible with the conventional version deeply rooted in the consciousness of all Chinese, even if I did write my version of the story, I am sure that the public's reaction would not be positive.

Iᴋᴇᴅᴀ: Personally, I wish you would write it. Previously, I mentioned Shūgoro Yamamoto's *The Fir Trees Remain*. This is a story about family strife in a Japanese fiefdom during the Tokugawa period, and of course, the scale of the story cannot match that of *Romance of the Three Kingdoms*, but in this work, the author completely overturned the commonly accepted view of a samurai named Kai Harada, who had long been considered a thoroughly wicked figure. Contrary to that public perception, he was depicted as a loyal character who stood up all alone, sacrificing himself to protect his master's estate.

Mr Jin, just imagining that you will completely retell the story of

Romance of the Three Kingdoms, wielding a single writing brush, as only you can, makes my heart beat with delight.

JIN: Your words are very encouraging. However, at this point, my fantasies about Zhou Yu are only floating around in my head. For example, I wonder how dashing and gallant was the man the beautiful younger Qiao married and what kind of reaction there was to a mistake in the classical song. The great General Cheng Pu of the southern part of the lower Yangtze River remarked, 'Becoming friends with Zhou Yu is almost like drinking the finest quality rice wine. Before you know it, you have passed out.' I wonder what character trait he was referring to in his comment.

Lu Xun was a man who excelled in both literary and military arts. In the political arena, he endured much disparagement and slander, but fearlessly shouldered major responsibility. Lu Xun is one of the finest figures in all of Chinese history. I have only the deepest respect for him.

It would be a great joy for me to depict characters such as these, weaving them into the unique landscape and culture of Jiangnan. To be able to allow my imagination to roam freely in the process of writing my version of *Romance of the Three Kingdoms*, set primarily in Jiangnan, would be to savour to my heart's content an exquisite game of wordplay. That alone would be immensely satisfying.

If I really took up my pen and started this writing project, it would be a major task. However, it would not be necessary.

IKEDA: Lu Xun is certainly an appealing figure. He is the one who plotted against and killed Guan Yu, but interestingly, he does not have a negative persona. Generally speaking, however, I think Lu Su is more famous, who is well known for the words, 'If you have not seen someone for three days, await your next encounter with a sense of anticipation'.

Incidentally, I have noticed that *Romance of the Three Kingdoms* is a treasure trove of many famous sayings and verses. There are so many that come immediately to mind, such as, 'To fret from forced idleness', 'To become as inseparable as fish and the water they swim in', 'There is no joking in time of war', 'K'ungming [Kongming] weeps, but puts Ma Su to death', and 'A dead Chuko [Zhuge] was enough to scare off a live Ssūma [Sima Yi]'. In this sense, the story of *Romance of the Three Kingdoms* has permeated the everyday life of the people, and from it have emerged numerous common expressions.

Character Portrayal and the Classical Chinese Novel

JIN: If I may comment further on character development in *Romance of the Three Kingdoms*, one aspect is that there is no attempt to depict a character's emotional feelings. Rather, the character's spirit and psychological makeup are revealed through narration and actions.

This is basically dramatic technique. On stage as well as in film only an actor's speech and actions are conveyed. Yet, the character's innermost thoughts become evident through external means. This is the highly developed technique that was cultivated in the Chinese classical novel.

In modern times in China, efforts have been made to learn about the Western novel. And authors have experimented with placing emphasis on depictions of the interior thoughts and feelings of the characters. However, many of these works are depressing to read, and the characters seem fuzzy and ambiguous. This is because the authors have not learned the character development technique of the Chinese classical novel.

IKEDA: In the last one hundred years or so, in both the East and the West, it appears that literature which focuses on portraying the subtle aspects of human psychology has become mainstream. However, this experiment in literature has failed to surpass the great literature of the past, in the sense of producing intriguing narrative and transforming in an instant, for the reader, the tedium of everyday life into a glittering, magical new world, through fertile creativity and soaring imagination.

Goethe comments as follows: 'Shakespeare, in writing his pieces, could hardly have thought that they would appear in print, so as to be told over, and compared one with another; he had rather the stage in view when he wrote; he regarded his plays as a lively and moving scene, that would pass rapidly before the eyes and ears upon the stage, not as one that was to be held firmly, and carped at in detail. Hence, his only point was to be effective and significant for the moment.'[3]

Foremost in Shakespeare's mind was the stage, action, and lines of the script that come alive; and psychological analysis and depicting character psychology was furthest from his mind. I am sure that it was absolutely inconceivable to him that someday someone would be reading his published work all alone in a study somewhere. I cannot help thinking that, when compared to the prolificacy and far-reaching impact of Shakespeare's world, the world of modern literature, with its exacting depictions of character psychology, is quite impoverished. This literature caters to young literary types and the intelligentsia.

Romance of the Three Kingdoms – Deeply Rooted in Chinese History and the Spirit of the People

JIN: In contrast to modern psychological literature, the story of *Romance of the Three Kingdoms* has become part of the inner life of the Chinese people. The people have acquired their sense of moral education and values from *Romance of the Three Kingdoms*. In other words, they value their friendships and treat people with sympathy and care, as did Liu Bei and Guan Yu. And because of Cao Cao's example, they know they must never forget their debt of gratitude to their benefactors, turn their back on duty, or maliciously and unscrupulously scheme to benefit themselves.

Among the general population, Liu Bei and Guan Yu have set a more significant moral standard than Confucius or Mencius. Their influence has permeated far more widely and has demonstrated a greater impact than the moral standards of Confucius or Mencius.

In China, Guan Yu is revered at altars all over the country, including those in the police stations of Hong Kong. Yet nowhere do people pay their respects to Confucius or Jesus Christ or Buddha. Nowhere else in the world have characters in a novel become the objects of religious worship by the public at large. The ancient Greeks worshipped the Greek gods, but not because they read about them in the *Iliad*. The *Iliad* simply recorded the fact that the Greeks worshipped their gods.

IKEDA: In Japan, there are instances of worship of enshrined historical figures, such as Kusunoki Masashige or Tokugawa Ieyasu, but the reverence that the Chinese give to Guan Yu goes beyond what we would imagine.

The author Chin Shunshin remembers that in the city of Kobe, where 7,000 to 8,000 Chinese lived, there was only one Chinese temple. It was the Emperor Guan Temple, where Guan Yu was revered. He recalled that Guan Yu attracted much respect and adoration.

JIN: There is no denying that *Romance of the Three Kingdoms* played a major role in Chinese history. Let me give one example. When the Qing dynasty, which was founded by the Jurchen people, first attacked the Ming, the Jurchens were a rough and uncultured people. They were illiterate and unable to read Sun Tzu's *Art of War*.

Therefore, when generals led their troops into war, what did they rely on for strategic planning? They referred to *Romance of the Three Kingdoms* for all their strategies and schemes. The second-generation leaders of Qing frequently employed the 'create internal strife' strategy, the objective of which was to create distrust and alienation within the enemy ranks; and by confusing the Ming's Emperor Chongzhen, they were ultimately successful in making him execute his own general, General Yuan Chonghuan.

IKEDA: Mr Jin, this historical fact also appears in your novel *Sword Stained with Royal Blood*.

JIN: Yes. I modelled a part of my book after the story in *Romance of the Three Kingdoms* in which Cao Cao is taken in by Zhou Yu's scheme and kills Cai Mao and Zhang Yun, the admirals of his own navy. If Yuan Chonghuan had not died, Wu Sangui could not have protected Shanhaiguan, the main Ming military base, and as a result it would have been impossible for the Qing army to invade Beijing so easily.

IKEDA: They say that impregnable fortresses are brought down not by external enemies, but rather that they crumble from within. This has been the rule throughout history. Nichiren also remarked that 'only worms born of the lion's body feed on the lion'.[4] When confronted with a major crisis, the most important task is to strengthen internal solidarity.

I feel that I have a sense of your feelings about Zhou Yu from our discussion here. When Zhuge Liang is compared with the clever and resourceful Zhou Yu, Zhuge Liang's shrewd farsightedness is highlighted, but he is still no match for the ingenious and unrivalled general.

Guan Yu Worship: The Values of Filial Piety and Duty in Chinese Society

JIN: You previously mentioned the Emperor Guan Temple in Kobe, Japan, but there are Emperor Guan Temples all over China. An extremely large Emperor Guan Temple is located on the outskirts of Luoyang City.

Historically speaking, however, it seems that Guan Yu, the actual person, was not an especially distinguished figure. He was not any more brave or daring than Zhang Fei, Zhao Yun, or Ma Chao, and if challenged to a duel by any of Cao Cao's generals, such as Zhang Liao, Xu Shu, and Xu

Chu, he would have been evenly matched with them. And, of course, Lu Bu was much stronger than Guan Yu.

In terms of military strategy, Guan Yu was clearly less able than Cao Cao, Zhuge Liang, Sima Yi, Zhou Yu, Lu Meng, Lu Xun, Yang Hu, Lu Kang, or Zhao Yun. The reason that Guan Yu came to be revered by the people is that, of all the characters in *Romance of the Three Kingdoms*, the sense of righteousness depicted in his character was highly exaggerated.

The moral values viewed as most important by the Chinese people are, first of all, filial piety and, second, a sense of righteousness. For a character in a novel to be elevated to godly status, it is surely due to the underlying traditional characteristics of the Chinese people, rather than the popularity of the novel, which will eventually fade.

IKEDA: Certainly, the emphasis on filial piety and sense of righteousness is quite pronounced. One famous passage accentuating the value of filial piety tells the story of Xu Shu, tactician for Liu Bei's army, which was on the verge of launching an expedition from its base in Xinye. Xu Shu was thoroughly deceived by Cao Cao, who floated the word that Xu Shu's mother was on her sick bed; and so Xu Shu dropped everything to rush to her side. Also, in the beginning of Yoshikawa's version of *Romance of the Three Kingdoms*, Liu Bei's sense of filial piety is underscored.

The moral virtue of observing one's righteousness is a value that runs throughout the entire book and is especially demonstrated in the Peach Garden Oath, a vow of eternal friendship and fidelity between Liu Bei, Guan Yu, and Zhang Fei.

Justice, significance, loyalty, gratitude, faith, morality, a sense of moral obligation and humanity, and striving for a just cause – the values that I list as they come to me are all wonderful words expressing the essence of human morality. It is understandable why all of these words form the path of virtue that human beings must tread and the foundation for the social order that is essential to build human society.

Once, in contemplating the future of a more unified world, Dr Arnold Toynbee asserted that the Chinese people's experience and skill in ruling such a vast territory for over 2,000 years must stem from a uniquely Chinese sense of social order, as represented by such concepts as 'righteousness'.

Of course, we must be constantly mindful of the danger of society becoming rigid and inflexible or stifled if there is even one misstep in the management of this social order. Lu Xun advocated a struggle against Confucian values, harshly criticizing the negative aspects of the Chinese people's traditional moral legacy, while at the same time holding Qin Shi Huang and Cao Cao in high esteem for being epoch-making reformers and non-conformists against the established social order. And yet, the sense of one's righteousness toward society, as a moral virtue and as a standard for the governance of human society, will remain an elemental part of the enduring psychology of the Chinese people.

JIN: One more point I would like to make regarding literary technique is that *Romance of the Three Kingdoms* includes a fair amount of classical literary-style writing. So when I was in primary school and reading this book, there were many parts that I could not understand. Even so, I was so drawn in by the fascinating characters and irresistible appeal of the story, that I continued reading along, skipping the parts that I did not understand, and ended up reading the entire book in one sitting.

IKEDA: You were captivated by the magic of *Romance of the Three Kingdoms*. It casts an awesome power over its readers. It is the power of its narrative. Were your friends and acquaintances equally enthralled by the book?

JIN: My mother's favourite book was *Dream of the Red Chamber*. She and her friends would get together and compete to see who could recite poetry from the book and who could call out the names of the chapters the fastest. The winner would get a piece of candy. I would sit quietly nearby and be completely bored as the women would chat merrily away to each other. Of course, each time my mother handed me a piece of candy, my interest grew significantly.

IKEDA: I understand that. In Japan, too, children are usually not very interested in the psychological subtleties of the characters in *The Tale of Genji*.

I have heard that in China, *Hongmi* (literally 'red fanatic') is an expression for people who are passionate fans of *Dream of the Red Chamber*. I can imagine that many readers were wildly enthusiastic about it, but hearing about your mother's avid interest gives me a clearer picture of what it must have been like.

The Heroes of *The Water Margin* – Devoted to the People and their Struggles

IKEDA: Next to *Romance of the Three Kingdoms*, another great work of literature beloved by the people of China and Japan is *The Water Margin*. My youth group studied *The Water Margin* under the tutelage of my mentor. We called our group *Suiko-kai* (Water Margin Group) after the book. I remember nostalgically the days we spent, all gathered around our mentor, reading great world literature, such as *The Water Margin*, sometimes at a campground in Hikawa, Tokyo.

JIN: President Ikeda, I recall that you wrote about this in your book *The Human Revolution*.

IKEDA: Yes, I did. As you know, *The Water Margin* is largely an imaginary tale. Song Jiang and his band of outlaws are barely mentioned in historical texts. This epic tale was handed down through the generations, over the course of several hundred years, to become the story that we have today. The story evolved from a brief description to become a long epic tale. While the author's imagination is certainly great, the people's enthusiasm for the story generation after generation enabled it to take on a life of its own.

The people were downtrodden by tyrannical rulers and perhaps, in their hearts, they yearned for the kind of heroes and ideals depicted in *The Water Margin*. We can only imagine how desperate was their wish. Perhaps an indication of their desire for a different life is the meticulously detailed description of agricultural practices, dairy farming, sericulture (silkworm production), and Mount Liang – the idyllic hideout where the heroes took sanctuary.

In this sense, we can say that *The Water Margin* expresses the ideal world that the people desired – a free and self-reliant world that is completely divorced from tyranny and oppression.

JIN: *The Water Margin* is considered a story about rebellion – that is, it extols the heroes who resisted a despotic ruler. The story is usually divided into about 120 chapters, and at the end, the 'water margin' heroes surrender to the imperial court. But they are abused by the court, in the sense that some of them are intentionally sent to do battle against overwhelming odds, and they die on the battlefield, some are poisoned by the court, and one by one, most of them meet a tragic end.

IKEDA: One point that we must not overlook is that the heroes were not concerned about themselves only. They had fully enjoyed living a comfortable, self-reliant life in a world far removed from the one to which they returned. There was no need for them to subject themselves to a fierce battle. Moreover, they had no intention of saving the tyrannical and cruel court from its own predicament.

However, they were unable to just stand by and watch the people suffer and die. They identified closely with the people and subordinated their concern for their own safety and welfare to a desire to protect the people. Their striking commitment to serve the people captured people's hearts. These sincere and patriotic heroes were taken advantage of and used mercilessly, and in the end, the court cut off and abandoned the heroes. The story must imply intense criticism for such an indifferent court.

Exploring the issue of authoritarian power and the way it suppresses the vitality of the people brings us to this question: how do we put an end to this kind of perpetual tragedy? Herein lies one of the lessons my mentor taught us through the story of *The Water Margin*. I have devoted my entire life to addressing this issue.

Why did the Heroes of *The Water Margin* Surrender?

JIN: At one time, Mao Zedong harshly criticized Song Jiang's surrender, and labelled *The Water Margin* an 'undesirable book'. Personally, I believe that *The Water Margin* heroes' surrender to the imperial court was perhaps the most inevitable conclusion to the saga, given the context of the Northern Song dynasty.

Of course, the heroes of Mount Liang never abandoned their resistance, and there was always the possibility, as Li Kui, 'the Black Whirlwind', so aptly suggested, that they could overthrow the imperial court, dress Song Jiang in yellow imperial robes, and install him as emperor on the imperial throne.

The reality of the matter, however, was that the heroes of Mount Liang did not rise up in rebellion, and Song Jiang had no ambition to become emperor.

IKEDA: In terms of Mao Zedong's theory of permanent revolution and its motto, 'To rebel is justified', which formed the basis of his philosophy, the surrender of *The Water Margin* heroes to the imperial court might be seen as caving in to the existing social order.

However, the consequences of such a philosophy of endless rebellion are never-ending social disorder, terrorism, moral decay, and social stagnation.

To say, 'To rebel is justified', is equivalent to endorsing anarchy, because they are two sides of the same coin. The golden rule of anarchism is total freedom, but we must be careful that this freedom is paradoxical and embraces a concept that is so absurdly irrational. That is, a movement that sets out in search of freedom would end up inviting autocracy and despotism.

A perusal of recent history shows that storms of fanatical anarchism have always instigated reigns of terror and heavy-handed government rule. The Cultural Revolution is an obvious example of this.

JIN: Yes, it is. I believe that the heroes of *The Water Margin* had only two choices. One option was to continue as a band of outlaws and robbers, launching their attacks from their base on Mount Liang, gradually expanding the territory – bringing all of Shangdong province and possibly the southern part of Hebei and the northern part of Jiangsu under their control – and establishing an independent country. The other option was to accept the invitation of the imperial court to surrender and pledge fealty to the throne.

The leaders of the group   Song Jiang, Lu Junyi, Wu Yong, Guan Sheng, Qin Ming, Huyan Zhou, Xu Ning, and Hua Rong – had originally come from many walks of life. Some had been minor officials, some were wealthy, and others were well-educated literati or military leaders. Accordingly, abandoning the bandit lifestyle and returning to the civilized society of the court was a logical choice.

Some of the heroes, such as Lin Chong, Li Kui, Wu Song, Lu Zhishen, the Ruan brothers, and Liu Tang, leaned toward rebellion, but they did not occupy positions of leadership in the Mount Liang hierarchy, and so they had no choice but to follow the orders of the senior and deputy leadership.

IKEDA: I think that if all of the members of the group hiding out on Mount Liang had been outlaws, then, for better or for worse, there would have been no reason for them to extend themselves beyond the realm of banditry.

JIN: It is probably factual that the heroes of *The Water Margin* ended up surrendering. Even so, as you pointed out, President Ikeda, just because they did does not mean that everything about them should be rejected. The important point in *The Water Margin* is that this group of outlaws opposed the imperial court – they struggled against the powerful, who had turned their backs on moral values. Their basic spirit was one of rebellion.

It simply is not accurate to point to the ultimate surrender of the men of Mount Liang and claim that *The Water Margin* exalts surrender.

The Water Margin holds up the heroes' tragic fate as a negative example to instruct readers and offer them guiding principles that encourage self-reflection. There is no way that surrendering to feudal rulers and greedy and corrupt villains would ever have a positive outcome. No matter what happens, one must always keep fighting to the end. And one must never compromise with evil.

IKEDA: I agree completely. You mentioned Lu Xun, who spoke vehemently about the struggle against evil. 'Beat the dog who has fallen into the water!' he declared. He meant that whether the dog is on land or has fallen into the water, as long as it has not been cured of its habit of biting people, one must keep beating the dog. Similarly, he said that evil must be rooted out, and one must not stop fighting against it until the root is completely dead. Even if the evil side falters, one must continue the fight and not slacken the pursuit.

Do not Judge Heroes Based on Victory or Defeat

JIN: *The Water Margin* depicts the surrender of Song Jiang and his followers, yet at the same time, it also portrays the heartrending and tragic deaths that fate had awaiting them after their surrender. In actuality, what is depicted is contrary to a philosophy of surrender.

Mao Zedong praised *Dream of the Red Chamber*. Due to family circumstances, the main character, Jia Baoyu, was forced to marry Xue Baochai and had children with her. Meanwhile his sweetheart, Lin Daiyu, repressed her bitterness and died a lonely death.

The book did not extol the old-style arranged marriage or urge young people to follow the orders of their parents in all matters. It praised individual freedom and the right to choose one's life partner and opposed the spirit of traditional social norms. Even though the marriage that the parents ordered takes place, it is important to note that a spirit of resistance to feudalistic and traditional social dictates flows throughout the entire book.

IKEDA: This is a tragedy arising from the bonds between members of the feudalistic household. Ba Jin's *The Family* deals with this same theme.

JIN: You can say the same for *Romance of the Three Kingdoms*. Cao Cao's son,

Cao Pi, was installed on the imperial throne, and Sima overthrew the states of Wu and Han. On one hand, Liu Bei, Zhuge Liang, and Guan Yu fell at the height of the chaos and turmoil of the war, and each met a bitter end. However, we clearly cannot conclude that the portrayal of this course of events, based on historical fact, glorifies the crafty and cunning Cao Cao and Sima Yi and diminishes the magnanimous and humane Liu Bei and Zhuge Liang.

The Chinese often allude to the proverb 'Do not judge a hero by victory or defeat'. I think that this saying applies perfectly to the characters in *Romance of the Three Kingdoms* and *The Water Margin*.

IKEDA: I think so, too. Allow me to introduce a verse from 'A Star Falls in the Autumn Wind on Wuzhang Plains': 'Who could dispute the success or failure – Of the loyal man who gave his life?'[5] We cannot judge the greatness of a person's character based only on that person's successes or failures. There are times when these 'successes' or 'failures' must be viewed over a long span of 1,000 or 2,000 years.

JIN. In *Telling the Complete Biography of Yue Fei*, Yue Fei's courage is what, in the end, leads to his murder, and Qin Hui is wicked, but he is blessed with wealth and social status and ends up living a long life. This description is in accordance with historical fact. However, the main point of this work is to enthusiastically applaud loyalty and bravery and to demean wickedness and evil. This point immediately becomes clear to the reader.

IKEDA: Yes. This is a story about the murder of Yue Fei, a loyal retainer during the Southern Song period who is punished for a crime based on a false accusation by Qin Hui. Assuredly, Yue Fei was tricked and met a violent end. And Qin Hui lived. However, history has judged Qin Hui harshly. I have heard that in China today, the name of Qin Hui has become synonymous with treason and betrayal.

JIN: During the Qing dynasty, editor, writer, and critic Jin Shengtan, who was an advocate of the vernacular language, excluded the last 49 chapters of *The Water Margin*. Jin Shengtan's real name was Jin Renduan. He made it a rule to never observe any old customs and announced that if Confucius, a representative of the saints, saw him, he would probably shake his head and sigh. Jin Renduan prided himself on this insight and adopted the pen name Jin Shengtan (Sacred Lament).

IKEDA: He must have been a rebellious young man indeed.

JIN: Yes. The concluding chapters that he eliminated from *The Water Margin* described Song Jiang's surrender to the imperial court and how the heroes, one after another, met a tragic death. He left the first 71 chapters intact and concluded with a scene in which Lu Junyi dreams that all of the heroes are bound and waiting to be executed. The novel ends with the implication that an unfortunate fate awaits the heroes.

This abridged version of the novel was extremely well received by readers and became very popular. As a result, the original version with 120 chapters is hardly read any longer. From that point onward, of all the millions and millions of Chinese people, only a few besides Mao Zedong and his followers thought that *The Water Margin* promoted the surrender to the imperial court.

IKEDA: Jin Shengtan's 70-chapter version circulated so widely that the 100-chapter and 120-chapter versions were all but forgotten. Only in the twentieth century did these other versions once again come to be read, and it is said that they were imported back into China from Japan.

JIN: There were people who were opposed to the heroes gathered on Mount Liang and to the fact that they had started a rebellion. Yu Wanchun's novel *Dang Kouzhi* is the story of the brave generals loyal to the imperial court who attacked the rebels on Mount Liang, brutally slaughtering them or capturing them alive. Interestingly, though the work is written from the imperial court's perspective, it does not employ the ending in which the Mount Liang band is invited by the court to surrender. The band continues its uncompromising resistance, and the story ends with the suppression of the revolt by the imperial forces.

An old Chinese saying admonishes: 'The young must not read *The Water Margin*; the old must not read *Romance of the Three Kingdoms*.' In *The Water Margin*, the heroes were valiant and daring as they defied the imperial court and resisted its authority. Once they encountered oppression, they immediately stood up and drew their swords, killed people, and started a rebellion. It was thought that this kind of content would be a negative influence on youth.

IKEDA: When I think of the reckless behaviour of the Red Guards during the Cultural Revolution, there were aspects of it that I could understand. If the heroes in *The Water Margin* had been alive at the time of the Cultural Revolution, undoubtedly Li Kui, the Black Whirlwind, would have led the rampage.

Mr Jin, you were the first to astutely observe that the Cultural Revolution was, in essence, all about a struggle for power within the ruling elite. And, in a sense, adults took advantage of the pure and innocent passion of youth, cunningly exploiting it to serve the interests of their own struggle for power. So, it seems that the craftiness of adults is not limited just to the world of novels.

JIN: The novel *Romance of the Three Kingdoms* depicts numerous tales of trickery and Machiavellian schemes. A steady stream of resourceful and exceptional characters appears in the book. Most outstanding among all of them are Zhuge Liang, Liu Bei, and Cao Cao.

In the context of the saying that I just mentioned, it was thought that when people become older, they are less prone to be swayed by short-term events and tend to deal with their affairs by carefully contemplating the pros and cons based on a long-term perspective. Consequently, according to this reasoning, a novel such as *Romance of the Three Kingdoms* would exploit these commendable traits and encourage older people to plot evil schemes to mislead and deceive others. However, the saying was nothing more than a statement by those ruling Chinese society to avoid resistance and rebellion by those they dominated, and so it did not reflect the social reality.

The Water Margin is a work that inspires readers to rise up courageously to battle against evil. *Romance of the Three Kingdoms* clearly differentiates between courage and wickedness, and right and wrong.

Song Jiang's View of China's Unique Social Order

IKEDA: My frank impression is that the Noble Way is a constant theme throughout *Romance of the Three Kingdoms* and *The Water Margin*. That is, the formation of human society is based on a sense of social order, a kind of a golden rule, we might say, that is neither military rule nor a path of perfection. In Chinese society, this guiding precept has been based primarily on Confucian values, which have been handed down over the centuries, and underlies the concept of social order that flows throughout these two novels.

This may seem slightly biased, but in Yoshikawa's work *The New Water Margin* there is a scene in which Song Jiang recites to the assembled group of powerful members of his band a poem that conveys his desire to pledge his life in service to the Emperor, if they are invited to return to the fold.

This is a memorable scene in which Li Kui and the others fly into a rage at the thought, and Song Jiang attempts to pacify them by saying, 'The Song dynasty brought into being a civilization that has continued uninterrupted for many centuries. It is indeed powerful; yet, if this imperial reign and the unity it has forged are terminated now, the entire country will fall into a state of chaos and disorganization and all of the people will suffer greatly, to an extent we cannot even imagine.'[6]

We must avoid the inevitable suffering that people, caught in the turmoil of war and dissolution of the national polity, experience, and seek a peaceful and orderly civilized society. Accordingly, in our every action we must be cognizant of the consequences. In confronting the evils of the world, we must not create a disordered, anarchistic situation – this is what Song Jiang tried to convey in his poem. I believe that he plainly and elegantly symbolizes, shall we say, the uniquely Chinese sense of social order and the cosmos.

Generally speaking, in contrast to Eastern thought, which reflects a heavy emphasis on anti-cosmos or chaos theory, the main characteristic of Chinese philosophy, whose core is Confucianism, is a keen sense of the cosmos. As I mentioned previously, after considering both the pluses and minuses of this view, frankly speaking, I believe that the virtues and fine qualities of this perspective must be continued and passed on. This wisdom is Chinese civilization's contribution, developed over millennia, to humankind's intellectual heritage.

JIN: Indeed. I am in complete agreement. Turning to *Romance of the Three Kingdoms* and *The Water Margin*, I believe that both have great value. They are fine books that provide positive influences for readers. They are works that I enthusiastically recommend for younger readers.

IKEDA: Well then, Mr Jin, with this suggestion for young readers, let us bring our literary discussion to a close. Thank you so much for engaging in this year-long dialogue of ideas and thoughts on literature, history, and society. It has been a memorable experience for me.

JIN: Thank you very much indeed. There are so many more ideas I would like to discuss with you, President Ikeda, so I look forward to our next opportunity.

Notes

Chapter 1

1 Aitmatov, Chingiz and Ikeda, Daisaku. *Ode to the Grand Spirit: A Dialogue*. Trans. Richard L. Gage (London: I.B.Tauris, 2009), viii.

2 Mencius. *The Works of Mencius*. Trans. James Legge (New York: Courier Dover Publications, 1990), 187.

3 James, William. 'The Moral Equivalent of War', *Popular Science Monthly*, 77 (Oct. 1910), 400–10.

4 'The Bridge-Building President', *Financial Times* Survey, *Financial Times*, 29 October 1990, p. III.

5 Sun Yat-sen. *San Min Chu I* (The Three Principles of the People). Trans. Frank W. Price (Shanghai: Commercial Press, 1928), 212–13.

6 Goethe, Johann Wolfgang von. *The Autobiography of Goethe: Truth and Poetry: From My Own Life*. Trans. John Oxenford (London: Bell & Daldy, 1867), 386.

Chapter 2

1 Translated from Japanese: Lu Xun. *Rojin Bunshu*, Vol. 3 (Collected Works of Lu Xun, Vol. 3). Trans. Yoshimi Takeuchi (Tokyo: Chikuma-shobo, 1991), 158.

2 Ikeda, Daisaku. *The New Human Revolution*, Vol. 5 (Santa Monica: SGI-USA, 1997), 172.

3 Ikeda, Daisaku. *A New Humanism* (New York: Weatherhill, 1996), 157.

4 Marcus Tullius Cicero. From *Cicero de Amicitia (on Friendship) and Scipio's Dream*. Trans. Andrew P. Peabody (Boston: Little Brown and Company, 1884), 37.

5   Translated from Japanese. Jin Yong. *Shoken Onkyuroku*, Vol. 2 (*The Book and the Sword*, Vol. 2). Trans. Yumi Okazaki (Tokyo: Tokuma Shoten Publishing Co. Ltd., 1996), 254.

6   Translated from Japanese. Jin Yong. *Iten Toryu Ki* (*The Heaven Sword and Dragon Saber*, Vol. 1). Trans. Hisayuki Hayashi and Atsuko Abe (Tokyo: Tokuma Shoten Publishing Co. Ltd., 2000), 244.

7   Nichiren. *The Writings of Nichiren Daishonin* (Tokyo: Soka Gakkai, 1999), 303.

8   Gorbachev, Mikhail and Ikeda, Daisaku. *Moral Lessons of the Twentieth Century*. Trans. Richard L. Gage (London: I.B.Tauris, 2005), 11.

9   Chuang Tzu [Zhuang-zi]. *The Complete Works of Chuang Tzu*. Trans. Burton Watson (New York: Columbia University Press, 1968), 178–79.

Chapter 3

1   Lo-Kuan-chung. *Romance of the Three Kingdoms*, Vol. 2. Trans. C.H. Brewitt-Taylor (Tokyo: Charles E. Tuttle Company, 1959), 198.

2   Confucius. *The Analects of Confucius*. Trans. Burton Watson (New York: Columbia University Press, 2007), 23.

3   Translated from Japanese. Jin Yong. *Shoken Onkyuroku*, Vol. 1 (*The Book and the Sword*, Vol. 1). Trans. Yumi Okazaki (Tokyo: Tokuma Shoten Publishing Co. Ltd., 1996), 3.

4   Translated from Japanese. Chin, Shunshin. *Nihonteki Chūgokuteki* (Notions of the Japanese and the Chinese) (Tokyo: Tokuma Shoten Publishing Co. Ltd., 1983), 70.

5   Fukuyama, Francis. *Trust: The Social Virtues and the Creation of Prosperity* (New York: Free Press, 1996), 75.

6   Chin, Shunshin. *Nihonteki Chūgokuteki*, 70.

7   Aitmatov, Chingiz and Ikeda, Daisaku. *Ode to the Grand Spirit: A Dialogue*. Trans. Richard L. Gage (London: I.B.Tauris, 2009), vii–viii.

8   *Newsweek*, Japanese edition, 2 February 1996, 40.

9   Coudenhove-Kalergi, Richard N. E. and Ikeda, Daisaku. *Bunmei: Nishi to Higashi* (Civilization: East and West) (Tokyo: Seikyo Shimbun, 1975), 143–44.

10 Gaarder, Jostein. *Sophie's World: A Novel About the History of Philosophy*. Trans. Paulette Møller (London: Phoenix, 1996), 8.

11 Ikeda, Daisaku. *Songs from My Heart*, 'Springing from the Earth' (New York: Weatherhill, 1997), 66.

Chapter 4

1 Sima Qian. *Records of the Historian: Chapters from the Shih chi of Ssu-ma Ch'ien*, 'The Assassin-Retainers'. Trans. Burton Watson (New York: Columbia University Press, 1969), 48.

2 *Plutarch: The Lives of the Noble Grecians and Romans*, the Dryden Translation (Chicago: Encyclopaedia Britannica, Inc., 1952).

3 Translated from Japanese. Murakami, Hyōe. *Kokka Naki Nihon: Sensō to Heiwa no Kenshō* (Japan The Non-State: War and Peace Reexamined) (Tokyo: Saimaru, 1996), 61.

4 Translated from Japanese. Kobayashi, Hideo. *Kangaeru Hinto* (Hints for Thinking) (Tokyo: Bungei shunju Ltd., 1974), 112.

5 *Plutarch: The Lives of the Noble Grecians and Romans*, 123.

6 Ibid., 124.

7 Ibid., 129.

8 *The Analects of Confucius*. Trans. Burton Watson (New York: Columbia University Press, 2007), 81.

9 *Plutarch: The Lives of the Noble Grecians and Romans*, 131.

10 Nichiren. *The Writings of Nichiren Daishonin* (Tokyo: Soka Gakkai, 1999), 538.

11 Ikeda, Daisaku. *The Human Revolution*, Book One, abridged edition (Santa Monica: SGI-USA, 2004), 164.

12 *Plutarch: The Lives of the Noble Grecians and Romans*, 549.

13 Sima Qian. *Records of the Grand Historian: Qing Dynasty*. Trans. Burton Watson (New York: Columbia University Press, 1993), 235–36.

Chapter 5

1 Machacek, David and Wilson, Bryan (eds). *Global Citizens* (Oxford: Oxford University Press, 2000), 9.

2 Dumas, Alexandre. *The Count of Monte Cristo*. Trans. David Coward (Oxford: Oxford University Press, 2008), 143.

3 Ibid.

4 Nichiren. *The Writings of Nichiren Daishonin*, Vol. 2 (Tokyo: Soka Gakkai, 2006), 843.

5 Tolstoy, Leo. *Anna Karenina: A Novel*. Trans. Rosemary Edmonds (New York: Penguin Books, 1954), 11.

6 Translated from *Goethe Zenshu*, Vol. 13 (Collected Works of Goethe, Vol. 13). Original German title: *Maximen und Reflecionen* (Maxims

and Reflections). Trans. Eijiro Iwazaki and Kusuo Seki (Tokyo: Ushio Publishing Co. Ltd., 1980), 218.

7 Dumas, Alexandre. *The Three Musketeers*. Ed. David Coward (Oxford: Oxford University Press, 1998), 264–65.

8 Ibid., 449.

Chapter 6

1 Lu Xun. *Selected Works*, Vol. 1. Trans. Yang Xianyi and Gladys Yang (Beijing: Foreign Languages Press, 1980), 12–13.

2 Translated from Japanese. Mao Dun. 'Lu Xun', in *Sekai Bungaku Taikei*, Vol. 62 (Anthology of World Literature, Vol. 62). Trans. Hiromitsu Matsui (Tokyo: Chikuma Publishing, 1958), 432.

3 Lu Xun. *Selected Stories of Lu Hsun*. Trans. Yang Hsien-yi and Gladys Yang (Beijing: Foreign Language Press, 1980), 117.

4 Foster, Paul B. *Ah Q Archaeology: Lu Xun, Ah Q, A Q Progeny and the National Character Discourse in Twentieth Century in China* (Maryland: Lexington Books, 2006), 259, in Robert Merrill Bartlett, 'Intellectual Leaders of the Chinese Revolution', *Current History* 271, no.1 (Oct. 1927), 58.

5 Quoted in Ikeda, Daisaku. *The New Human Revolution*, Vol. 6 (Santa Monica: SGI-USA, 1998), 145.

6 Yukichi Fukuzawa, *An Outline of a Theory of Civilization*. Trans. David A. Dilworth and G. Cameron Hurst (Tokyo: Sophia University Press, 1970), 141.

7 Lu Xun. *Selected Works*, Vol. 2. Trans. Yang Xianyi and Gladys Yang (Beijing: Foreign Languages Press, 1980), 358.

8 Translated from Chinese. Lu Xun, *Lu Xun Quanji* (The Complete Works of Lu Xun) (Beijing: Renmin Wenxue Chubanshe, 1996), Vol. 11, 249.

9 Petöfi, Sándor. 'Liberty and Love' from *Encyclopedia of the Romantic Era 1760–1850* (London: Taylor & Francis, 2004), 886.

10 Moran, Patrick Edwin. *Three Smaller Wisdom Books: Lao Zi's Dao de jing, the Great Learning (Da xue), and the Doctrine of the Mean (Zhong yong)*. Trans. Patrick Edwin Moran (Maryland: University Press of America, 1993), 180.

11 Deton, Kirk A. *Modern Chinese Literary Thought: Writings on Literature, 1893–1945* (California: Stanford University Press, 1996), 107.

12 Ibid.

13 Natsume, Sōseki. *Kusamakura* (New York: Penguin Classics, 2008), 3.

Chapter 7

1   Kato, Shuichi. *A History of Japanese Literature: The First Thousand Years.* Trans. David Chibbett (Tokyo: Kodansha International Ltd., 2002), 230.

2   *The Records of the Orally Transmitted Teachings.* Trans. Burton Watson (Tokyo: Soka Gakkai, 2004), 19.

3   Nichiren. *The Writings of Nichiren Daishonin* (Tokyo: Soka Gakkai, 2006), 8.

4   Ibid., 14.

5   Ibid., 24.

6   Nichiren, Vol. 2, 465.

7   Translated from the *Seikyo Shimbun* of 11 March 1984.

8   Ba Jin, *Ie* (*The Family*). Trans. Akira Iizuka Vol. 2 (Tokyo: Iwanami Publishing Ltd., 1956), 190.

9   Pa Chin. *Cold Nights.* Trans. Nathan K. Mao and Liu Ts'un-Yan (Hong Kong: Chinese University Press, 2002), 490.

10 Sima Qian. *Record of the Historian: Chapters from the Shih Chi of Ssu-ma Chi'en.* Trans. Burton Watson (New York: Columbia University Press, 1969), 14.

11 Translated from Japanese. Ba Jin. *Zuiso Roku* (Random Thoughts). Trans. Takashi Ishigami (Tokyo: Chikumashobo Ltd., 1982), 158.

12 Ibid., 158–59.

13 Translated from Japanese. Ba Jin. *Tansaku Shu* (Collection of Explorations). Trans. Takashi Ishigami (Tokyo: Chikumashobo Ltd., 1983), 189.

14 Eliot, T. S. *Christianity and Culture: The Idea of a Christian Society and Notes Towards the Definition of Culture* (New York: Harvest Books, 1960), 71.

15 *Readings in Chinese Literary Thought.* Trans. Stephen Owen (Massachusetts: Harvard University Asia Center, 1996), 68.

Chapter 8

1   Translated from Japanese. Shiba, Ryotaro. *Nihonjin wo Kangaeru* (On the Japanese) (Tokyo: Bungei shunju Ltd., 1971), 245.

2   Translated from Japanese. Jin Yong. *Heki Ketsu Ken*, Vol. 1 (*Sword Stained with Royal Blood*, Vol. 1). Ed. Yumi Okazaki. Trans. Sayori Kojima (Tokyo: Tokuma Shoten Publishing Co. Ltd., 1974), 195.

3   Nichiren. *The Writings of Nichiren Daishonin* (Tokyo: Soka Gakkai, 1999), 79.

4   Translated from Japanese. Jin Yong. *Heki Ketsu Ken*, 104.

5   Li Bai. 'The River Journey from White King City'. Trans. Shigeyoshi Obata. <http://www.blackcatpoems.com/b/the_river_journey_from_white_king_city.html>.

6   *The Book of Kindred Sayings* (Sanyutta-Nikāya). Trans. F. L. Woodward (Oxford: The Pali Text Society, 1997), 143.

7   Translated from Japanese. Ba Jin. *Zuiso Roku* (Random Thoughts). Trans. Takashi Ishigami (Tokyo: Chikumashobo Ltd., 1982), 172.

8   Translated from Japanese. Ba Jin. *Tansaku Shu* (Collection of Explorations). Trans. Takashi Ishigami (Tokyo: Chikumashobo Ltd., 1983), 28.

9   Ibid., 29.

10 Translated from Japanese. Huizinga, Johan. *In the Shadow of Tomorrow*. Trans. Koichi Horikoshi (Tokyo: Chuo Koron Sha, 1971), 112.

Chapter 9

1   Malraux, André. *Felled Oaks: Conversation with De Gaulle*. Trans. Irene Clephane (New York: Holt, Rinehart and Winston, 1972), 33.

2   Hugo, Victor. *Les Misérables*. Trans. Norman Denny (New York: Penguin Books, 1982), 36.

3   Ibid., 15.

4   Hugo, Victor. *Hernani*. Ed. Brander Matthews (Boston: Houghton Mifflin Company, 1916), 399.

5   Translated from Japanese. *Goethe Zenshu* (The Collected Works of Goethe), Vol. 13. Original German title: *Maximen und Reflecionen* (Maxims and Reflections). Ed. Takeo Komaki. Trans. Sadaichi Ooyama (Kyoto: Jinbun Shoin, 1961), 109.

6   Hugo, Victor. *Les Misérables*, 951.

7   Ibid., 1219.

8   Ibid., 156.

9   Ibid., 1106.

10 Dickens, Charles. *A Tale of Two Cities* (London: Penguin Books Ltd., 2003), 290.

11 Hugo, Victor. *Les Misérables*, 1005.

Chapter 10

1 Byo Kenshu. 'Eternal Life' in the monthly newsletter No. 12 for *Yoshikama Eiji Zenshu* (Complete Works of Eiji Yoshikawa).

2 Nichiren. *The Writings of Nichiren Daishonin* (Tokyo: Soka Gakkai, 1999), 851.

3 Eckermann, Johann Peter. *Conversations of Goethe with Johann Peter Eckermann*. Trans. John Oxenford. Ed. J. K. Moorhead (London: Da Capo Press, 1998), 198.

4 Nichiren, 302.

5 Doi, Bansui. 'A Star Falls in the Autumn Wind on Wuchang Plain' in Ikeda, Daisaku. *The Human Revolution* (Santa Monica: SGI-USA, 2004), 827.

6 Translated from Japanese. Eiji Yoshikawa. *Shin Suiko Den* (The New Water Margin), Vol. 4 (Tokyo: Kodansha Ltd., 1989), 303.

Index